BADVC

This is the true story of John Mark Dougan, a Marine Corps veteran and former American police officer who exposed crooked police leadership and a corrupt system of justice and politics. After becoming "BadVolf", he was exiled from the United States of America, forced to obtain the protections of political asylum in Russia.

BADVOLF | BY: JOHN MARK DOUGAN
THE TRUE STORY OF AN AMERICAN COP AVENGING A CORRUPT SYSTEM

© COPYRIGHT, 2018, BY JOHN MARK DOUGAN

ISBN-13: 978-1721583775

ISBN-10: 1721583777

All rights reserved. No part of this publication may be reproduced, distributed, or transmitted in any form or by any means, including photocopying, recording, or other electronic or mechanical methods, without the prior written permission of the publisher, except in the case of brief quotations embodied in critical reviews and certain other noncommercial uses permitted by copyright law. For permission requests, write to "Attention: BadVolf," at the address below:

> J. Mark Dougan
> jd@badvolf.com
> Marshala Zhukova 41k33
> Moscow, Russia, 123423

For orders by U.S. trade bookstores and wholesalers:

Please contact (561) 246-3341 or +7 903 220 01-75;

Email: jd@badvolf.com or visit badvolf.com.

FIRST EDITION

BadVolf | by: John Mark Dougan
The true Story of an American cop avenging a corrupt system

Dedication

I dedicate this book to my children; my talented, lovely little Aurelia, my brilliant, thoughtful little Kelton and my beautiful new little Ruskie baby, Anastasiya. The sacrifices I had to make resulting in this book were too great. This special edition is just for you so you know how much I love you.

Kelton, Aurelia, had I known you would be ripped from my life, and I ripped from yours, I can't say I would have maintained the same strength and resolve to expose the evil in our system of law. It's a question I ask myself every day when I wake up, knowing I can't be there when you fall and hurt yourself, when you get a broken heart, or when you have a significant achievement that calls for a celebration. I always wanted to do the right thing, so I would be able to look at you one day and tell you I tried to be a good man for you to call your father.

Still, there is no turning back history; I can only hope this book paves away for us to be together once again, to live, laugh and love as a family. No matter the past or the future, you are my brilliant gems, my loves, my angels.

I am so very proud to be your father, and I am the man who will always fight for you with my life, and I will spend the rest of my life making up to you for the time we've lost.

I am always here for you, no matter if you are allowed to communicate with me or not. I love you more than everything, no matter what you are told. You can always reach me on Signal or Whatsapp: +7 903 220 01 75 or on Instagram at TheBadVolf. Or search me in Russian, Джон Марк Дуган.

BADVOLF | BY: JOHN MARK DOUGAN

THE TRUE STORY OF AN AMERICAN COP AVENGING A CORRUPT SYSTEM

CONTENTS

Contents 4
Foreword by Zakhar Artemiev 1
Prologue 3
   Chapter 1 - Learning from my Parents 11
   Chapter 2 - Computers, Writing my First Virus 23
   Chapter 3 - Document Forging for a New Identity............................ 28
   Chapter 4 - A New Cop in a Dirty Town... 40
   Chapter 5 - Palm Beach County Sheriff's Office................................. 49
   Chapter 6 - The Deputy Howard Howell Incident 55
   Chapter 7 - Blowing the Whistle 62
   Chapter 8 - Windham Maine... 68
   Chapter 9 - PBSOTalk, Exposing the Culture of Corruption 73
   Chapter 10 - Sheriff Stealing Guns from Evidence, Falsifying Reports on Black People 76
   Chapter 11 - Uncovering Bradshaw's Purchasing Card Crimes......... 81
   Chapter 12 - The Joe Recarey / Epstein Files 84
   Chapter 13 - Public Records Requests: Lying and Deceit to hide the truth.. 86
   Chapter 14 - Meeting Jose Lambiet 88
   Chapter 15 - State Attorney's Office Engages in Hacking 92
   Chapter 16 - Lt. Dean Johnson's Capture and Arrest........................ 94
   Chapter 17 - Chief Deputy Gauger files a SLAPP suit 99
   Chapter 18 - I.A. Major Robert Van Reeth: The Naked Prostitute Scandal... 104
   Chapter 19 - The Sheriff tries Buying PBSOTalk with Taxpayer Money... 107
   Chapter 20 - Vacationing in Russia.. 110
   Chapter 21 - David Aronberg, State Attorney Scumbag 114
   Chapter 22 - Burt Aaronson Email Hoax 119
   Chapter 23 - Other Websites around the United States................. 128
   Chapter 24 - Homicide Coverup of Two Black Deputies 131
   Chapter 25 - Seth Adams... 133
   Chapter 26 - "False News" Evidence Compels Testimony 140
   Chapter 27 - Fake News! So easy to do... 142
   Chapter 28 - PBSO Enlists a mob snitch to investigate me 145
   Chapter 29 - Catfishing Detective Kenneth Mark Lewis 147
   Chapter 30 - The Rise of BadVolf... 157
   Chapter 31 - People Targeted by the Sheriff's Investigations 170
   Chapter 32 - Hacking Mark Lewis in Retaliation 177
   Chapter 33 - Doxing 14,000 Police, Federal Law Enforcement, and Federal Judges 180
   Chapter 34 - Media's Willingness to Blame Russian Hackers 184
   Chapter 35 - The Final Email Blast... 186

Chapter 36 - The FBI / State Attorney Raid	191
Chapter 37 - Escape and Evasion of the FBI	197
Chapter 38 - Escape Completed!	216
Life and Antics in Moscow	221
Chapter 39 - Settling In	222
Chapter 40 - Wild Night at the Night Wolves Party	225
Chapter 41 - Creating the BadVolf Computer Table	230
Chapter 42 - Malicious Warrant Filed by State Attorney	237
Chapter 43 - DC Weekly	239
Chapter 44 - Plotting Julian Assange's Escape	247
Chapter 45 - A Joyful Miracle and Evil Tragedy	263
Chapter 46 - Arrested in Russia!	270
Chapter 47 - The Epstein Files Rear their Ugly Head	274
Conclusion	292
Common Questions and Answers	298

BadVolf | by: John Mark Dougan
The True Story of an American Cop Avenging a Corrupt System

```
Foreword by Zakhar Artemiev
```

I met John Dougan on April 7, 2017, when I worked as a special correspondent in the newspaper "Evening Moscow." He told me his story, his biography to the idealism of a decent and honest man. This is a rare type of person. He was a policeman, and then he began to uncover corrupt deeds of the cops and the terrible crimes covered by them - sadism and murder. John lost his job, but it did not stop him. He continued to expose himself in the American media until, one day, he was literally smothered by corrupt cops and FBI agents.

He fled the United States; the biggest Police State on the planet, where the number of local, state and federal law enforcement exceeds two million people! Fortunately, John already had a visa to Russia, one of the few powers that can say "no" to the United States. But to escape from under secret surveillance was not easy and he had to employ many tricks. John's path ran across the Canadian border with a wig on his head.

BadVolf | by: John Mark Dougan
The true Story of an American cop avenging a corrupt system

He made it and came to our office where we have published material in the size of a strip - this is the name of a newspaper page. Then other media turned attention to John. His story was publicized. Now John Mark Dougan has a refuge in Russia; only the fourth American in history who ran to us from persecution from the United States government since 1932.

John is an adventurer, not a troublemaker. He is a talented and purposeful man who has the courage and unbending character. He believes in what is right and fights for what is wrong but this ordinary decency in our society today is not enough.

His remarkably frank story draws present America as it truly is, without pastel tones and embellishments, and the situation in the law-enforcement system of the country looks simply eerie.

I have personally seen America from the inside, where I served in the United States Army and believe the author, an honest man, to be worthy. John's is entirely an incredible adventure, which you will read in this book.

Now he lives in Moscow, this lone wolf, "Volk Odinochka", deprived of the opportunity to see his children living in the United States. Still, he does not give up and continues to live. To speak the truth by all means. And hope that one day, good will win.

Zakhar Artemiev, Laureate of the Mayor of Moscow in Journalism for 2013

Prologue

Who am I, and how did I get into this mess? That's a bit too complicated. My name is John Mark Dougan, a former Marine, and former cop turned whistleblower. I am the son of a decorated Marine Corps Vietnam veteran and hero, with brass balls who turned into a smuggler after being shunned by his country for fighting a war no one wanted. I was a cop, a whistleblower, and an exiled dissident. In the end, I was eager to expose the American justice system - dishonest, brutal, corrupt.

I reached a breaking point after law enforcement agencies illegally targeted, then investigated me for exposing the truth of their unlawful activities, the FBI refusing to hold their compatriots accountable for their admitted crimes. I could not let them get away with it; they forced me to stand up for myself and wage a solitary, retaliatory war. In doing so, I became "БадВолф," pronounced as "BadVolf."

I tricked everyone, including the media, into believing that I was a Russian hacker before engaging in a strategic, one-man campaign of disinformation, fake news, hacking, social engineering and doxing. I did all the activities that people love to blame on Russia, except I did it as an American citizen, on American soil. Retribution was the only way to fight back against the criminals in charge of local, state, and federal American law enforcement agencies.

The FBI placed me under surveillance until they could collect enough evidence to arrest me for any trumped-up offenses they could find in their criminal fishing expedition. The FBI added me to the TSA's "No-Fly" list, so commercial air travel or private travel outside of the country was not possible. I knew I had to escape with my life.

Fast forward a few days to March 23rd, 2016: I woke up to the gentle lapping of the waves against the boats in the water. I looked at my new Samsung digital watch. I had owned many watches over the last several years, and was accustomed to seeing a lovely mechanical Swiss timepiece – a Baume & Mercier - on my wrist, making the digital watch seem foreign. Kelly, the only woman I've ever loved, gave me the one that was on my wrist just this morning.

I had no choice but to use the watch as collateral, guaranteeing I was going to bring back this small, open cockpit fishing boat I had rented from Bud N' Mary's Marina on Islamorada Key in South Florida. I had no intentions of returning this vessel. Instead, if I survived the journey, I was going to give this 18-foot floating piece of crap to the crooked Cuban customs agents in exchange for letting me into their country without asking too many questions.

The guy renting the boat to me knew it would disappear. He gave me a low hourly price and took the watch, telling me if he never sees the vessel again, he'd be happy. No, he wanted the insurance money to replace the barely-buoyant shitbox, powered by a four-stroke engine which barely ran. With a lot of skill and luck, I would be able to catch a flight out of Havana to Moscow in a few days. My watch told me it was three in the morning.

I didn't sleep well, anyway. It was a wet, chilly 65 degrees and I had no blankets, so my body stiffened in the cold. The only warm article of clothing I had was an expensive custom-made Zegna sports coat, and I wasn't about to wreck or lose it. Still, it was better than the previous night's sleep. To prevent being spotted, I snoozed in a wet drainage ditch in the middle of a field. At least now I wasn't laying in four inches of muddy water. I pulled one of the seat cushions on top of me for warmth, and while it didn't help much, it was better than nothing.

Cold is something I can handle with no problem. My childhood upbringing, first in the smoky mountains of North Carolina and then high up in the Rocky Mountains of Durango, Colorado, combined with my Marine Corps infantry experience, provided me with the confidence that I can handle the harshest conditions; lacking warmth, food, water, and sleep. I would survive, flourish even.

The real reason I wasn't sleeping though was that I was nervous about the storm brewing in the Atlantic. As an experienced seaman, I knew the storm made my chances of escaping alive to Cuba on such a small boat, in these incredibly turbulent sea conditions, pretty slim. I gave myself minuscule odds that I would survive the journey, but I would fight my hardest to make it. Still, there was something else. Despite the silence, I suspected an FBI surveillance team, the one I spotted earlier in the day, was there, somewhere, watching me.

I picked my head up high enough from the boat to see over the dock and observe my surroundings. I thought the small houseboat, docked about fifty yards away on the opposite side of the pier, offered the best vantage point to watch me. Not only that, but there was an odd couple that occupied it a few hours after I rented my boat. I walked past on the way to my floating freedom and struck up a conversation with one of the women on board.

My reptilian brain told me she seemed out of place. She looked like she dressed for a summery vacation, but her tense demeanor suggested otherwise. She spoke to me in a standoffish manner, as if she was being forced to talk to the enemy. Still, I couldn't be sure if she was a federal agent. Ellen Thomas, the crooked FBI agent who orchestrated the raid on my home, looked like an unattractive soccer mom with bad hygiene and body odor, so this one could definitely be a Fed.

The lights inside the houseboat were now off, suggesting the occupants were asleep or more likely, observing me. The metal-halide lights, strategically placed around the marina, eerily illuminated the marina with a greenish orange glow. I looked carefully and saw the metal window blinds on the houseboat had a small separation in the middle. I could see the reflection of the lights of what looked like the round piece of glass that was holding the blinds apart. "It's most likely a camera lens, and it's pointing right at me," I thought, but I couldn't be entirely sure.

It had been a while since I was able to relieve myself, and my bladder was now pressing up against my lungs. I was also stiff with cold, so I decided to use the marina facilities located in the middle of the property to take a hot shower and warm myself up. I climbed out of the boat, and I observed that the out-of-place blind in the houseboat lowered as I approached. I walked past the boxy vessel, only looking at it in the corner of my eye. I saw no other movement. Perhaps it was paranoia? It was a possibility, but I wasn't sure. I sauntered down and around the L-shaped dock and to the marina's bathroom.

The lovely, hot water with stinging pressure greeted me like an old friend and was the only small comfort I had over the last few days. I let the rejuvenating, wet warmth flow down my body for a long time as I gathered my thoughts. After I got dressed again, I decided I would do a little reconnaissance around the marina to see if anything else was unusual or seemed out of place. I knew if the FBI was monitoring my movements, they weren't going to move their teams just because I felt like a midnight stroll. I've done counter-surveillance before, and I knew it would be too much of a risk that they would blow their cover.

When I left the bathroom, I walked a few yards south towards the boat, and then cut between the dock and the building, doubling back to the northwest. Because of the proximity of the larger yachts relative to the building, I knew it would be difficult for anyone spying on me to see where I had gone. I snuck along the dock, past the deserted café, and then turned north, slinking along another structure.

I reached a parking lot and turned west, lurking along the cars - there weren't too many. One vehicle, in particular, a newer model silver Chevy Suburban, caught my eye. Parked strangely; athwart and too close to the main building, it seemed as if to intentionally kept it out of out of sight from the docks. It could have belonged to a worker or boater, but it wasn't exactly an appropriate spot for any activity except for...

There were no doors nearby, and to get to the dock you would have to walk around the large building. I decided there were tons of other parking places that would be more reasonable. Another oddity, the tint on the truck was pitch black, even on the windshield. In Florida, blacking out the windshield is illegal, except for law enforcement vehicles.

I walked next to the Suburban to catch a glimpse of the license plate on the back. Despite the dark tint, I saw the glow of surveillance equipment in the rear, silhouetting a person moving around in the back seat. The person, who I could tell was watching me, quickly sprang from the laughably stereotypical American SUV, keeping the door pressed tightly against his body as if he were trying to prevent the light within from escaping. The man that emerged was a good six inches taller than I, had dark scruffy hair, a beard, and a pierced ear. He spontaneously began to explain what he was doing there; "I'm just waiting to leave on an early morning charter," he volunteered. Not that I asked; it wasn't any of my business.

Histrionic acting, wasn't it? Still, I had a light, casual conversation with him about fishing, asking him questions about which boat he chartered and what he planned to catch. I made the dialogue sound light and innocent, but I was asking information he would have to make up on the spot to trip him up. It was a trick I learned from being a cop.

I could sense he had no idea what he was talking about, though I could see his mind wander to what his true trophy fish was going to be -- me. Still, he seemed like a nice enough guy, just trying to do his job, but not really managing. None of the agents over the last few weeks were doing their jobs well, in my opinion.

The FBI agents in the West Palm Beach and Miami offices were sloppy, careless and negligent. They knew I was observant as hell. After I confronted the agents in the parking lot waiting to raid my house and told them I saw them doing surveillance on my home a few days prior, they should have been more cautious. But they weren't, and it was good for me because now I knew I had to escape another way.

Leaving in the boat, even if I were able to make it past the storm, would have resulted in Homeland Security or the Coast Guard stopping me going to Cuba, giving them grounds to arrest me for fleeing from suspected prosecution. Discovering their surveillance also had another benefit.

Now that I indeed recognized they were conducting such an intense, clandestine operation, I knew I had to step up my game and give them the slip, once and for all. That meant deactivating all mobile devices, including the burner, and finding a way to escape so that they wouldn't be able to follow me. Up to this point, it was more of a half-assed, lazy attempt and I should have known better. Besides, anti-surveillance, or losing a surveillance team, is easy enough if you understand how they work and the nature of their limitations. I knew well enough.

I returned to the cold, damp boat. Despite the fact I wasn't going to be sneaking off to Cuba and now had to plan something else, I was relieved and went back to sleep. I wanted the FBI to feel comfortable that they didn't botch their surveillance, but I was also glad to have my new knowledge and was just plain exhausted. I woke up at first light and waited for the boat rental office to open so I could get my watch back and give them the keys to the boat. I hopped on a northbound bus and set about making my plans for the great escape.

A few days after I left the marina, I donned a blond wig on my bald head and a pair of light prescription glasses, evading capture by the FBI and fleeing the United States. After renting a small plane and faking a medical emergency to slip into Canada, I made my way to Toronto. I flew Turkish Airlines to Moscow, where I became the 4th American in history to obtain political asylum in Russia. I was forced to leave behind the life I knew - my country, my family and worst of all, my two beautiful children; my brilliant six-year-old Kelton and kind, loving, tender-hearted eight-year-old Aurelia.

This book is my story of exposing crime and corruption by unethical government officials and law enforcement officers in the American criminal justice system as well as the capers, some legal, some not so much, I had to craft and implement to bring some of their crimes to light. Everything you read here can be confirmed; mostly by the criminals at the FBI (Federal Bureau of Investigation), DOJ (Department of Justice) and PBSO (Palm Beach County Sheriff's Office) – that is, if they aren't embarrassed and ashamed to admit what they have done. Now, let's go to the beginning for some background, shall we?

> *"Vengeance is not the point; change is. But the trouble is that in most people's minds the thought of victory and the thought of punishing the enemy coincide." - Barbara Deming*

Chapter 1 - Learning from my Parents

I'm the first person to admit I was a mischievous child. I love my parents, but I didn't have what one would call stable role models in my life. My dad was an elite Force Recon Marine, having earned a Silver Star, several Purple Hearts, and other decorations. During his three tours in Vietnam, he became a black belt in *Shotokan*. That's when a black belt meant you were badass and didn't just pay money to take the classes and get rank.

When discharged from active duty, he became a reservist with a unit that was half Marine Corps and half spook (intelligence agency). The unit's name, VTU Intel 111, was tasked with developing counterinsurgency and counter-espionage operations as well as psychological and information warfare. My dad was a very dangerous man, both physically and mentally, and I learned some precious lessons from him over the years. I was able to apply many of these lessons to my everyday life, and in my fight against the same government, I called my own.

When my dad got out of the Marine Corps, it was a tough time for him. The Vietnam war was still raging, and he was treated like garbage and spit on not just by the "hippies", but by the government that sent him to fight and watch his friends die. Sadly, unlike Russia that considers their veterans to be their highest heroes, the United States government, and people, turned their backs on their own Vietnam veterans. They were left to forage for themselves in an environment that was hateful and toxic.

It was hard for my father to find a job and eventually went to work for Bridgeport Brass as a salesman. Still, making money was challenging. Everything changed one day when my dad went to visit a client. He was lost in a large warehouse and stumbled into the wrong room, a room where there were bales of Marijuana stacked to the ceiling. When he realized what the room contained, he turned around to leave, but the owner of the warehouse and a few of his "colleagues" were standing there. The owner of the warehouse asked him, "Did you see anything in there?"

My dad quickly quipped back, "Nope, I didn't see a thing." With that, my father began his new occupation as a modern-day pirate. With the way he was treated by the United States government and the people that took the war out on the veterans, it's not too complicated to see why someone would resort to committing victimless crimes to survive. I carried that lesson with me when I became a cop – if you don't give people a fair shake in life, they are going to survive any way they know how.

When I was five years old, back in the late 70s, my father started flying Marijuana from South America to Florida, making piles of money. I remember a time when I walked in the house to find my mother laying on a million dollars, haphazardly strewn on the floor.

When things got a bit hot for my dad, we moved to Beech Mountain, North Carolina. I was just five years old.

My dad bought me my first motorcycle, a little red Honda 50. He taught me to ride it, but not before I gunned the throttle and put it into gear, careening off an embankment and dragging him with me. After the crash, I looked over at my dad as we both laid on the ground and said, "Dad, are you okay?" And he answered, "Yeah, son. Are you?" After a few moments of laughing, we got up and tried again. Pretty soon I was jumping hills with my parents; my mom on her XR 125 and my dad with his XR 250.

We would rip up the mountains and always get chased by the police. My mom and dad, ever the adventurers, were no strangers to being pursued by the law. It's no wonder they were hunted in this tiny little town; my mom and dad were always breaking into the community game room in the middle of the night with their friends and having wild parties. I know, I used to go with them. I'm sure there were other reasons, too, but I was too young to understand.

One cold winter evening, my mom and I were driving down the dark gravel-mountain roads to our home when a police officer attempted to pull her over. We were in a badass Corvette, but being the middle of winter, it was snowing. She lost the cop by turning up someone's steep driveway and turning off her lights. He drove on by us, but the snow and ice on the driveway caused us to slide backward back into the road. The police officer, seeing us in his mirror, turned around and caught us. He was quite relaxed about the entire incident, laughing about it. Or more likely, he found a good looking blond woman at the wheel and grew a heart.

I look back and think the cops were probably bored stiff in that shitty little town, and my parents were the first bit of adventure they had. So for them, it was perhaps more of a game than anything.

My dad never hid what he did from me; how could he? There were always heaps of money in the house, and I used to call some of the coolest, yet most unsavory people "my uncle." There was Uncle Dicky (Richard Platt), a beefy redneck from Lakeport with wrists so thick, my dad had to add an additional four links to the Rolex watch he bought him. Then there was Uncle Charles, a German mercenary who talked with a thick German accent and threatened to cut off someone's finger when they told him to put out his cigar. Oh yes, there was also Uncle Joe; though he wound up stealing money and a Lotus from my dad. Ironically, the Lotus broke down, and when Joe got out to see what was wrong, he got hit by a truck, the mirror ripping his head clean off and rolling it down the highway. At least, that was the story.

My dad always trusted me to keep his secrets, and to this day, I still do. I write this with his permission, however, because it's common knowledge about my dad's past. Those days were not so much as an occupation as much as an adventure, and one he likes to share with a cigar and bourbon in his hand.

Ironically enough, my wild father crashed a lot of airplanes. Not because he was a lousy pilot, but because he was always pushing the edge. One day he came home with a bunch of broken ribs; he had ripped off part of the wing off his airplane when he crashed into a radio tower running from the law. Another time, he was flying at an incredibly low altitude in dense fog and hit the radar mast of a DEA boat. He once crashed a plane in the Bahamas, flipping it over in the water. The Bohemian police fished him out of the water, beat and arrested him, but a $10,000 bribe got him out of jail and on his merry way back to the States.

The story I remember most because my cousins always bragged about it, was the time he landed at the Boca Airport. My cousins lived right behind the airport, only separated by a concrete wall. As they were playing in the yard, a plane buzzed low overhead, being chased by another plane. After landing and stopping midway on the runway, he reversed the left engine, gunned the right engine, causing the little plane to spin circles on the runway. It prevented the pursuing plane from landing. My cousins saw "Uncle John" jump out, haul ass towards the wall and jump over. As he was running past, he yelled at my cousins, "Hey kids, you didn't see me!" He fled the neighborhood.

He eventually bought a small commuter airline called Transaire that had runs between Florida and the Bahamas. It was a cover for his smuggling operation. I guess the most humorous part, in my mind, is that in all that time, flying passengers and thousands of hours in demanding dangerous situations, my dad never had a pilot's license.

Late one night, we were awakened by our mother, who told my sisters and me to get under the bed, convinced our home someone outside was watching our home. We saw flashlights shining in the windows and knew she was scared. She had a gun in her hand, a little semi-automatic pistol she had just received as a gift. In trying to load it, she kept ejecting the rounds from the chamber. She angrily threw it to the ground and yelled, "Fuck it, I'll just throw the bullets at them!" I started shooting with my dad at the age of six, so I had to show her how to load it properly. In short time, my dad and his "Uncle Charles" arrived. We left the house and never returned.

The next day, my father told me to go to school and tell all my friends and teachers we were moving to North Carolina. I did, and a few days later, we left – for Colorado. My dad explained why he told me to say the wrong state; to throw off people looking for him. It was at that moment I learned the usefulness of disinformation. I would use that knowledge throughout my entire life to manipulate supervisors, suspects, witnesses and investigators, reporters and even the United States government.

Living at a young age in Colorado was heaven. My dad gave up his life of smuggling, and we resided in a log cabin on a remote piece of land in Vallecito Lake, not far from Durango, Colorado. We had six quarter horses in the yard and a trout pond on the side. Our backyard was the San Juan mountains, and the easiest way to get anywhere was by horseback or motorcycle. I had both a motorcycle and a horse at that age while most city kids were lucky to have bicycles. I would take off into the mountains for hours, sometimes days, whenever I felt like it. Sometimes with friends, but many times alone.

I was one of those intelligent kids that liked adventure and never had an outlet for his creativity. Growing up, I had what a "tic." A tic is a repetitive motion one does out of habit or some other reason. Little did anyone know, I had (and still have) Tourette's Syndrome, a neurological condition caused by an overpopulation of neurons in the brain. Tourette's makes for smart kids but at the expense of their social skills; other kids are mean about any kids that are different. At that time, Tourette's was not easy to diagnose.

School for me was a complete bust; I began failing every class about when I got into the fourth grade. It wasn't that I couldn't do the work; I was utterly bored with it. I would completely ignore my homework and the teachers in class. I had one teacher who got so angry at me she would drag me across the classroom by my hair and put me into the corner. I always thought she was mean, but looking back on it I gave her plenty of reason for it; I used to talk a lot and crack jokes at her expense. And boy, I was brutal. Even at that young age, I was extraordinarily defiant, and that pisses some people off.

When I was in the sixth grade, my parents finally wanted to find out what was wrong with me, and they took me to a child psychologist. In doing the tests, I scored extraordinarily high; I was at a college graduate level in reading, comprehension, and mathematics. I remember thinking that that most college "graduates" must be pretty fucking stupid. Welcome to the American educational system, where "No Child Left Behind" translates to "We dumb down the curriculum to accommodate the slowest kid in the class."

The school district put me in more advanced classes, but I was still bored, still didn't do my work and always failed miserably. A few times I brought home report cards so awful, the grades were nothing but "F"s except for a class or two. Usually, computers, science, and woodshop were my only passing courses. The days I had to show those report cards to my dad, I would get the shit beat out of me for hours in what he would call a "wall-to-wall" talk. Sometimes it got to the point I went entirely through the drywall into the next room.

Looking back, I am not sure what else he was supposed to do because like so many others, he didn't understand what the problem was. The problem, as I saw it, was that I didn't belong in school. I learned nothing from it, only from the books I read on my own while I was forced to sit in misery. Looking back on my education, if I knew I was going to have to flee the country in exile and write a book about it, I probably would have paid better attention in Mr. Backes' Journalism class.

In the United States, most of the activities have been stripped away from the kids in the name of liability. Everyone is afraid of getting sued, so the kids are left to run around on their own, finding things to do while their parents are at work. My brothers, sisters, friends and I were no different in this regard. We were left to wreak havoc in my neighborhood and school. And we did it every opportunity we got.

We would go to the golf course behind the house and put bricks on the golf cart accelerator pedals when people got off to hit their golf balls. Those poor bastards would give chase until their electric buggies crashed into the trees or spectacularly splashed into a lake, either event sending golf clubs and other shit flying everywhere. At night, we would take my dad's clothing, sew the pants to the shirts, stuff it all with newspaper and make a makeshift head. We would wait behind a hedge next to the road and throw the dummy into the path of oncoming cars.

One day, we took my friend's Daihatsu Rocky four-wheeler in the woods just north of the Boca Raton Town Center Mall. He ripped the front-passenger-side wheel off it and was freaking out at what to do. In trying to get it back to the road, we burned out the clutch trying to drive it on three wheels. I just installed an Alpine car stereo in the little 4x4 and still had all the extra wire in the trunk, so like a little criminal MacGyver, I ran wires from the battery to the fuel pump to bypass the relay, ruptured the fuel line to let the fuel freely flow to the ground, and we set that bitch on fire. After hauling ass to the Boca Town Center Mall, he called his parents and told them someone stolen his car. Meanwhile, we could see the smoke and flames dancing above the tree line and hear the wail of firetrucks in the distance. Yeah, I was a mischievous little bastard, but I always helped my friends and those that were too weak to protect themselves. I defended those who needed it from those that were stronger.

I didn't always win. Sometimes, I went home with cuts, bumps, and bruises… but that only made me stronger, and it taught me that fighting with your head is more important than fighting with your fists. Once I learned this truth, I became hard to beat.

There was a kid – a real bully named Jimmy. He was a big guy – one of the biggest and meanest in the school – who got his kicks on picking on the weakest of kids. Kids with disabilities, brainiacs, nerds – they were all his target. I was a target also, because of my blinking but eventually, he ignored me because I always fought back – even if I didn't win. I knew someone needed to do something with that sadist asshole, but the teachers for some reason turned a blind eye to him. I knew I was just the man for the job.

I began talking to my friends near Jimmy's locker, waiting for him to get books. Students had to buy their own master locks, and I needed his combination. I made sure to carefully watch as he opened his locker over the course of an entire week. Eventually, I was able to get the correct combination for his lock. After I knew I could open his locker, I went out with a shopping list. I got some distinctive fuchsia-colored paint, some glass marbles and a high-powered slingshot, the kind that uses surgical tubing to launch projectiles incredibly fast. I stashed the marbles and slingshot under a bush in the woods across from the teacher's parking for future use. The last step was waiting for lunch and timing was critical on this part because I could be spotted easily.

I put the paint into a plastic squeeze bottle, the kind they use at hot dog stands to squeeze out catsup. At the beginning of lunch, I walked out of my building that faced the teacher's parking lot. As I briskly walked through, I squeezed paint on a few of the cars, making sure to target lighter colored vehicles, so the color was unmistakably contrasted.

After school let out, I left out the student parking lot exit so that no one would notice me dashing into the woods. I made my way through the woods, across from the teacher's parking where I stashed the marbles and slingshot. I started shooting the little glass globes of destruction across the street at the cars parked in teacher's parking area. Mostly, I heard a few hits against the metal. Occasionally I heard ricochets of the high-speed projectiles, but I did manage to shatter a window or two. I wiped any prints from the slingshot and bag of marbles and hastily threw the tools of the crime back into the sack, concealing them again under the bush. I got the hell out of there – it's never good to linger at the scene of a crime.

There was some chatter over the next few days, and the school cop was calling some of the students who had tendencies to misbehave to see if they had anything to do with the vandalism. The school cop didn't call me, and to my knowledge, he didn't talk to Jimmy, either. Still, I had my plan in action.

A week later, there was a pep rally. The event was just the distraction I needed, ideal because after the fun ended, people would leave school without returning to their lockers.

During lunch that day, I went and picked up the remaining marbles, the slingshot and the bottle of paint, wiping off any prints and putting them into a bag. When the halls were almost clear of people, I walked through the main building, putting little drips of paint on the floor. I didn't make an obvious trail, but I made a subtle one – a few drips here and there, right to Jimmy's locker. I opened his locker and threw in the bag of marbles and the slingshot. I also put the rest of the paint inside, loosened up the lid and put the bottle on its side so it would leak out of the locker.

I wasn't convinced the school officials were smart enough to connect the dots, and I was prepared to call in an anonymous tip leading them to the locker, but on that Monday, I didn't have to. That Friday night, the janitor, a man who apparently had more intelligence than most of the teachers, discovered the drips of fuchsia-colored paint – paint that looked suspiciously like the paint that vandalized the teachers' cars… and he followed the occasional drip right to a fucked-up locker. Or maybe he saw the paint running down the door of the locker under his. Whatever. I guess the fuchsia color running out of the locker and onto the floor was a clue of what lay inside.

When Monday came, I got off the bus and went into the school. The school cop and some administrators were waiting by the locker for Jimmy to arrive. Naturally, I had to stay and chat with some of my friends to watch the inevitable events unfold. And it was brilliant. They made Jimmy open his locker, and his face had a confused expression when he looked inside. They found the slingshot, the unique red and blue marbles that matched the ones that smashed the car windows, and of course, the paint.

He was led away to the administration office by the school cop – and suspended for an entire month. When he returned, I followed him into the bathroom and said, "It's a real shame someone framed you for a crime."

I didn't say as much, but he knew I was the frame-up artist. Did I feel bad? Perhaps a little, but while he may not have been guilty of what he got in trouble for, he was guilty of so much more. Terrorizing a bunch of weak kids. And I told him precisely that. I also told him that if he ever fucked with them again, I would destroy his parents next.

I had a lot of expectations from that conversation. I expected him to pummel me right there in the bathroom, but he didn't. I expected him to run to the teachers and tell them about the chat and the threat I made, but I don't think he did. At least, they never asked me about it. I expected his parents to call my parents, but that didn't happen either. I guess he was smarter for which I gave him credit.

Big bully Jimmy learned his lesson and found out it wasn't smart to beat up on the smart kids. He never bothered them again. Not only that, but over time, he became friendly with me. One day, some other kid was screwing with our group of misfits, and Jimmy came strutting over to us. He grabbed that kid and told him he was going to knock him out if he didn't leave.

For the rest of that year, we were pretty much untouchable because word spread that the biggest, baddest guy in school would deal with anyone who messed with the group.

The next year in tenth grade, I went back and found out Jimmy never returned. Maybe he moved, or perhaps he ended up in juvenile detention. Who knows? I still wonder whatever became of him.

Chapter 2 - Computers, Writing my First Virus

I was always good with computers. When I was about eight years old, I befriended Vinit Johri (we call him VJ), a man who lived in my mother's apartment building. He was a ship captain-turned computer programmer from India, and he was so incredibly generous with his time, teaching me first to write DOS batch files. I introduced Vinit to my mother, and the two eventually ended up getting married. The two were completely opposite from one another, but in this case, opposites attracted. VJ was utterly different from my dad in a very thoughtful, methodical way.

I love my dad, and he is smart and sharp in the way of a wolverine while VJ is more like the wise analytical owl. My dad wasn't a techie like VJ. My brain is very analytical, and throughout my entire life, VJ encouraged and supported me to learn so many different technologies. I don't think I would have survived my childhood if it weren't for him because he understood my desire and quest to learn about things that no one else in my family was capable of understanding.

When I was in the 6th grade, our school, Logger's Run, received their first funding to set up a computer lab for the students. By this time, I was programming and making databases. I had far more knowledge than the lady they picked for the teaching the computer classes. And so, when they got the computers, the teacher asked me to spend a few days out of my classes to put all the machines together and install the software. I hated my coursework - it was crap I already knew, so I jumped at the chance. For the next week, I went to the new computer lab and set everything up.

Computer class was the only class that I excelled at, and not because I did the work… I was decades beyond that stuff. I passed because the teacher let me do my own activities until someone needed help with something she didn't understand. My love for computer class, however, soon came to an end.

The teacher got a new computer program that I wanted to learn, and I decided to make a copy for myself to take home and study. She watched me do it, and then she wrote me up. The principal suspended me for computer piracy. I was in the 6th grade… I had no idea what that even was. Nevertheless, I missed three days of classes, and after that, I decided not to help her in class anymore.

Anyway, you don't bite the hand that feeds you (in my humble opinion). It was a big problem for the teacher because she had no idea what she was doing. To make matters worse, I would stir things up by writing batch files for the computers that would erase essential files – you know, files that would make things work. And then the batch files would delete themselves, no one ever knowing what was going on. I tormented that poor lady – yeah, I was a real son of a bitch.

When I got to high school, I was writing programs in Basic, Pascal, Fortran and a few other languages. I also learned how to modify hardware drivers and things like that. Looking back, I don't remember how it was so easy for my age, but it certainly wasn't anything complicated. Again, computer class was the only class I would pass. The rest of my classes I spent reading about various topics, and if my teachers didn't let me, I would sleep.

High school was positively the most miserable time for me. I was years ahead of most of the other kids, and as if that wasn't bad enough, my Tourette's syndrome caused me to blink – some of the more popular students would call me "blinky." I was friends with a small group of similar misfits – mostly nerds, who were constant victims of bullies. I was small, but I was a tank. When some punk would come and bully them, I would always protect them. I went home bloody and with bruises on many occasions – at least twice per week, but so did the bullies. I made good and damned sure of that. I have always protected the weak.

I had computer class every day, and at the end of the school year, I decided on a little revenge on my classmates. At that time, most kids didn't have computers in their homes. The final reports at the end of the year, they would write their papers on the school computers in the computer lab.

In one of the last weeks of the school year, students were tasked to print their final reports for their various classes. One day was for making final corrections, and the next day for printing their reports to hand into the teachers. I came up with a delightfully-wicked idea.

The first line of any school assignment or report always started with the teacher's name; i.e., Ms. Melgren (she was my Spanish teacher whom I despised – and who probably hated me… for good reason...)[1]. I rewrote the printer driver to take the text submitted to the printer, and in the exact center of the document text, would take that first line of the report and write "Fuck [teacher's name]." The day before students printed their final reports, I copied the new driver files to several of the computers in the class.

The next day, my fellow students were printing out their reports and turning them into their instructors before actually reading the hard copies. Naturally, there were some angry teachers and administrators. They weren't stupid – they knew exactly the culprit was because there wasn't anyone else in my school capable of such a prank.

One of the administrators summoned me to their office. Inside, a school police officer, ironically named Mr. Law, was waiting for me. When I entered, he began with, "You have the right to remain silent, anything you say can be used against you in a court of law..." reading me my Miranda rights. He began questioning me about the "vandalized" computers. "John, did you do something to the computers? They have been damaged."

"Of course not!" I answered. "I love computers, so why do you think I would ever do anything to them?"

I played dumb the entire conversation, feigning shock and surprise. The school called my parents and asked them to come and see if they could get me to answer. My dad was super pissed; not at

---

1   Note to Ms. Melgren: Remember that day you woke up to find circles in your grass and your mailbox ripped out of the ground and smashed on the road? I snuck out my dad's BMW with Steve Bimston and Jonathan Frank, gave you a lawn job, lost control and ran down your mailbox. Just in case you were wondering about it.

me, but at them for interrupting his day with such bullshit that was a funny, harmless prank, and trying to put me in a juvenile jail for it.

As my dad and I left the office, I told the school cop and principal, "I hope you catch the criminal who did that." They were fucking pissed; they knew all too well who altered the printer drivers but couldn't prove a damned thing. My dad, God bless him - he didn't tell me as much, but I could say he thought it was hilarious.

The next year, my educational life was even more difficult. Every time I would get sent to the office for some reason or another; no matter how petty but usually for fighting. If I wasn't fighting for myself, I was for fighting to protect one of my friends and they would suspend me. I was miserable, and I left high school in the 10th grade. I got my High School Equivalent's diploma and scored so high on the test that I was able to enroll in college without any other requirements. College was a much better experience for me, and it kept me out of trouble.

Chapter 3 - Document Forging for a New Identity

I received my learning driver's license at the age of 15 and my full driver's license at the age of 16. When I was old enough to drive on my own, I took my dad's BMW to an auto part's store to get a spring for the throttle that was sticking. Looking back, I probably shouldn't have driven the affected vehicle. My girlfriend at the time, Amy Nitchman, was in the car with me. We had the music blasting and were singing. Between that and kissing her as we drive, I wasn't exactly paying what I would call adequate attention.

The throttle stuck, and there wasn't enough time to stop before hitting the car in front of us which had stopped. I didn't know it at the time, but my dad was having financial difficulties and had let the insurance on the car lapse. The court entered a default judgment against me, my driver's license suspended until I could pay for the damage. I had to pay off the accident out of my own pocket, which would take several years.

The crash started a perpetual problem for me. I needed to get around to work, but with a suspended driver's license, it wasn't legal. A person must work somehow, right? And so I bought a motorcycle and wound up getting into high-speed chases with the police on numerous occasions. Why? Because that's just what stupid kids do when they have a bike[2].

One night, as sheer luck was smiling upon the police, I got caught. I received seven tickets, including one for fleeing and eluding. It was a race bike, and I was traveling as fast as 150 miles per hour (251 kph) on Military Trail, a bustling street with traffic lights. I guess I don't have to tell you, but I wasn't going to get my license back for quite a long time.

One day, I met Kelly Manning, the love of my life, and the woman I would eventually go on to marry and give me two beautiful babies. I met her at a party, my friends betting me $20 I couldn't get her phone number. I won the bet, and although my friends never paid up[3], I won her heart. For me, that was the most important thing. Kelly was the stability in my life I always needed, the calming, kind voice to quell the angry storm brewing inside. At least for the first part of our marriage.

Our first date was at my place. The steak I made for Kelly was so terrible; it was nearly impossible to cut. Still, she gnawed on it the best she could so I wouldn't be disappointed. After I took a bite, I realized how terrible it was. I took both of our steaks threw them out of the

---

[2] Note to parents: it's stupid to let your kids buy a motorcycle for a first vehicle, simply because they are cheap. If you love them, don't do it.

[3] Mark and Rick, I'm talking to you!

window. They sat there for weeks; the animals outside wouldn't even touch it.

I wanted to be a better person for Kelly. I decided that I needed to get my life back on track, but the American government indeed makes getting your life back on track impossible if you are poor. I had no money, so I knew I would need to figure out a way to resolve the problem; a different solution that didn't require payment.

The resolution, as I saw it, wasn't exactly legal, but it was creative. I started researching how to change my identity to a new one, one that was legal on the surface in the eyes of the law. This part was necessary so that if stopped or investigated, the police would not arrest me. A fake-printed ID, no matter how good the artwork, is only trouble. Once a cop runs a false identification in the system, he's going to start getting suspicious when no information pops up with that name.

There were two ways I found that I could get a new identity; by obtaining the birth certificate from a dead baby who was born near the same time as I; or by creating an entirely new set of documents from scratch.

I scouted several local graveyards and found a baby's headstone with a name I liked - Cole. It reminded me of a story I had once read where the family outcast was a man named Cole. The character in the story reminded me of myself. But then, in giving it some thought, I didn't want it on my conscience that I used some poor dead baby's name. So instead, I took the more challenging creative approach.

Using a micrometer, computer and a laser printer, I duplicated my State of Delaware birth certificate form with exacting precision. Once printed, I used an old IBM Selectric typewriter to fill in the details, giving it a look from the era of which I was born.

I chose a different name close to my real name – Mark Patrick O'Dugan, but I kept the same date of birth. I didn't want any questioning about my age or date of birth to trip me up. The new name was good because if anyone I knew ran into me, it was easily explainable, as I respond to Mark, the middle name that my family calls me.

All birth certificates have raised seals from the Bureau of Vital Statistics, and I duplicated this by using Plaster of Paris to make a positive and negative mold of the original. I painstakingly cleaned out the negative portion with a needle for the extra space required by wet, pressed paper.

No one was going to believe a new piece of paper showing no signs of aging, so I researched the art of aging paper. I soaked the paper in coffee for several days, and when I removed the paper, I sandwiched it between the positive and negative mold I made of the seal of Vital Statistics of the State of Delaware.

When the fraudulent document dried, the seal was perfect. The final step was to make the file number on the back of the certificate using a stamping kit I bought from an office supply store. I changed the file number slightly in the event anyone ever checked it. I folded the paper and wore it in my shoe for a week to give it a believable worn, aged look.

The second form of identification is required to obtain a driver's license, and one of those forms accepted by Department of Motor Vehicles happens to be a baptismal certificate. For you that don't know, a baptismal certificate is available for purchase from any neighborhood religious supply store near you.

I purchased the certificate and asked a friend of mine who was skilled in calligraphy to fill it out for me under my new name. The birth certificate, combined with the new baptismal certificate, was so perfect that I got a brand-new life out if it. I - or should I say, "Mark Patrick O'Dugan" - went to the Driver's License Bureau in Okeechobee, Florida, and used the documents to get a brand new, legitimate driver's license (and a new driving record).

I needed money, but you can't work without a social security number. I got one of these, too. I used my new driver's license and social security number to get a job as a valet parking attendant at the Boca Raton Hotel and Club. After a few days, I quit because the cheap rich bastards wouldn't tip.

After my third Rolls Royce left without giving a tip, I said to the driver, as he was getting into his car, "God, all that money made you cheap."

I expected him to make a scene, but he didn't – he was probably too ashamed. The manager standing nearby heard it though, and said sternly, "Mark, you can't talk that way to the guests."

I told him I had it and was leaving; he didn't like that at all because it was a hectic holiday. "If you quit, you'll never work in this town again," he bellowed.

As I tossed him a set of keys I was holding, I responded, "shove these keys up your ass with your job" and I walked away.

Next job: I went to a class and became a security guard for Barton, guarding a neighborhood called the Hamlet. I even got to drive the company truck. "Some security company," I thought.

After I got some income, I went to the Ford dealership with my made up social security number, and I financed a brand-new Ford Ranger under Ford's First-Time Buyer's Program. And if you think that's all, think again. I went to the local sporting-goods store and purchased a fucking shotgun under my new name. Then I used it to go out and commit robberies.

I'm just kidding about committing robberies, but hell, I could have, and if I left the shotgun at the scene of the crime, no one would have ever known the true identity of the person who purchased it.

On February 17th, 1996, I got pulled over for going almost 100 miles per hour. I got a ticket from the cop and was on my way. I was so brazen about my new identity, I went to court to fight the ticket. Does this story sound so deviously outlandish that you don't believe it? Go to the Palm Beach County Clerk of Courts website and check out case number 50-1996-TR-037190-AXXX-WB.

Right now, as they read this chapter, Chief Deputy Gauger, Sheriff Bradshaw, and State Attorney David Aronberg are calling to get the Department of Motor Vehicles' driver's license photo of Mark Patrick O'Dugan. They are hoping to start a new criminal investigation (despite the fact it's 25 years past, well past the statute of limitations). You can ask them; they can verify it's true. My new identity was entirely legitimate[4], and no one knew the wiser. If I recall correctly, I never did pay the traffic fine.

In March 1996, I was out drinking Boone's Farm with my friends. I loaded them up into the back of my truck and was driving like a little maniac. In doing a J turn[5], I wound up flipping the truck

---

4   Well, other than the fact I committed a crime to get it…

5   A "J-turn" is where you drive in reverse very fast, cut the wheel and flip the front around to drive the other way. My dad taught me that maneuver during my driving lessons. You know, you never know when you will need some maneuver like that in your everyday driving.

in the parking lot of the community pool where my dad lived. I was scared to death at first, hoping I didn't kill anyone. Thank god no one was seriously hurt, although some chick who was with us broke her arm. We all flipped my truck back over on the wheels, and I got out of there. It was an incredibly stupid thing to do.

I drove to the end of my dad's neighborhood, a T-shaped intersection. I looked left and saw lights from the police cars and ambulances coming. I made a right and went the opposite direction until they turned into the neighborhood. After they had driven past, I turned around and drove the smashed heap of metal to my friend's repair shop. Oh yeah, the truck was completely fucked. I crushed the roof, and it looked like I participated in a demolition derby.

I left the mangled truck parked behind my buddy's body shop and cut through some fields back to my dad's place, navigating my way stealthily up the canals to avoid detection. When I reached home, I snuck in the back door, went into my bathroom and looked; my forehead was bleeding from the small shards of broken glass embedded in my skin. I picked out the glass and took a shower. When I stopped the water, I could hear my dad in the living room talking to someone - the police. After the cops left, I went into the living room to talk to my dad. We ended up arguing about it all, but I couldn't blame him for being pissed.

Luckily for me, Boynton Beach Police Department didn't do any follow-up investigation. My neighbor had the identical make, model and color truck and the cops thought it was the vehicle that had been in the accident. Since there was no damage on it at all, they just said "fuck it" and left.

Ford Finance company called me after a few months, complaining I hadn't made my payments for the truck. They wanted to come to repossess it. I told them it was at a body shop, where it had been there for a few months because it had been in a severe crash. The collector asked why I hadn't let them know about the accident, and asked if my insurance was going to fix it. I told him I never bothered getting insurance... I can still hear him screaming over the phone. "You didn't have insurance? Do you know what this is going to do to your life? You are finished. We are going to sue you blind!"

I just laughed and began taunting him to the point that he told me to fuck off, slamming down the phone. While it was at my buddy's body shop, it was racking up storage fees. The total sum of the charges were far higher than what the now-crunched vehicle was worth on paper, so the finance company just gave it to them. They fixed it for a thousand bucks or so and sold it for a nice profit.

A month later, when knew my life wasn't going anywhere, I decided to try and fix my real driver's license. I still had many legal troubles from that wreck when I was 16, running from the police, not having a driver's license and driving with a suspended license, and the judge was going to give me ten days in jail. I went to court and told the judge if we were to put me in jail, I would be unable to join the Marine Corps. The judge said, "You want to join the Marine Corps, young man?"

"Yes sir," I replied.

"Well, boot camp is worse than any jail, and it might just be good for you. I'll tell you what, I will drop the charges if you promise me you will join the Marine Corps."

And the judge did; he dismissed the charges on my word I would join. By the way, I always wanted to thank the judge for that, and I even tried to find him several years later, but to no avail. A few weeks later I got my real driver's license reinstated. I dropped the driver's license of Mark Patrick O'Dugan into the sewer and never spoke about it again.

I can hear Gauger telling all his two friends and contacts at the media what a terrible little criminal I was, and maybe he's right. I'm not going to deny that a hooligan I was as a kid and young adult, but I grew out of it. With a little guidance, I pulled myself out and straightened up my life. Gauger, on the other hand, is a crooked cop that serves as an officer of a for-profit probation corporation, a scam responsible for extorting fees and money from countless indigent people, putting them in jail when they can't pay. People like Gauger are worse than the most unsavory of criminals. It makes me sad that I don't believe in a heaven or a hell; if I did, I would be comforted by the fact Gauger - as well as most other law-enforcement leadership - would be going to the latter.

I left for Marine Corps boot camp a month later as a member of the infantry. After boot camp, Kelly and I spent every day together during my 10-day leave period between boot camp and my primary MOS school. Wouldn't know it, but she got pregnant. We discussed it and she decided to have an abortion. We were young and afraid of raising a child.

Looking back on it, it's one of my few regrets in life. I am pretty much an atheist, and as such. I view the miracle of life to be much more powerful than of being created from some god somewhere. After seeing my beautiful babies, I always think back and ask, "Who would he or she be?" it's a very haunting question for me. I don't ever wish for my children to suffer this torment and I would urge them to consider their options and know that things happen. Sometimes these things are not ideal, but nevertheless, we can deal with the cards we are given.

My primary MOS was DRAGON[6] missile gunner and demolitions. You know, blowing up bridges, making improvised explosive devices, all that awesomely cool stuff. People knew I had a very high ASFAB score and word quickly spread that I was good with computers, so I wound up working with the Company Clerk as the Training NCO.

I wrote the Marine Corps' first digital morning roster database program in MS Access to keep track of Marines that were present, sick, or AWOL (Absent Without Leave). It was also very convenient to keep all their personal, emergency and other information that the company office could access with a few mouse clicks. The database was a hit, and I gave the program to several other company clerks, and no doubt they passed it along, as well. It would reduce the morning count from several hours to just a few minutes as all the defaults were set and only a few moments were needed to make changes. Me and the company clerk, Joel Dudley, became best friends and were always causing some problem or another. Usually, it was in the form of waking up late and not having our room ready for inspection.

I spent my last year in the Marine Corps competing on the Marine Corps Rifle and Pistol team, finishing in the top ten for both rifle and pistol for my entire division. I received an Honorable Discharge at the end of 1999. I was married to Kelly in 1997, so I decided to go home to Florida and live as a husband and wife should.

When Kelly and I first met, she was working for two of the top criminal defense attorneys in Florida, and we always had heated

---

6   The Dragon was a shoulder-fired wire-guided piece of garbage missile system that would break the wire and malfunction frequently, flying uncontrollably before impacting wherever and detonating

debates about the merits of the legal system. To her, her clients were victims of the police, who would lie to put them in jail. I always believed this to be liberal bullshit, until I later became a police officer and saw it firsthand. As usual, she was right. Not only was she right, but it's an epidemic.

After being discharged from the Marine Corps, I was incredibly bored, living with a wife whom I had never lived. It was a culture shock. Kelly was pretty lazy about cooking, her idea of a good meal being Burger Helper or Mac and Cheese, or something along those lines. And god, she was an awful cook. If I wanted a good meal, it was up to me to make one. I'm not knocking her – some people aren't good at math. Some aren't good at mechanics. She just happened to be a lousy cook. Also, she wasn't exactly an extrovert. Okay, she was downright boring. But I still loved her.

To combat my boredom, I started a horse-shipping company. I was shipping horses for some of the biggest names in the Hunter-Jumper and Dressage world. People like Norman Dello Joio, Margie Goldstein, Tara Stegan… I had one lady pay me $10,000 to go pick up her horse from the quarantine station in New York on New Year's Eve 1999 because she was worried the Y2K bug was going to crash all the computers and leave her horse stranded at the quarantine station. After a few years, I got tired of shipping horses, and so I decided to do what all sons of former drug smugglers do; I became a cop. It was quite the family joke; that I followed my dad's career path up until the Marine Corps until I drastically veered off course.

And why not? At the time, my wife was working for the Palm Beach County Public Defender's Office – as the assistant to the elected Public Defender. I decided I was going to get the bad guys off the streets and send them to her office. I thought she would cringe at the idea, but she has always been very good at supporting my rational decisions (though not so much the irrational ones). And even though we had a small amount of money, she came up with enough to send me to the Police Academy. Kelly was always loving and supportive in that way.

Chapter 4 - A New Cop in a Dirty Town

I went to the Indian River Police Academy where I was made the 1st squad leader. The police academy was a complete joke, and I firmly believe anyone with a little common sense and a sense of morality could go through it in a week. If they can't, there's no reason they should be a cop. You don't teach ethics to people… people are either ethical, or they are not. Anyway, at the end of the academy, there was one afternoon of academic testing and the next afternoon, physical fitness testing.

I decided to have a good meal before the educational testing, so my cadet friends and I went to the local buffet and gorged ourselves into a stupor. You can imagine our surprise when we returned from lunch, and they decided to switch the days of testing for whatever reason. We had to run three miles right after eating. Still, I came in second place in the three-mile run; the other Marine in the class (Brent Winneka) and I decimated everyone else by several minutes (although Brent still kicked my ass by a good 30 seconds). I didn't vomit, but I wanted to. Many of the other cadets did.

I was the "top shooter" of the class, not just that class, but every class that had ever gone through the police academy. I never missed a shot. Ever. I know I am bragging a little, but it's true, not many people in the world could shoot better than I could when I was in my prime. And they still can't.

After the police academy, I joined the Mangonia Park Police Department. Mangonia Park was this little run-down shithole of 1400 people, about 800 of them convicted felons. The demographics were 90% black and about 10% Hispanic - mostly Guatemalan. We used to call them GTMs – Guatemalan Teller Machines because they would get drunk on payday and get robbed by the black people in town. There was one white man who lived in the city, but he bought that home in the 1950's when Mangonia Park was an upscale white neighborhood.

The town, whose area was only one square mile, was rife with crime. Drugs were a huge factor. And the culprits? Most were the relatives of the mayor and city councilmen. We had one black police officer (other than the Police Chief), Dalmino Simmons. He's a twin, so we all just called him Twin.

Twin had been working there for a few years when I got there, and frankly speaking, he was one of the best cops who taught me a lot, and we became best friends. Every other cop that wasn't a sergeant was either scared of his shadow, scared of liability or just didn't want to write any reports. My Field Training Officer's name was Sgt. Luis Colon, an extremely funny short little Puerto Rican who was a contradiction. On the one hand, he hated any paperwork, but on the other, he was a very skilled cop who knew how to find trouble and man, could he run!

I am a pretty fast runner, a good ten years younger than Luis. I have longer legs than Luis, and I am a few inches taller than he. One day, we went chasing a drug dealer… I was hot on the guy's heels, but that crazy Puerto Rican blew right by me and tackled the guy. It was terrific; I would have never known Luis had that kind of speed in him.

During the training portion of my employment, I was terrible at hearing the radio. To this day, I still can't quite figure out why. Maybe hearing loss from shooting missiles and blowing stuff up in the Marine Corps, or perhaps I wasn't paying attention. And each Field Training Officer had his own trainee. Sgt. John Shaver. Shaver initially hated me and used to look for reasons to be a dick. I think it was because he viewed me and his own trainee, Fred Chidsey, as competition.

Chidsey and I were soon released from the FTO program and were fully-fledged road cops. When that happened, I was making arrest after arrest of bad guys, getting into foot chases, and never backing down from a fight with the worst people. Chidsey was lazy as hell, and it drove Sgt. Shaver nuts. Nevertheless, it surprised me when Det. Sperbeck was giving me some shit about violating the chief's order about not arresting the drug dealers, only to have Sgt. Shaver come to my defense. Sgt. Shaver told Det. Sperbeck to keep his nose the hell out of out of road-patrol business.

After that incident, John and I became fast friends. Another unusual thing about John that I liked, he always treated the bad guys with respect. Most cops don't do that. They look down their noses at everyone and treat them like street trash from the very beginning. But not John. Shaver was a thoughtful guy, an upstanding cop, and would give the drug dealers respect, as long as they returned the respect. He would arrest them and still treat them like human beings, and not animals unless they acted like animals. Out of all the police officers I know, he is one of three that I thought were very decent cops from whom I wanted to learn.

Best of all, Sgt. John Shaver wasn't scared of the police chief, Chief Rodney Thomas. Chief Thomas would give the order to stay away from the Dixie Fried Chicken or park in the parking lot and do nothing, so the children of the mayor and town council could deal their drugs. Sgt. Shaver didn't care, and we would arrest them anyways.

Every time we would make an arrest, Chief Rodney Thomas would be on the phone with the mayor, apologizing and kissing his ass. It was quite pathetic to see a grown man with no pride, no backbone and no intelligence trying so hard to suck off the mayor so he could keep his position.

The way I saw it, black people fought and overcame so much for their freedom and rights in the last hundred years only to have a puppet like Rodney Thomas act like a slave to his masters. It's probably a good thing Thomas didn't have enough pride to feel humiliated.

A little history on the issue – when the previous chief resigned, the mayor appointed then-sergeant Rodney Thomas at the police chief because he was the only black officer at the time, despite the fact Thomas severely lacked intelligence or common sense. The mayor thought it would bring the community together. That's not me saying it – Thomas himself would tell it to the department.

The kids of the mayor and town council, along with their friends, would always sell drugs in front of the Dixie Fried Chicken. We would arrest them regularly, and at the town council meetings, the chief would get threatened to lose his job. The mayor and town council members were all sick of us arresting their kids. It wasn't like making an arrest made a dent in drug sales; you would capture them one day and the very next day they would be selling drugs in the same place. They were also worried that rival drug dealers were going to gun down their kids. To prevent such a "travesty," Chief Thomas sent out a standing order that we were to park in the parking lot of the Dixie Fried Chicken and not make any arrests for drug sales.

As a brand new officer, it was a lesson in humiliation, because the drug dealers were slinging crack and heroin in front of us like we were their protection. After a few weeks of doing that shitty assignment, I said fuck it, got out of my car and arrested some piece of crap drug dealer that I chased for ten minutes on foot. The game was on after that, and there was no stopping us.

Twin and I started doing sneaky foot patrols, going up behind buildings and whatnot. One of us would park at Channel 12, cut through the woods, and watch for transactions and would give the information over the phone to the other one, who would sneak up behind the Dixie Fried Chicken and make an arrest. Sometimes I would wear my ghillie suit to do surveillance. We were defying the Chief's orders, but we didn't care. We weren't going to be anyone's drug protection. When the Chief realized he was going to have a mutiny on his hands, he backed off and was forced to tell the town council there was nothing he could do; that the law was the law. And the town council? They were pissed.

Not only was Chief Thomas a dirty cop, but he was a wife beater. One day, I was sitting at the Mangonia Park Police Station when cops from the Riviera Beach Police Department knocked on the door. They were looking to arrest Chief Thomas for punching his wife in the face. The chief knew the cops wanted him and that they would come looking, so he didn't bother coming to work for several days. He called the on-duty supervisor and told him to cover for him. He remained in hiding for a few days, until his wife cooled down and recanted her story of domestic abuse. The chief was a moron. Captain Nicholson (Captain Nickelback, we used to call him, because he was notorious for kicking back reports for the slightest mistakes) was pretty much a good guy when he wasn't micromanaging. He was in line to be police chief, but got passed over by the town council in favor of Thomas – the town council wanted a black police chief, no matter how inexperienced or moronic, simply appease the people.

After two back-to-back hurricanes, there was a curfew in Palm Beach County. I was standing in the office with Capt. Nicholson; there were a total of four people on duty, and Chief Thomas wanted us to direct traffic at major intersections. After Thomas barked his orders out over the radio, Nicholson said, "Uh, Chief, that's going to require a minimum of 12 people. We only have four." To which Thomas replied, "Exactly. Get it done."

I am not sure what Thomas was expecting. Maybe he wanted us to go out and hire some of the town felons to direct traffic. Perhaps he wanted us to be in three places at one time. Nickleson and I gave each other a WTF look, and then we completely ignored the impossible order given by Thomas.

When working in Mangonia Park, I saw first hand what drugs and AIDS did to people. There was a family that lived there, a mother, father, and their 18-year-old daughter. They all had AIDS; all were heroin users. The mother and father used to pimp out her daughter to get drugs, and after talking to the daughter, I had found she was being pimped out for drugs when she was younger than 15. It was one of the most terrible things I had ever heard.

Out of all the incompetent people working at Mangonia Park, the biggest was Sperbeck. He was the department "Detective" that I don't think ever successfully caught even one criminal because of his "investigations." He was a pretty smart guy, very knowledgeable about the law, but would criticize any arrest of which he wasn't a part. Sperbeck was incredibly jealous of Twin and me because we made arrest after arrest for all types of crimes and he was incapable or arresting anyone. So when he wasn't spending time blowing off investigations in his office, he spent his time trying to burn other cops who were trying to make a difference in the community.

Seriously – he would try to investigate Twin and me on a regular basis. He even began an investigation on me for pulling out my Taser on a passenger that jumped out on a traffic stop. I wrote the guy a seat belt ticket, but Sperbeck spent months trying to find something.

He even wrote the manufacturer of the truck to see if that year truck came equipped with seatbelts. When the Internal Affairs interview came around, Sperbeck had my attorney and me in the conference room for eight hours. He was trying to get me to trip up on why I wrote the guy a ticket. The interview process was so disgraceful, my attorney, Garry Lippman, told the chief he was going to sue the department for harassment. At that point, the chief grew some balls and told Sperbeck to knock it off.

Poor Sperbeck – he was always trying to get in on our sting operations, but he was so annoying, so idiotic about things, we would plan any activities when he wasn't working, or when he wasn't available. No one wanted to be involved with the guy because he was toxic to teamwork.

Still, being a cop could be fun and was always interesting. There was some guy who had a dirt bike, and man, he was probably one of the best riders I had ever seen. He taunted us mercilessly, doing wheelies past us and running from us when we chased him.

One day, however, his luck ran out. Sgt. Marinuzzi[7] and I were walking through a parking lot near where the drug dealers would hang out; this guy saw us walking, started up his bike and started doing donuts around us. He began to do wheelies past us… and the bike stopped. The damned fool forgot to turn on the fuel petcock, and it ran out of gas. He jumped off the bike and started running away, but I tasered him, and he dropped to the ground like a 200-pound sack of wet diapers.

Probably the funniest thing that ever happened while being a cop came when I was doing surveillance across the street from the drug dealers. At the end of the day, the DEA was jumping out on the drug dealers. I was wearing a ghillie suit and covered in camouflage face paint. My job was to monitor their actions, tell the jump-out teams what direction to come in from and to coordinate the units in making their approach.

There were about ten drug dealers in front of the Dixie Fried Chicken when the unmarked DEA vans rolled up, and the agents jumped out. It was complete chaos; drug dealers running in every direction. One drug dealer got away from the agents and ran across the street into the woods where I was hiding. As he approached my location, I jumped up, blocking his path. He was utterly terrified – I am sure he wasn't expecting the forest to become alive like a scene from a Predator movie. He let out this blood-curdling scream and passed out as a grabbed him. When he fell to the ground, I handcuffed him and let the DEA know to send a van over to pick him up.

---

[7] Marinuzzi's fellow officers called him "Sgt. Liability" because he was petrified of getting sued. Women had a different name for him. They called him "Sgt. Horsecock" or "Dino the Impaler"; you can probably guess why.

A white van arrived, and I loaded the drug dealer inside the back. I climbed into the passenger seat, and we began riding back to the station. A smell hit us – the DEA agent driving the van looked at me and asked, "Jesus Christ, did you fart?"

"Oh god no," I responded in disgust, "I was just going to ask you if it was you." I turned to the drug dealer in the back of the van and asked, "Hey man, did you fart?"

He looked at me with indignation and mumbled, "Man, I didn't fucking fart."

We pulled in to the Mangonia Park police station and brought the prisoner inside. The agent put him against the wall and pulled down his pants to make sure he wasn't hiding any drugs inside, and that's when the real smell hit… I began laughing hysterically because literally, I made the drug dealer shit his pants!

The most bizarre incident? There was a bum who was huffing lacquer thinner in his tent in the woods to get high, and at the same time, he was masturbating. Yeah, but that's not the only thing he was doing – he was also smoking a cigarette. For those who have worked with lacquer thinner, you probably know how explosive the vapors are. And for you that haven't, well, now you know.

Someone had called in to say there was a fire in the woods. The raging fire, fueled by a five-gallon can of lacquer, wholly incinerated the cloth of the tent. When I arrived, I saw his corpse smoldering in the middle of the burning field. That bum exploded from the inside out and died while holding his willie.

Chapter 5 - Palm Beach County Sheriff's Office

I left the tiny, 12-man department of Mangonia Park for the Palm Beach County Sheriff's Office, a 4,000 person agency I thought would be a better change. And in some ways, it was. But in other ways, it indeed wasn't. For one, they were stuck in 1976, technology-wise. Literally – I was riding in a car with a terminal purchased for them in 1976. To put it mildly, their technology was horrifying. Deputies were writing probable cause affidavits and log entries by hand. I went out and bought my own laptop and portable printer because I can't stand writing.

But the patrol area was massive compared to Mangonia Park which meant you didn't have supervisors breathing down your neck. And the training, it was much better. Still, I learned that in a typical police agency, such as the Palm Beach County Sheriff's Office, they stuff the ranks with liars, cheats, and criminals. Not everyone mind you; I mean about twenty percent. Still, that's enough to have a bad apple or two in every squad, if not more. The majority of the department who were good cops always knew who to stay away from and did their best to do just that.

> *"Wherever the topic of police brutality comes up, people always say, 'it's just a case of a few bad apples.' But the expression is not 'a few bad apples are really annoying,' or 'one bad apples make the others look bad.' It's 'one bad apple SPOILS the bunch.' That's why farmers get rid of bad apples. They don't defend bad apples. They don't give bad apples promotions. They don't let bad apples take early retirement with full pensions. They throw them out to protect the good ones. If police departments want the respect of the public, they have to earn it by showing us they actually care about their product. Until then, it's perfectly reasonable to assume the whole barrel is spoiled and the farmer doesn't care." -- Jeremy McLellan*

The worst part of the problem is, not only do all the senior supervisors and administrators know about the bad apples, but for the most part, they cover for them.

During my tenure at the Palm Beach County Sheriff's Office, I was on the PBSO Honor guard, having been hand-picked from thousands of deputies. I was also the road patrol liaison to the technology department and was supposed to provide feedback to the software company that was implementing the new in-car computers. After a few months, however, I quit that assignment. The Sheriff's Office was paying several millions of dollars for a computer system developed for the Charlotte, NC police department and they refused to tailor it for the needs of the Palm Beach County Sheriff's Office. They expected to change a few fields and workflow models to bilk millions from PBSO in the name of annual licenses. I told the IT department it was a disgusting sham and whoever hired them was not only a disgrace to PBSO, but should be fired.

Working on the road, I could always find trouble at PBSO, and it was usually always interesting. Getting into car and foot chases became a weekly routine. One day, I chased this neo-Nazi asshole who had just burglarized a house. While he was fleeing from me, this skin-headed genius jumped a big fucking chain-link fence. That chain link fence happened to be preventing two extremely nasty pit bulls from leaving the yard and eating people. When that guy got to the other side and made it over the fence, and it was a miracle that he did, he looked like a bloody chew toy with flaps of skin hanging off him everywhere.

The Palm Beach County Sheriff's Office eventually absorbed the Mangonia Park Police Department. Chief Rodney Thomas was demoted to a lieutenant. Lt. Thomas' blowing the mayor and town council got even worse. Thomas was still an ass-kissing piece of crap who would lie about his fellow cops to appease the Mangonia Park leadership so they would insist on PBSO keeping him there.

One sunny day, I arrested the town's most prominent drug dealer. I fought with the guy for several minutes, rolling around with him on the ground, and finally was able to arrest him thanks to the help of a passing good Samaritan who worked in the city's industrial zone. I handcuffed the criminal and went to put him in the back of my car.

Lt. Thomas came to the scene, telling him to sit down in the back of the car. I was later called to the office because I had been written up for insubordination. Lt. Thomas had written a complaint to Internal Affairs that he ordered me to stop trying to push the drug dealer into the car. He said I slammed the guy's leg in the door after refusing to obey his orders, claiming I was insubordinate.

Luckily, I had my own video recording with audio, proving Lt. Thomas was a lying sack of dogshit. The video demonstrated I was quite polite and reasonable with the suspect. Lt. Thomas was trying to have me suspended for insubordination by lying, an offense for which Thomas could have, and should have, been fired. Did Thomas get into trouble for it? Not really, but luckily, Lieutenant Carris, who was doing the investigation, wrote, "There are two versions of what happened here, Lieutenant Thomas' version and then the version that actually happened." Maybe Thomas didn't get fired, but at least the other guys knew what a lying slimeball he is. To this day, I think Thomas was probably on the Mangonia Park drug dealers' payroll.

In police work, like at the Palm Beach County Sheriff's Office, it wasn't just the criminals you had to watch. There was lots of backstabbing happening, and the detectives loved stealing the credit from the road patrol guys. For example:

On June 16, 2006, I responded to a report of a burglary in Loxahatchee, and during a canvass of the neighborhood, someone told me one of the nearby neighbors who had just moved into the home with his grandmother and he was acting strange, going out at all hours of the night to meet with cars that would stop and leave. I decided to knock on the guy's door and ask him a few questions.

The door was answered by his grandmother, who said her grandson, Michael Vaneron, was out but was going to be home any moment. I told her about the concerns of other neighbors, and she told me he had all sorts of new property but didn't have a job. Vaneron also had a drug problem. Vaneron came home, and I said I wanted to talk to him. I patted him down for officer safety purposes, and there was a heroin needle in his pocket. I arrested him and found a pawn receipt for an Apple iPod. The serial number on the iPod wasn't listed as stolen, but I called the Apple store and got the name of the owner. The owner of the iPod was just a victim of a robbery a few weeks prior.

Over the course of a week, I took my four days off, and I spent them in the Wellington substation, researching every burglary that happened in the area within the last few months. Without any confession from Vaneron, I was able to link dozens of burglaries to him and his friend.

I arrested Vaneron on my Friday, and over the next four days, I spent the time in the Wellington substation reading hundreds of police reports, making calls, following up on leads and such. There were over fifty burglaries that the detective bureau was incapable of solving, but I handed everything to them on a silver platter. The investigation. The name of his accomplice. The research linking a bunch of burglaries together. The only thing that the detectives had to do after that was to match up the recovered property with the rightful owners and file a few more pieces of paper with the courts to charge the suspects.

The Sheriff's Office, those cheap motherfuckers didn't even want to pay my overtime for all the work I did to link all the burglaries, so you can probably imagine my surprise when I walked in one day to Detective Cassie Kovacs getting Deputy of the Year for "solving" those burglaries.

I don't know who was worse; her supervisor, Sgt. Matlack, for writing her such a glowing bullshit commendation to make his department look good, or Kovacs, who knowingly took credit for work that wasn't hers. Either way, I was pretty pissed off about the entire thing. That incident was a good indicator of the dishonesty taking place within the ranks but was only the tip of the iceberg.

Chapter 6 - The Deputy Howard Howell Incident

But the biggest problem at PBSO is that they have some bad apples. Unfortunately, more-often-than-not, the agency would cover for the bad apples to shield the Sheriff from liability or for political reasons. One such incident was in 2007, where a deputy named Howard Howell was DJ'ing a party. The music was so loud, a neighbor half a mile away made the complaint.

Dispatch asked us to go to the home where the loud music was located and ask them to turn it down. I had a police explorer with me, Adam Avey, an ambitious kid who was very determined to become a cop (he's currently a Sergeant with the Sheriff's Office – CONGRATULATIONS!). My zone partner, Deputy Matthew Wood, met me in the driveway of the house from where the music was coming. We heard Two Live Crew playing - I liked Two Live Crew from my childhood – but this was so loud, I could hardly hear Wood talking to me when we met.

The homeowner, a smiling lady, greeted the three of us at the front gate. She knew the music was much too loud. I told her in a jovial tone that if I weren't on duty, I would probably be at the party also, but since I was working, I had to ask the DJ to turn it down a bit. Anyone who knows me knows I love a good party, and there was complete truth to my statement.

As I was talking to the homeowner, Deputy Wood started up the walkway to the backyard to ask the DJ to lower the music. The DJ, as we found out later, was an off-duty deputy named Howard Howell. He was dressed like any ordinary citizen would be dressed.

Now, at the time, I had no idea who Deputy Howard Howell was, but deputy or not, these kinds of calls are usually very standard. A deputy shows up, the music gets turned down, and we leave, happy to help the public. Sometimes the music gets turned up after we clear the call, and we have to go back and "remind" the people that it's too loud. It's done by almost every deputy dozens of times every year. But no such thing took place.

Just a little side note here… Some cops, generally the bad ones and regardless of the color of their skin, think the law doesn't apply to them when they get a badge. Howard Howell was one of them. He was a black deputy that had a history of race-baiting white police officers with some of his friends. Howell and his group of police friends got off on putting themselves in suspicious circumstances to make white cops question them or act so that they could scream racism.

This isn't to say it's a black cop thing – it's not. Some of the best cops I know are black, Dalmino Simmons. Danta Manuel was another – they would have never pulled that shit. No, it's not a black cop thing. It's an asshole cop thing. I just wanted to be clear on that before some white supremacist cop asshole starts praising my statements as being in favor of white cops.

One of Howell's friends that were present at the party, a Palm Beach County Sheriff's Office corporal named Clinton Cohen, was watering his lawn in the middle of drought restrictions. When the neighbors called the police, and the police went to his house, they told Cohen he was setting a bad example by violating the law, thumbing his nose at his neighbors, with a Sheriff's patrol car parked out front.

A good cop, no matter the color of his skin, would have been embarrassed. But did Clinton Cohen say he was sorry for setting a bad example? No, he told the officers they were picking on him because he was black. Then slammed the door in their faces.

Another one of Howell's friends that happened to be there was a deputy everyone used to call Shaq (short for Shaheed). Shaq and his fellow deputies on the task force used to sit in an unmarked car near burglar alarms so that they would get stopped and questioned by cops "because they were black."

To this day, I can't understand the point of trying to stoke racial tension between cops in police work. White cop, black cop – everyone should just be trying to do their work, and shouldn't be making the job any harder for one another. Anyway, back to the DJ story…

The homeowner and I walked up the path to the DJ booth where Deputy Wood had gone and was talking to the DJ, who was spinning the records. One thing I can say for Howell, he was doing a hell of a job as a DJ. Howell was yelling at Wood with a very aggressive look on his face. Now, the music was indeed loud, but if a cop shows up, it's not that hard to turn down the music to hold a normal conversation.

As I got closer to Deputy Wood, the DJ, who never identified himself as a deputy, told deputy Wood to fuck off. I saw the DJ's fists balled up and he was leaning forward. "This is going to be bad," I thought to myself. Deputy Wood was new on the job, and I was sure he was about to get punched by Howell.

I am five foot seven inches (172cm) and weigh about 165 pounds (74kg). Wood was a few inches taller than I am but had a more lithe, slim build. Perhaps 155lbs? Howell, in contrast, stands over 6 foot tall and weighs over 240 pounds. Had Howell punched Wood, it wouldn't have been pretty. And that was my fear.

I got involved in diffusing the situation, telling Howell, "Look, man, we are just asking you to turn the music down." Howell leaned forward like he was going to strike me with his fists, so I pepper sprayed him.

Maybe he was drunk (he was), but only after he got hosed with pepper spray did any of the other off-duty deputies, like Cohen or Shaq, step forward to tell us Howell was a deputy. That's right – my off-duty colleagues sat back thinking the entire incident was hilarious. At that point though, it didn't matter. We were trying to do our jobs and get the music turned down quickly so we could eat but when you start those kinds of problems, and it turns into a physical altercation, being a deputy isn't going to save you. Also was the fact a deputy would act so horrendously was a complete surprise to both Wood and me.

But the crazy situation didn't end there. Cpl. Cohen, Shaq and several other people at the party blocked us from getting to Howell. Cpl. Cohen took on his supervisory role, preventing us. "Get your sergeant on the phone, now!" The music was still insanely loud, so he and I walked down to the front of the property to contact the supervisor, Sgt. Porath.

While I was talking to the sergeant on the phone and explaining what had happened, Deputy Wood, who was standing near the house, shouted something about a gun. As I looked up, I saw a crowd of people behind Howard Howell, who was about five meters from Deputy Wood, his hand outstretched towards Wood. There was something in his hand, though I was too far away to say it as a firearm definitively. As I began to run towards Wood, several people grabbed Howell and dragged him into the house.

Deputy Wood came towards me, still holding his pistol and visibly shaken. "Howell came out of the house and shouted 'I'm going to kill Dougan.' He pulled a gun on me!"

While I didn't get a good look to say it was a gun in Howell's hand because of the lighting and distance, I saw… something. And Deputy Wood, who spent five years in the US Army protecting a general, would have undoubtedly known if Howell was holding a pistol. For this, I have absolutely no reason to believe Howell was holding something else other than his gun.

A short time later, the place was swarming with detectives from Internal Affairs, captains and others. Deputy Shaq had hauled ass before anyone arrived. Detectives contacted Shaq and ask him where he was, and he said he went home. The Captain who came to the scene ordered Shaq back to return, but he didn't make it back for several hours, despite his home being a mere five minutes away. During that time, investigators were unable to locate Howell's service weapon. The speculation was that Deputy Shaq took off with it and hid it, so Howell would be able to deny there was a gun.

I arrested Deputy Howell, and Internal Affairs towed his patrol car. During a search of Howell's police cruiser, Internal Affairs found an unauthorized pistol in his trunk, a cheap pistol. These types of weapons also known as a "throw-down" gun and bad cops use them to plant on unarmed people they shoot.

After the jail released Howell, he was ordered to turn in his duty weapon. He brought it to Internal Affairs; the handgun had been wiped clean of fingerprints. However, there was Howell's DNA on the duty weapon, along with the DNA from a second, unknown source. The source was believed to be from Shaq, but he refused to provide his DNA for comparison, and the Sheriff's Office didn't feel like getting a warrant.

By now, you are probably wondering if Howell was fired. Of course not! Sheriff Bradshaw had just been successfully sued for one million dollars from a black employee. The employee rightfully alleged discrimination where black officers were disciplined more heavily than their white counterparts. Not wanting to look like they were harsh on Howell, they reduced his punishment to two days of suspension and Anger Management classes. And since the paperwork just sat on the Captain's desk for 180 days, Howell didn't have any disciplinary action at all.

Naturally, when Howell later sued the Sheriff's Office for being pepper sprayed and wrongful arrest, he told the jury he didn't even get reprimanded or disciplined for the incident. During the trial, I was positively shocked at what never made it into evidence or to the jury's hands.

The original statement given by the homeowner said I was smiling and pleasantly conversing with her – but for the trial, she changed her account to say I was hostile on arrival. The PBSO attorney never played those recordings for the jury.

The homeowner's husband? Initially, he gave a statement that he had to drag Howell away by force because he was violent. But the day of the trial, he never showed up, despite his subpoena. The PBSO attorney decided not to bother without such a crucial witness. Shaq, the detective from OCB? Well, he was in prison during the trial because he got caught using his PBSO uniform to illegally evict people from their foreclosure homes and renting those homes out to people on Craigslist. The jury never heard that, either.

I wholeheartedly believe the jury felt at least a little sorry for Howell and awarded him $275,000. It was a pity the jury wasn't allowed to read the Internal Affairs report on the incident because they would have been horrified. If you are interested in reading the Howard Howell Internal Affairs report, it's in the document section of PBSOTalk.

Chapter 7 - Blowing the Whistle

Before, I mentioned Sgt. Brent Raban, who was running around beating minorities; it was such a disgusting situation. One day, I was forced to use my baton on a guy, and I whacked him so hard in the stomach, he fell to the ground. I felt terrible even though I was entirely justified.

Sgt. Raban came up to me and said, "Good job, Dougan. That's what we like to see." And then he invited me to hang out with him and his crew, an invitation I decided to ignore. I declined because Raban was running around with his team beating the tar out of people. The worst part is, people higher up in the chain of command knew about it and ignored it.

The Lieutenant in the district, Lt. Reilly, was a real piece of shit and let them do whatever they wanted. Lt. Reilly was placed in Belle Glade as punishment for getting caught committing fraud or embezzlement, by selling overtime details, or some shit like that from the Palm Beach County Sheriff's Office. Knowing what I know now, I see why they only transferred him; as it turns out, the Sheriff was openly defrauding PBSO also. Maybe he was punished for cheating PBSO and not giving the Sheriff a cut.

Oh yes, back to Sgt. Raban. He and his subordinates would openly brag in the lineup about who they had beaten the previous night and talk about how to find people to beat on the current night. Without thought of consequence or common sense, Raban and his crew would take photos of who they had beaten and post them to Facebook, where they would make comments about them falling down the stairs and other egregious statements.

Sgt. Raban and his group of guys would regularly show up to work out of uniform, instead of wearing tactical gear and a knit cap that had the word "Punishment" written on it. Sgt. Raban would be at calls with Lt. Reilly, who would completely ignore the breach of protocol. Still, to this day, I don't know if Reilly liked the fact that Raban's crew was terrorizing the residents of Belle Glade, or if he was just such a lazy supervisor that he didn't want to get involved. It could have been both, though either one is inexcusable.

One day I got to a call where Sgt. Raban and his men were already on scene. They had a Hispanic guy sitting on a gravel driveway in handcuffs. As I got out of my car and started walking up, Raban yelled at the guy, "Don't fucking look at me!" He grabbed the man and slammed his face into the gravel leaving it quite scraped up. Raban told me to charge the guy with possession of a stolen firearm. The guy did, in fact, have a firearm in his car, and it was, in fact, stolen, but when I asked him where he got it from, he told me he bought it from a friend of his for $300. The price he told me at the time was reasonable, so I had no probable cause to charge him with possession of a stolen firearm as the elements of the crime were not present. Sure, I could have ignored that fact and charged him with it anyway, but that isn't the way our criminal justice system was designed to work.

Not only does it contribute to clogging up the system, but it places a burden on a man who may be innocent of the crime. Many cops have the wrong idea about police work. They think it's "Us vs. Them," that they are the first line of putting people in jail. They are wrong. Law Enforcement officers are supposed to be the first line of determining the truth, and if someone is possibly innocent, that needs to be taken into consideration.

It was enough that the man was going to jail for misdemeanor domestic battery, and I found it repulsive to throw a felony charge on the guy for circumstances that didn't warrant it.

I transported the suspect to the county jail but defied Sgt. Raban's order to charge him with the weapons felony. The jail asked me what happened to the suspect's face and demanded I fill out an injury report. Generally in such reports, cops write some shit like, "Suspect fell while fleeing" or "Suspect slipped on a Banana peel upon my arrival," but I wasn't going to lie for those guys. I didn't put into the injury report that Sgt. Raban beat the fuck out of him; that would have been career suicide. But I did state in a very roundabout way for anyone reading the report that it happened from Raban's actions or at least call me in to ask what happened. I also sent an email to an assistant public defender, T. Mahoney, the arrestee's lawyer, telling him his client had been brutalized (see appendix).

I finally had enough and knew that Raban was bad news, and I couldn't just sit on my hands and turn a blind eye. I knew it would likely be the end of my career, but there comes a time where a man must be a man and do what's right. It was a tough decision because I had a beautiful baby girl at this point. After considerable thought on the matter, I decided I've always been good at spitting in the eyes of authority… I might as well keep doing what I know best.

I took Raban's Facebook page where he and his friends were posting photos of their beatings and sent it anonymously to Internal Affairs. Internal Affairs, instead of doing anything to Raban, tracked the anonymous tip back to my father's company. They made my working life a living hell, starting internal investigations for anything they could find. They even investigated me for helping a pregnant lady remove a car seat from her car that was being repossessed. The reason? They claimed I violated policy by getting involved in a civil matter. I filled out my own Internal Affairs complaint regarding the retaliation, and they transferred me to another district.

I knew I had to resign, so I submitted my resignation and quit. Still, Internal Affairs at that point didn't do a damned thing to Brent Raban, so I send the Facebook postings and photographs I took of Sgt. Raban in his Punisher hat to the Palm Beach Post, who broke it in a story and forced the Sheriff's Office to start an investigation into Raban. Did Sgt. Raban get fired for it? Hell no! He was merely demoted a grade and transferred to another district. They tried to move him to Royal Palm Beach, but when the Royal Palm Beach mayor found out about it, he said "hell no!" and told the Sheriff he wasn't going to have Raban work in his town.

Ironically, Raban was eventually fired, but not for torturing minorities; they terminated him for being rude to a white woman by yelling at her over his patrol car's PA system.

I still had the frivolous Internal Affairs complaints lingering over my head. One complaint was from Sgt. Mack Coleman, who claimed I was insubordinate for refusing to return potentially stolen property (a fat bag of jewelry) back to a suspect. The suspect had told me he said he "found in the grass" the day after a Smash and Grab robbery of a jewelry store.

Sgt. Coleman told the investigator some bullshit lie to make his case for insubordination. Little did anyone know I had written a report on the entire incident and had an audio recording of it all. When I pulled out the recording, I played it for Lt. Reilly, who told me I didn't want to use the audio as it would open up a can of worms. I demanded it to put on the record despite his objections. To prevent a scandal, they couldn't close the investigations while I was working there and they knew I was leaving, so PBSO left all of the investigations open, and they remained open for over a year after I had left PBSO.

It was their final "fuck you" to me for ratting out their bunch of goons in green - they don't have to pay the money they owe you if there are pending Internal Affairs investigations.

I wrote PBSO's chain of command dozens of emails demanding the money, yet they always had some excuse about why the reviews were not closed, despite the PBSO policy that clearly states all investigations are to be closed within 90 days; and a law declaring that after 180 days, the probes are without consequence.

When the media finally got around to breaking the Raban story, I wrote PBSO a letter and told them I was planning on giving an interview to MSNBC about their retaliation for turning in Raban. They quickly sent me my money after that. By this time, I was working at the Windham Police Department in Maine.

The Sheriff and Chief Deputy Gauger are keen to claim that I was fired or was going to be fired from the Palm Beach County Sheriff's Office. He also tells people I was a substandard deputy. They were going to try and have me fired for being a whistleblower.

As far as being substandard, my arrest statistics were usually twice as high as the next closest deputy. I wrote my own program to manage all of my paperwork, and I bought my own printer for my patrol car, so it took a fraction of time to do the paperwork that other deputies would waste half of their shift completing. I worked on my days off, doing investigations and interviews, usually not asking for overtime. I solved a lot of cases that way, and my supervisors all recognized it. My dedication to doing the job, and doing it right earned me a lot of written letters of commendation from both civilians and my supervisors, but neither the Sheriff nor Chief Deputy Gauger will ever tell people that.

Nor will Chief Deputy Gauger admit to signing six of my letters of commendation, as well as my Deputy of the Month award for 2008.

In December 2008, right before I left the Sheriff's Office, my commander, Lt. Rich Burdick, stated:

> *"John's primary duties were patrol, but I also used him as one of my 'go to guys'... when something needed to be done I would go to his Sgt. and he would have John take care of it. When he was asked to do something, he would do it without question. His work was beyond satisfactory. John got along well with his Sgt. and co-workers, but with a large department, there are going to be personality conflicts. He was part of the team and a team player. He is a very honest person."*

Why don't they tell people about my many successes? Bradshaw and Gauger are liars; coverup artists. Telling the truth would be bad for their version of the story. Instead, they paint me as a disgruntled, angry man with an ax to grind. It's not true at all, but hey, if that's what makes them feel better, if that's what makes them sleep better at night, then I encourage them to continue. They are responsible for the public good, and I would hate for them to do it with little sleep; they would make even worse decisions than they do now.

Chapter 8 - Windham Maine

Everyone makes mistakes; bad decisions. Mine was moving to Windham, Maine and taking a police job there after I left the Palm Beach County Sheriff's Office.

I wouldn't exactly say it was like working with a bunch of inbreds, but Jesus Christ, they were some of the dumbest, most clueless people I've ever met. In fact, the cop bragging about having the highest aptitude test in the Windham police department scored a 52 on Maine's law enforcement aptitude test. I scored a 66. Though I don't know how the scoring works and no one could ever explain it to me, it's supposedly a logarithmic form of scoring, meaning the people at the Windham Police Department were dumber than a box of rocks.

The K9 sergeant told me the other cops were intimidated because I was intelligent. It seemed ridiculous, but hey… these weren't logical people.

When I got hired, the polygrapher, Gerard Brady, told Windham I was a perfect candidate. He told them if they were dumb enough to pass on me, to let him know so they could hire me at the Cumberland

County Sheriff's Office. I moved to Maine in January 2009 and went to work for Windham. I passed field training in just two weeks.

My evaluations had said things like:

"Dougan showed outstanding conflict resolution skills during a call regarding an unruly juvenile female. Dougan was able to get through to both the daughter and the mother and created a peaceful resolution."

and

"Dougan showed exemplary professionalism and patience in dealing with an intoxicated and distraught female at Wal-Mart. Dougan was able to talk to her and brought her from a hysterical state down to a level of calm where he was able to ascertain that she did not have the police or medical emergency, and arranged for a ride for her and her daughter from the store. Dougan continues to do an excellent job of adding narrative notes to all calls for service that require them."

and

"Dougan handled a residential burglary complaint demonstrating good officer safety, as well as exemplary customer service and investigatory skills. Dougan, after speaking to the homeowners, decided to tactically clear the building since the timeframe of the burglary was unknown. Dougan did an excellent job of clearing the home and then proceeded into the investigation."

And then just after a few short weeks, they waived the rest of my training, putting me on the road myself with this letter:

"…Mark's Officer safety skills were superb and he handled the subjects in a calm professional manner. In speaking with Officers' Andrews, Cote, and Cook, they made the following observations. Like I stated above his Officer

safety skills are excellent and are surpassed only by his smooth, professional demeanor with the public.

At this point in Mark's field training program, I do not see any reason why he should not be cleared for regular patrol activities."

And so I went on to road patrol. During this time, I was stuck working with the most dangerous cop I ever met, Danielle Cyr Nelson. Cyr was a 25-year-old petulant child who was keen to lie when she didn't get her way and was continually abusing good faith in dealing with the public. Not only that, but she routinely sloughed off work to sleep on duty in the firehouse or spend all night inside the dispatch area when her boyfriend was working.

To make matters even worse, she was a complete officer-safety disaster which was going to get someone killed, pulling right up in front of alarms and walking around checking structures with her hands in her pockets. I wrote several letters explaining what a dangerous liability she was, so one day she decided the best way to get rid of me was to claim sexual harassment. She, her sister and her dispatcher friends made up a bunch of ridiculous allegations, so ridiculous, they alleged my "harassment" started a full five months before I even lived in the state.

I was a probationary officer, so the police chief decided it was easiest to fire me, despite recordings and other evidence I had that showed they were, in fact, lying their asses off. It didn't help that PBSO's Chief Deputy Gauger, who was pissed off that I send the Brent Raban photographs to the media, called Chief Lewsen and told him I wasn't a cop that would abide by the Thin Blue Line and protect other cops. But so what? I'm proud of that.

I filed a lawsuit with the Maine Human Rights Commission and sued them, and they settled out of court. The real problem for them, however, was the can of worms they opened. Seeing how easy it was to get an administration to bend to her demands, Officer Danielle Cyr turned around and made sexual harassment allegations against half the department, including her own friends that lied and covered for her, and then she sued the Windham Police Department for creating a hostile work environment.

During the Cyr's lawsuit against the department, I talked to Chief Lewsen, who was apologetic and claimed it was a mistake on their part to fire me. I had plenty of documents and audio recordings showing Cyr was a liar. I also had correspondence between her and her attorney showing her attorney was assisting her in coming up with a false story to have a case. Her attorney, a real lowlife, gave her the names of some of her clients and told her to talk to them. This way, she could get her story straight and could come up with some juicy allegations that would get her a bigger payday.

I gave these documents to the Chief, but he asked me if I could release them and taint the jury in the case. Instead, I published a recording of Chief Lewsen's request for jury tampering. Fucking scumbag. That guy cost me a $325,000 house, and he didn't expect me to burn his ass when I had the chance? What a fool.

As a side note, I am now very skeptical of women who claim sexual harassment. This incident, admittedly, jaded me and now I just don't believe that most claims to be authentic. Instead, I profoundly suspect most allegations are a convenient way for the "victim" to get ahead as a substitute for talent or good work.

It's such a shame; people like Danielle Cyr cry wolf and wreck the system for women that legitimately need protection.

By this point, Kelly and I had started growing apart in 2007. I can see why – when you are young, you want different things in life.

As you start to get older, what you want changes. I wanted adventure and Kelly wanted a quiet, reclusive life. A life that I was unable to provide her. Not only that, but she was just cold to be around. She didn't even want to scratch my back.

Kelton was just born and she was a good mother, and that's really all that mattered.

Chapter 9 - PBSOTalk, Exposing the Culture of Corruption

When I returned to Florida, I was so angry at getting what I considered a "raw deal," I

founded PBSOTalk.com, exposing the Culture of Corruption in Palm Beach County. I started the site after I found out the moderator for another site (LEO Affairs) was censoring critical posts about the Sheriff's Office. I knew why; the head of Legal Affairs for the Palm Beach County Sheriff's Office was the moderator of the Palm Beach County Sheriff's Office forum. He was making sure that dirt wasn't exposed about PBSO and was protecting the guilty.

I wanted the truth to be known and uncensored, and I wanted to protect the good cops who feared for their families and careers. I built my own server, downloaded forum software and modified the source code heavily to prevent anyone's identities from being logged. I began to post on LEO Affairs that a new site was up allowing people to be critical. Shortly after, the entire Palm Beach County audience from LEO affairs stopped posting, and the traffic moved to my site.

Good cops were very happy to have an outlet to complain without fear of being outed. Meanwhile, the guilty were on the site defending themselves. One of the most prominent targets at the Palm Beach County Sheriff's Office was Chief Deputy Michael Gauger, a corrupt, power-hungry, obese little man with a striking resemblance in physical appearance and behavior to the Italian fascist Benito Mussolini. There was good reason for the criticism; Gauger spent his entire career stabbing people in the back while giving promotions to his friends. He was also infamous for making deputies out of criminals with histories of violence and narcotics, against the wishes of Human Resources.

Gauger positively hated the site, and almost since the site started, he had me under criminal investigation. Various organizations in law enforcement went out of their ways to do everything possible to bring down the site.

Gauger took a handful of postings and went to Kelly's boss, the elected Public Defender Carey Haughwout. Carey basically told him, "Hey, freedom of speech..." and all that. Still, the site had been up and running for a few years before Kelly even found out about it.

Journalists tried to find out why they were investigating me on numerous occasions, and PBSO always told the journalists they couldn't talk about ongoing criminal investigations. It's an illegal and very Orwellian method to blanket-investigate anyone you want, solely for the fact you don't like what they have to say. But the Palm Beach County and the federal government did just that.

I teamed up with Rick Sessa, a former commander with the Riviera Beach Police Department, and the host of the Cop Talk Radio program. Sessa's show was about supporting the great cops, but he often did segments on stories about crime and corruption committed by police officers. We frequently traded inside information from our sources, and he did a hell of a good job exposing the Sheriff and his band of thugs.

The Sheriff's Office hated Sessa and his show, so they went around bribing and threatening his business sponsors to stop advertising on his program. Bradshaw sent a deputy from the administration into Palm Beach Harley Davidson, offering the contract to service the PBSO Harley Davidson motorcycles at a higher rate than they were currently paying in exchange for dropping Sessa's show. Eventually, Sessa lost all of his advertisers and had no way to pay for the show.

Another man, a medic with the fire department, started a Palm Beach County news blog. He often posted news that would anger the Sheriff. Chief Deputy Gauger had one of his goons call the medic's place of employment and threatened their standing with the county if it didn't stop. When he went to work, they told him if he kept posting on his blog, they would find a way to fire him.

To the Sheriff and Chief Deputy Gauger, Bullying, intimidation, and bribery are mere tools in their toolbox to attack the free speech of the People. This unchecked abuse of power is now an epidemic plaguing most law enforcement entities.

> *"I'm not violent, I don't believe in killing people, but standing up for yourself, speaking out against injustice, is another form of vengeance."* - Eva Gabrielsson

Chapter 10 - Sheriff Stealing Guns from Evidence, Falsifying Reports on Black People

Not long after I launched the PBSOTalk, I had numerous people that wanted to send tips but didn't want to do it electronically. I set up a mailbox so they could submit any documents anonymously. One day, I went to the mailbox, and there was a thick manila envelope containing a sealed deposition. Receiving this information became my first "Eureka!" moment for the site.

The deposition was testimony by Chief James Gabbard, the police chief of the West Palm Beach Police Department where Ric Bradshaw worked before he was the Sheriff.

The deposition made bombshell revelations into the stunningly unethical, immoral and criminal behavior of Sheriff Ric Bradshaw when he was a high-ranking Major at the West Palm Beach Police Department. It was an old deposition, from the mid-1980's, but it gave insight into the lifetime Bradshaw spent being a criminal in uniform.

According to the deposition, Bradshaw ordered that Use of Force reports were not to be done. Chief Gabbard speculated it was to prevent them from being obtained by subpoena. It also revealed how then-Captain Bradshaw was carrying around a "Bite Book," a book used to document the injuries to suspects sustained in the process of getting bitten by police dogs. Bradshaw wasn't in the K-9 unit but liked showing the gruesome photos off to friends. In the deposition, Gabbard stated, "…there was a bit case at Peacock Radiators, I think it was the first one, and there was a black guy standing in the parking lot there on the west side of Peacock's, and he was -- and I can't remember the officer, but there was a dog there. And the guy was standing there with his pants down, and his testicles ripped out." He continued, "His testicles were actually hanging out of a sac. And he was standing there. basically. Pretty gruesome. actually. "

Gabbard went on to say he didn't know what Bradshaw's motivation was for showing the book. He thought perhaps that Bradshaw was just proud of the injury inflicted on the black men. Shortly after, an inspector named Bill Eaton told Bradshaw he needed to get rid of the book before someone found out about it and it caused serious troubles one day. The scandalous deposition continued, segueing to the topic of police reports. The plaintiff's attorney in the deposition asked Chief Gabbard if he had ever heard Bradshaw, who had attained the rank of Major at that point, "direct police officers to change the sequencing of fact contained in [their] police reports." If you don't know what this means, it's a huge deal. For instance, in the simplest of examples, if a million dollars goes missing from a bank, and then you enter, you aren't a suspect however if you left the bank and then it was missing a million dollars, you would have a lot of explaining to do. To this question, Chief Gabbard answered that he had, in fact, witnessed this. He stated,

> *"Bradshaw and I were in the Detective Bureau together. I worked an armed robbery that I went to Babcock Furniture at the top of the hill from the police station. He and I responded from the police station. The guy had come in and snatched some money out of a bag and taken off. We tracked the guy and went into the house down there on Datura street, someplace in the 600 block. It was either Datura or Clematis Street address. It was in the alley. We arrested some individuals for the offense or at least one individual. We got to the police station; there were three officers writing reports about the incident… and they said to me that Bradshaw wanted them to change their police reports to indicate the bag of money was found closer to the suspect, actually on the opposite side of the room than where it was."*

I have always been a fan of getting the bad guy, but if you can't do it by telling the truth, you'll get him another day. Making up a story to fit the narrative is not just illegal and unethical, but can cost an innocent man his freedom or life.

There is far too much of a "winning" attitude in police work in the USA, where police officers and prosecutors want to win no matter what they have to do or what lie they have to tell so they can get their man. That's not the way the system was designed to work. The cops and prosecutors should want to get the guilty man, and if there is evidence pointing to someone's innocence, then rightfully so, that information needs to be included, analyzed and used to provide the real truth, not just the facts the police and prosecution would like to sell to the public.

There were other bits of scandalous information regarding Ric Bradshaw when he became the Chief of the West Palm Beach Police Department, like shredding his disciplinary file to prevent the public from ever seeing it, but the last big bombshell in the deposition was when Bradshaw had been caught stealing guns from the evidence room.

Gabbard testified that he was a captain at the time. Captain Mann's called him to his office, where Gabbard was informed there was a serious problem. Capt. Mann didn't know who else to tell.

According to Gabbard's testimony, the evidence custodian, Bob Linton, had witnessed then Major Bradshaw enter the evidence room and when he came out, a gun that had been placed into evidence was missing, along with the evidence cards, property receipts, etc.

The evidence custodian went to Capt. Mann, who found out the case number was a "found property" case, the property being a 9mm Smith and Wesson pistol. Everything regarding the case was missing; the reports, the evidence sheets, and the pistol were stolen. The chief at the time went to the command staff and told them, "I've caught Major Bradshaw with his hands in the cookie jar and I am going to suspend him for five days, and the matter is closed."

When the chief asked anyone if they had a problem with it, Capt. Gabbard told him Bradshaw was a thief. The chief later said to him, "I know he was going to steal the gun. I am going to save him. He has a lot of time invested here, and I would hate to see him ruin his career over this."

Saving people from an innocent, good faith mistake is one thing. But protecting a thief from a multitude of felonies, a thief that happens to be wearing a badge - it's a sin that perpetuates a culture of corruption, a culture that blossomed under Sheriff Bradshaw and his dirty administration after Bradshaw was elected to be the Sheriff.

That election, as it was, should have never happened. Before the vote, Bradshaw, who once had been in the Marine Corps, filed a document with the Florida Department of Law Enforcement and the Palm Beach County Sheriff's Office saying he had a dishonorable discharge and a dishonorable discharge disqualifies you from carrying a gun or holding public office. When I made a public records request into the matter, I received an edited version from PBSO where it was crossed out and initialed by the personnel clerk. In his file was an Honorable Discharge certificate that anyone can order on an internet website called Sgt. Grit. No actual military discharge paperwork (DD-214) was ever placed in his file, contrary to the law.

Chapter 11 - Uncovering Bradshaw's Purchasing Card Crimes

Not long after I received the deposition in the mail, I started getting tips here and there. I requested the purchasing cards for Joe Bradshaw, the head of legal affairs (no relation to Sheriff Bradshaw) and Carol Verdigi, the head of Event Management. I found tens of thousands of dollars of mismanaged, illegal spending. There were expensive purchases at home decorating stores, pet stores, and restaurants. I received an anonymous letter in the mail, saying that after I requested the purchasing card records, the Sheriff, afraid of what I was going to find, went to purchasing to fill out a fraud report, claiming someone stole his purchasing card. The tip directed me to wait a few weeks until Bradshaw received his new card and then make the request for all of his purchasing card records. Not just the last one, but for every card ever issued to Bradshaw. The tip also told me to ask for the fraud reports, because filling out a fraud report when no fraud took place, to cover up illegal spending, is a felony called Official Misconduct.

I waited and filled out the request like the tip had advised, and the results were shocking. There were payments to expensive restaurants and bars on numerous occasions. The fraud report showed precisely what the tip said it would; unlike another fraud report the Sheriff filled out, there was absolutely no documentation as to what the alleged fraud was to make Bradshaw cancel his card.

I filed a criminal complaint with the Palm Beach County State Attorney's Office, who "investigated" the incident and declared the complaint "unfounded" because he determined that it was used in a fraud. The investigator for the State Attorney's office knowingly lied, using the facts from a previous fraud report to clear the Sheriff of any wrongdoing. And that, unfortunately, is how the State Attorney's office works; not just in Palm Beach County, probably almost anywhere in the United States. They cover for the cops, and the cops cover for them.

I then directed my complaint to the Florida Commission on Ethics, who investigated the matter. The investigation found that Bradshaw had been wining and dining major campaign contributors on the taxpayers' dime. Even more startling was that some of them had ties to some of the most brutal criminal organizations in the country. For instance, one of his guest diners was a man by the name of John Stiluppi, a man with ties to the Colombo Crime Family. According to the FBI, Stiluppi was laundering money for them. A source told me that Bradshaw would purchase all of PBSO's patrol cars from Stiluppi's car dealerships in New Jersey at an inflated price in return for kickbacks.

The Florida Commission on Ethics found that Sheriff Bradshaw's shocking purchases were "improper performance of his official duties" but let him walk, saying that Bradshaw didn't know what he was doing was illegal. If only the law worked like that for the common people, the people without badges, the ones who are naturally more ignorant about the law. The irony here is black as coal and dirty as a New Jersey trash factory.

> *"In its purest form, an act of retribution provides symmetry. The rendering payment of crimes against the innocent. But a danger on retaliation lies on the furthering cycle of violence. Still, it's a risk that must be met; and the greater offense is to allow the guilty to go unpunished."- Emily Thorne*

Chapter 12 - The Joe Recarey / Epstein Files

In 2010, it was widely known in my county that I was the guy to give files you wanted to leak while keeping your identity a secret. It was also known I had protections in place to prevent the Sheriff from getting these files. I got a call from an old friend, Joe Recarey, who I hadn't seen since I was a cop a few years earlier. I worked district three in the Palm Beach Palm Beach County Sheriff's Office and he worked for the Town of Palm Beach. Technically, his jurisdiction was inside my district, so occasionally I would run in to him for overlapping cases.

Joe asked me to meet, and of course I told him sure. He came to my office on Olive Avenue with a cart full of boxes. One of the boxes was a bunch of DVDs – the blank kind that you record your own media on. They were labeled by date and spanned from 1994 to 2005 or so. I asked Recarey what they were, and he told me they were concerning Jeffrey Epstein, but he didn't elaborate.

He said he and the rest of the Palm Beach Police cops, didn't trust the Palm Beach County State Attorney or the Palm Beach

County Sheriff. According to Recarey, they had already sabotaged his original investigation and wanted to make sure he had copies in case they tried to make the originals disappear. My server collection was growing... I had a rack of servers in my office and a few at my house, and I had one with optical drives for bulk production of media, so for me, it wasn't a problem. I was able to copy the hundreds of DVDs from the box in a day and returned it to Recarey the next day.

I didn't actually pay any attention as to what was on the disks... it wasn't my business. But in the rare case I did open a video file it was always just a room covered by an old style 480 CCTV camera. You have to remember, in those days, CCTV was poor quality and some of the earlier files had the telltale signs that they were burned to the disks from VHS tapes. And I never say ay activity, because at the beginning of the tapes, it would be before people would have come into the rooms. So as far as I knew, they were just regular surveillance videos.

I put all of the videos into a TrueCrypt container (the software was discontinued in 2014 and taken over by Veracrypt) and the file sat on my server for years. I had forgotten about it, frankly. The encrypted container moved from server to server over the years, ensuring the data would stay fresh and there wouldn't be data loss. It would also go on my regular backup schedules – My wife, who is the Executive Assistant to the Elected Public Defender of Palm Beach County, would keep the rotational backups at her office for me, encrypted, along with the decryption codes.

If I am honest, I never gave the files a second thought, never was curious to explore them, and felt it was none of my business. I was merely acting as a digital safety deposit box for Recarey, and I did this for many other cases over the years. And so, I just kind of forgot about them. Later, the recordings reared their ugly heads.

Chapter 13 - Public Records Requests: Lying and Deceit to Hide the Truth

At the beginning of 2011, I got another tip that the Sheriff bought three very expensive BBQ grills. How expensive? We're talking a combined cost of $90,000, not including the trucks they bought to tow the grills around. I made numerous public records requests to the Sheriff, which they denied any records existed. Finally, PBSO relented and forked over the documents. The local media should have been outraged, but they remained silent.

Pretty soon, the Palm Beach County Sheriff's Office began getting tired of my public records requests. They would drag out the requests for the maximum time allotted by law, and rather than giving me the documents I wanted that showed their criminal activities they would flat-out deny the records even existed.

On June 30, 2011, I was given a tip by a reader that the Sheriff used taxpayer money to purchase 67 "Wyatt Earp" gold-plated western-style replica revolvers. On July 27th, I received a response from the Public Records department saying the records didn't exist. I made several other requests, and PBSO always denied the existence of the files. Still, I knew the replica firearms were given away to the other elected Sheriffs of Florida, too. I made a public-records request to the Martin County Sheriff's Office. They were incredibly kind, not only acknowledging they got the gun from Sheriff Bradshaw but sent me a photograph of the weapon. The response admitted it was handed to Sheriff Crowder directly from Sheriff Bradshaw himself.

I made a few more records requests to PBSO, still with more denials. Since I knew the manufacturer, thanks to Martin County's Sheriff, I contacted them directly. I told them I was with PBSOTalk and that I needed a copy of the invoice emailed to me. They were happy to oblige, showing the Sheriff wasted $12,631 or taxpayer money to give away as gifts. Again, the local media should have been outraged, but they remained silent.

Chapter 14 - MEETING JOSE LAMBIET

In Palm Beach County, the local media pretty much turned a blind eye to what the Sheriff was doing at the Palm Beach County Sheriff's Office. I was pretty new at getting records and such, so I turned to Jose Lambiet, the one journalist that wasn't afraid to write stories critical of Sheriff Ric Bradshaw and Chief Deputy Michael Gauger. Jose had written some pretty good bombshells in the past and exposed a lot of disturbing behavior performed by PBSO employees in the past.

One of his more salacious scandals that caused an uproar within the ranks of the Sheriff's Office was photographs of Internal Affairs Lieutenant Swank sleeping during a class. I know it sounds petty, but the Palm Beach County Sheriff's Office launched a massive investigation into which deputy took the photo and sent it to Jose.

Internal Affairs at the Palm Beach County Sheriff's Office began demanding to examine all the deputies' phones to determine who took the photo. This type of demand is a blatant violation of the

Constitution of the United States; Specifically, the 4th Amendment which guards people against illegal search and seizure.

The deputy in question went to his union, the Palm Beach County Police Benevolent Association, for help. It has long been known that the PBA and Sheriff Bradshaw are in cahoots; the Sheriff makes sure deputies pay their dues to the PBA or can find cause to terminate them. The PBA, in return, picks and chooses who gets good representation and who gets thrown to the wolves. It gets even worse; I am told by a very reliable source who is in the know that the Sheriff has his own PBA credit card that he can use for whatever he wants, as a kickback for letting the PBA make mad cash and not spend any of it on legal representation. Still, the deputy didn't think the PBA would be so unethical they would turn him in. Yet, that's exactly what happened. They drove the deputy to Internal Affairs and demanded that he give up his cell phone.

I made contact with Jose Lambiet, who told me he had previously received a call from Chief Deputy Gauger. Gauger tried turning him against me, claiming I was unreliable with my information and was under a criminal investigation for numerous crimes.

Jose began telling me of many of the allegations Gauger had made, and I put together a package of documents that systematically proved Gauger to be a liar. At that point, Jose and I started having a dialogue together, exchanging information. For me, breaking the news on my site wasn't important; I just wanted the information out there. When I would receive hot tips from sources, Jose or I would investigate them, and I would let Jose have the first decision as to if he wanted to publish a story regarding them. I would regularly give the Palm Beach Post second choice if Jose didn't want the story.

Jose and the Palm Beach Post got a lot of stories that way. The story about PBSO purchasing three BBQ grills for over $90,000, the purchasing card records, over 130 take-home cars for civilians that worked on Bradshaw's campaign, costing the taxpayers millions. All were hot tips from inside sources.

I stopped giving stories to the Palm Beach Post after Jane Musgrave wrote a patently dishonest tale about Gauger's lawsuit against me and the reasons for my termination from the Windham Police Department. Also, she tried to minimize the impact of my site, claiming I was a disgruntled ex-employee of the Sheriff's Office that probably didn't even have a job. Except she failed to mention that just weeks earlier, I met with three Palm Beach Post employees; Investigative Editor Joel Engelhardt, journalist Cynthia Roldan and another journalist whom I don't remember, who came to the office of the company that I owned, located on the top floor of a prestigious building in Downtown West Palm Beach.

The reason for such dishonesty became apparent when I spoke to a source of mine in Internal Affairs who told me that Jane Musgrave was at a PBSO Christmas party with Chief Deputy Gauger. According to the source, Gauger ordered Lt. Dean Johnson to get a file he kept on me for Musgrave.

Musgrave's motivation for such character assassination, according to my source, was that Chief Deputy Gauger was having an affair with Musgrave in exchange for information, feeding her hot stories before they were public to other news outlets. She's not a very good writer, so I assume that was her way of maintaining her competitive edge in a dying newspaper that hands out pink slips like candy on Halloween.

Perhaps the most ironic thing is when Musgrave contacted me, she asked why I would publish stories and why I didn't leave it to the professionals that make sure the facts were all correct. Mostly, I told her, is that the Palm Beach Post wasn't doing their jobs. A year later, Musgrave published a story about me, claiming that I had filed a lawsuit against the Sheriff's Office for coming to my home, taking my guns after I threatened to commit suicide.

The problem with her story, however, is that in her rush to assassinate my character even further, she failed to realize someone with a completely different middle name filed the lawsuit. I called her up, and she laughed about it. Like she had warned me, those little details can bite you in the ass; their paper had to print a retraction, and a rival publication did a big story on her seriously embarrassing lack of journalistic integrity and skill.

For the record, in writing this story, I reached out to Jane, telling her what my source had informed me about her affair with Gauger in trade for information for information. She replied to me and surprisingly, while she didn't clarify the allegations, she didn't deny them either. Interesting.

The story published by Musgrave about Gauger's SLAPP suit was the breaking point for Kelly. She asked me to move out of the house, which I did. I would come see my kids as much as possible, almost every day. But I was staying up in Vero Beach and it was a long trek. Eventually, I moved back in to be with the Kelton and Aurelia, but my relationship with Kelly was damaged beyond repair.

Chapter 15 - STATE ATTORNEY'S OFFICE ENGAGES IN HACKING

In early November 2012, some strange activity was happening with my website. I kept receiving messages that attempts to log in were failing. While I didn't log the IP addresses of readers and posters, I did write code that defines criteria to record suspicious information. This was suspicious, as it was the "Admin" username with an old password that I used when I was at the Palm Beach County Sheriff's Office, yet I was out shopping at the time.

I went back to the office, pulled the logs, and ran the IP addresses. They belonged to Palm Beach County's Information Technology department. I quickly made a public records request of the logs showing every user that went to PBSOTalk, as well as the times, so I could match up who was attempting to access the site.

In the first response, they denied anyone had been reading, posting or trying to access PBSOTalk. I wrote a response to the IT department, telling them it was not accurate and threatened to file a criminal complaint about denying the records I was entitled to under the Florida Sunshine Laws.

Finally, on December 7th, they responded, telling me they made a "mistake" and they provided a list of people that had been accessing PBSOTalk. The person in question who appeared to be trying to gain access to my site was a man by the name of Glenn Wescott, one of the investigators for the Palm Beach County State Attorney's Office, and a former PBSO deputy.

There were other names, as well. One name, in particular, was redacted; I think that name belonged to the then-elected State Attorney, Michael McAuliffe.

Jose Lambiet contacted Glenn Wescott at the Palm Beach County State Attorney's Office to get an answer as to why he was trying to break into my site. Wescott denied it and instead said he was merely posting responses on my website. In the article by Jose Lambiet, he had a good point: "While on taxpayer's time? Yep!"

Chapter 16 - Lt. Dean Johnson's Capture and Arrest

In January 2012, one of the most horrible cases that were attempted to be covered up by the Sheriff had occurred. A 46-year-old SWAT Lieutenant named Danial Burrows was caught forcing a fellow cop named Mike Collister, who was dying of cancer, to open his safe so he could steal his pain medications and guns. The dying Collister's wife had become suspicious when Burrows would show up to visit, only to find the Collister's pain medication would disappear from the nightstand. One day she left and returned a short time later. Michael Collister was forced by Burrows to walk to the safe in the garage and open it, meanwhile, in so much pain he was crying. Collister's wife had caught Burrows in the act and contacted the Palm Beach County Sheriff's Office.

Even the cover-up artists in Internal Affairs have a soul, and a limit to the depths of evil they will tolerate, and Captain Larry Easton wanted to have Burrows' head on a stick. He called Lt. Burrows to Internal Affairs and ordered him to take a urine test, to test for narcotics in his system. When Burrows showed up and was ordered to do so, he contacted his pal, Sheriff Ric Bradshaw, for help. Bradshaw went down to Internal Affairs and got into a confrontation with Capt. Easton, and ordered Easton to stop the investigation. The two had a heated argument about it, but the Sheriff, being the Sheriff, won the debate in the end. That, however, is not the end of the story.

Lieutenant Dean Johnson, who was privy to the argument, decided he wasn't going to stand around and watch the agency cover up for such a disgusting human being. He turned to PBSOTalk to give the information anonymously. The news made its way to Jose Lambiet at Gossip Extra, and it caused a massive scandal. The Sheriff and Chief Deputy were absolutely furious and ordered the higher-ups to find the snitch. The snitch, Johnson, was found, but not by any fault of PBSOTalk; he got caught because he had a big mouth.

There was a deputy, one of my informants and moderators, by the name of Anne Burke. I can use her name because she engaged with me in bad faith to trap Johnson, posting on PBSOTalk. Anne Burke had been a Captain with the Palm Beach County Sheriff's Office when she got into trouble. She kidnapped her lesbian lover at the FBI academy and held her captive with a knife. You can't make this stuff up. One would think, like any ordinary citizen, she would have been tossed in jail, but instead, she received a demotion to the rank of sergeant.

Angry at being demoted, Burke had a score to settle. She and I frequently communicated, and she would give me several tips regarding public corruption that turned out to be entirely legitimate. One day, however, Burke wanted to retire, but not as a sergeant. She wanted to retire as her old rank of captain. She approached Chief Deputy Gauger and struck up a deal to deliver an insider who was posting tips on my website in exchange for getting her former rank back right before her retirement.

Sgt. Burke worked in Internal Affairs with Lt. Dean Johnson, and she knew he was responsible for leaking information to my site. How did she know? Johnson told her. He had met Burke in a restaurant and knew Burke was one of my moderators. He asked Burke if it were possible to trace people posting on my site, and Burke told him it was impossible. Johnson discussed how to get rid of his phone and hard drive to prevent anyone from finding out. Later, Lt. Dean Johnson was arrested on five felony counts relating to divulging confidential information about an investigation as well as charges stemming from destruction and tampering with evidence.

I was reading the Probable Cause affidavit for his arrest, which talked about a "John Doe" who was under a criminal investigation so secretive, they wouldn't name him or pull a case number. Page 7 of the probable cause affidavit also stated that "approximately 0842 hours, the CI called the phone number he/she said belonged to John Doe." I looked at my phone bill and saw that on that day, and exact time, I had spoken to Anne Burke.

BADVOLF | BY: JOHN MARK DOUGAN
THE TRUE STORY OF AN AMERICAN COP AVENGING A CORRUPT SYSTEM

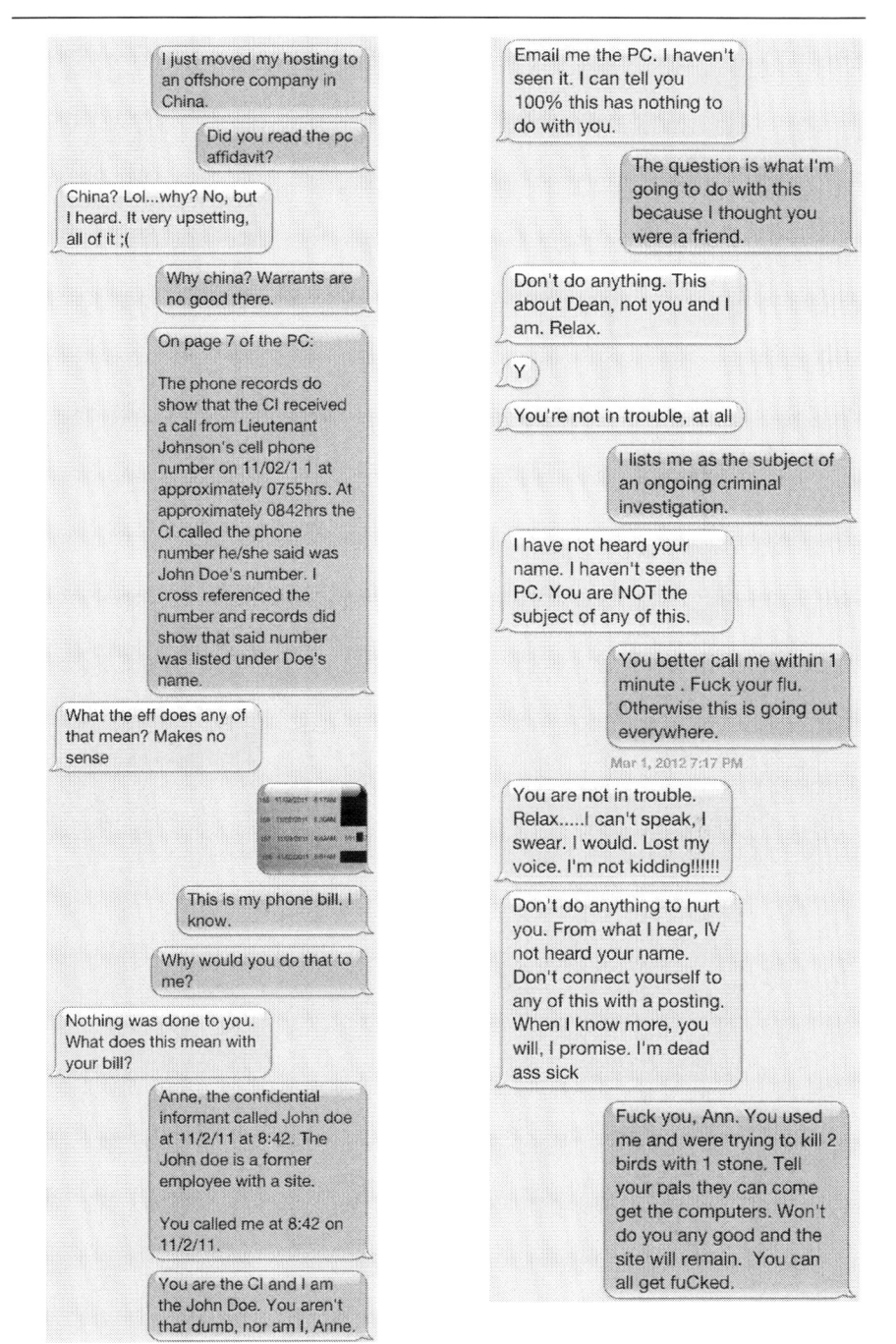

> I just moved my hosting to an offshore company in China.

> Did you read the pc affidavit?

< China? Lol...why? No, but I heard. It very upsetting, all of it ;(

> Why china? Warrants are no good there.

> On page 7 of the PC:
>
> The phone records do show that the CI received a call from Lieutenant Johnson's cell phone number on 11/02/11 at approximately 0755hrs. At approximately 0842hrs the CI called the phone number he/she said was John Doe's number. I cross referenced the number and records did show that said number was listed under Doe's name.

< What the eff does any of that mean? Makes no sense

> [image of phone bill]

> This is my phone bill. I know.

> Why would you do that to me?

< Nothing was done to you. What does this mean with your bill?

> Anne, the confidential informant called John doe at 11/2/11 at 8:42. The John doe is a former employee with a site.
>
> You called me at 8:42 on 11/2/11.

> You are the CI and I am the John Doe. You aren't that dumb, nor am I, Anne.

< Email me the PC. I haven't seen it. I can tell you 100% this has nothing to do with you.

> The question is what I'm going to do with this because I thought you were a friend.

< Don't do anything. This about Dean, not you and I am. Relax.

< Y

< You're not in trouble, at all

> I lists me as the subject of an ongoing criminal investigation.

< I have not heard your name. I haven't seen the PC. You are NOT the subject of any of this.

> You better call me within 1 minute . Fuck your flu. Otherwise this is going out everywhere.

Mar 1, 2012 7:17 PM

< You are not in trouble. Relax.....I can't speak, I swear. I would. Lost my voice. I'm not kidding!!!!!!

< Don't do anything to hurt you. From what I hear, IV not heard your name. Don't connect yourself to any of this with a posting. When I know more, you will, I promise. I'm dead ass sick

> Fuck you, Ann. You used me and were trying to kill 2 birds with 1 stone. Tell your pals they can come get the computers. Won't do you any good and the site will remain. You can all get fuCked.

I was frankly outraged at the betrayal. I blocked Burke from my site and told the bitch never to contact me again. I posted on PBSOTalk that Sgt. Ann Burke ratted out Lt. Dean Johnson, and for everyone to avoid her. She didn't like it very much and begged me not to do it, but screw her. She retired a short time later at the rank of Captain, costing the taxpayers hundreds of thousands of dollars.

You see, government, and not just Palm Beach County government; all government, they don't mind wasting hundreds of thousands of taxpayer dollars to silence their misdeeds, ones that cause them embarrassment or land them in jail. That's right. Generally speaking, the government, especially law enforcement, is as dirty as it gets. Bad cops commit, get away and even get promoted for engaging in crimes and coverups that would land ordinary citizens in jail for the rest of their lives. Welcome to America, Land of the Free, Home of the Brave, where justice is equal in the eyes of the law. What a sham.

It was this point I had my first shred of evidence that the Sheriff and his minions were trying to investigate me criminally, to try to shut down the site, and I knew I had to take action. The first thing I did was to move the site to an offshore hosting company in a country with strong privacy laws. I moved it to servers to Malaysia, a hosting company called Shinjiru. I paid them with a money order and put the site in a fake name.

Chapter 17 - CHIEF DEPUTY GAUGER FILES A SLAPP SUIT

In April 2012, Chief Deputy Michael Gauger filed an S.L.A.P.P. suit against me. SLAPP stands for Strategic Lawsuit Against Public Participation and is a lawsuit that is intended to censor, intimidate, and silence critics by burdening them with the cost of a legal defense until they abandon their criticism or opposition. Such lawsuits have been made illegal in many jurisdictions because they impede freedom of speech.

The typical SLAPP plaintiff does not normally expect to win the lawsuit, which is why Chief Deputy Gauger has let the lawsuit go on for six years now. The plaintiff of a SLAPP suit accomplishes his goals if the defendant succumbs to fear, intimidation, mounting legal costs, or pure exhaustion, abandoning the criticism. A SLAPP may also intimidate others from participating in the debate, which they have tried to enforce by telling people in the department when they uncover who is posting, they will be terminated. A SLAPP is often preceded by a legal threat, which Chief Deputy Gauger provided in 2011 when

I ran into him at the Office Depot as I was buying office supplies. Incidentally, that lying sack of shit wrote about that encounter in his court filing, saying I started a verbal confrontation with him in the store. It was Gauger that came up to me and told me not to "poke the sleeping bear," or I would be bitten.

In a SLAPP suit, there is a difficulty in that plaintiffs do not present themselves to the Court admitting that they intend to censor, intimidate, or silence their critics. Hence, the challenge in drafting SLAPP legislation, and in applying it, is to craft an approach which affords an early termination to invalid abusive suits, without denying a legitimate day in court to valid good faith claims. Thus, anti-SLAPP laws target tactics used by SLAPP plaintiffs.

Ordinary anti-SLAPP laws include measures such as penalties for plaintiffs who file lawsuits ruled frivolous and special procedures where a defendant may ask a judge to consider that a lawsuit is a SLAPP (and usually subsequently dismiss the suit). Florida, a state that has crafted legislation to allow politicians, police, and others in positions of authority blatantly break the law without repercussion, has no such requirement.

Admittedly, some of the PBSOTalk forum postings included allegations of child molestation and torturing of minority suspects. There was also a satirical photo I had on the website with Gauger's face on a picture of Mussolini, and Sheriff Ric Bradshaw's face on Hitler. Many PBSO deputies simply hate Gauger and there was no shortage of people willing to stab the guy in the back. Whether the worst posts were valid, I cannot say. Some of the stories about Gauger that were so detailed, so vivid, they I felt there was something to them; some factual basis on which the poster made the posts.

Nevertheless, I removed several of the postings myself, and in an email I sent to Gauger, I told him if anything published on PBSOTalk wasn't accurate, he should alert me so I could remove it. Naturally, I didn't want false or misleading information on my website. But Gauger never said a word, leading me to believe the allegations were indeed factual. It is my belief, and the opinion of many others that know him, that he filed the suit merely to silence me.

There have long been rumors about this stuff, stories told by several people that worked with him for many, many years. One very reliable source told me about his eye-witness account of Chief Deputy Gauger throwing a handcuffed black man off a bridge and into a canal to elicit a confession for a crime.

Hey, when there is smoke, there is fire. Who would have ever believed that Sandusky was raping all those kids? There were whispers, just like with Gauger. If my site had been available for Penn State, maybe it would have prevented some of those child molestations from taking place.

I had one of the best 1st Amendment attorneys in my corner, Thomas Julin, and he went to bat for me, taking my case *pro bono*. The civil suit went nowhere. Yes, they tried their best to collect evidence of who was posting on PBSOTalk, but when people looked at Gauger like the shady-ass character that he is, he could say, "Well, I'm suing that guy for defamation." It makes it easy to redirect allegations without actually denying them. Gauger took a beating on PBSOTalk after that, and I didn't give a damn. A parody advertisement used in a landmark Freedom of speech case from Huster Magazine vs. Falwell was recreated in Gauger's image and posted on the site and I left it there.

Another person opened up an account in his name on a gay dating site called Man Jam. They used his photos and made a very vile profile depicting him as a gay sexual beast. While many people thought it was hilarious, I don't think he did. The profile was soon taken down and no doubt he launched an investigation of who the culprit was. No doubt he blamed me, but it wasn't. In fact, some of the very worst posts, it wouldn't surprise me if it were Gauger or Bradshaw themselves, looking for an excuse to subpoena all of the records or get a warrant for the servers.

Gauger and his attorney, bigshot Jack Scarola, subpoenaed the IP addresses of people posting on the site. Naturally, I told them to get fucked because I made it a point not to log any of that information. But there was more. They wanted all the data from the hard drives that were in the server. Again, in a "fuck you" move, we told them they could have the data, but it would have to have it forensically cloned from the existing drives. The beauty of this is there are only a few places in the entire world with the ability to forensically clone an eight-drive RAID array, which I knew when setting up my server for PBSOTalk. As bad as they wanted the information, they weren't willing to pony up the $60,000 and a couple of years' time it would take to do it.

Eventually, the judge tossed out most of their lawsuit, deeming me a media defendant, falling under the Communications Decency Act and exempted from what others posted about Chief Deputy Gauger.

The judge didn't buy Gauger's claim that I made the postings which were why there were no IP addresses available. The judge in the case probably read my website and in so doing realized what a scumbag Gauger was, and understood why I had no choice but to not log IP addresses to keep whistleblowers safe.

In an almost comical turn of events, Gauger's attorney, Jack Scarola, later filed a complaint with the Department of Justice for the criminal brutality that was taking place at the Palm Beach County Sheriff's Office.

I needed an insurance policy; one that would stun Gauger in court if his S.L.A.P.P. suit ever made it that far and to be blunt, to get even with them. They were using taxpayer dollars, engaging in illegal investigations into me by using lies, so I decided they needed a taste of their own medicine.

I got another money order and paid Shinjiru to host a site called "ServantsOfLordGod.com," registered in the name of Phyllis Gauger and the guy who runs the that nutty Westboro Baptist Chuch. One would think it would be a far stretch to link the two together, but tales of Gauger's blatant racism posted to the site from when he was a young deputy, and the fact Gauger's kid was arrested after attacking a minority police officer while calling him a "nigga" makes it a pretty short leap.

I set up the site to pull posts from white nationalist websites, people like David Duke and the like. It was simply a move in a chess game, and I never knew when I would need it a year, two, or three from that time. It was a figurative bomb I was going to drop to a jury if the case ever went to trial. And how would he explain it? It wasn't morally or ethically right, I know, but nothing they did were moral or ethical. Gauger had lawyers and judges in his pocket, and being of a limited budget, I had to fight any way I could to win, even if it meant getting dirty to do it.

Chapter 18 - I.A. Major Robert Van Reeth:
The Naked Prostitute Scandal

I received a tip call from Gino diFonzo, a bartender from a golf course who asked to meet with me. He claimed to have damning photos of the head of Internal Affairs and some other cops. I was skeptical, but I invited him over. I viewed the pictures, and he was undoubtedly right – they were nothing short of explosive. They were photos of the Major of Internal Affairs, Robert Van Reeth, his underage son, his cousin, Joseph Van Reeth from the West Palm Beach, and Lou Penque, a treasurer for the Palm Beach County Police Benevolent Association. And what were they doing? They happened to be posing in the middle of a public golf course, groping a naked prostitute. A naked prostitute who was high on cocaine supplied to her by her pimp… in front of the cops.

One would think this story has to be fiction; a made-up tale, because no cop would be so stupid… but when I saw the photos, it showed with the utmost clarity in every detail. Now, cops would have arrested any ordinary citizen for indecent exposure, lewd behavior and not to mention delinquency of a minor and sex crimes for exposing your juvenile son to that kind of thing.

Gino, the bartender who gave me the photos, said it gets even better… according to him, a room was set up in the clubhouse where this prostitute was performing oral sex on the golfers for cash and cocaine. I would like to think little Jeffrey got sucked off, too… because how lame would it be for an "upstanding" man who judges morality for the entire department to get a blow job from a coke addict hooker without springing for the extra cash to get his own son in on the fun and games?

You can imagine what happened… I posted the photos on my website, and the story blew up. National media outlets from all over the country were covering the story, and Major Van Reeth became famous. The comments on my website were priceless.

One person wrote, "this is taken completely out of context, this woman was playing a round of golf when a gator attacked her, (no it was not Tim Tebow, so don't comment with juvenile jokes) tore off her clothes and was about to do bodily harm to her until these brave men came to her rescue."

Other comments, however, were either corrupt cops or the administration, posting in defense of Van Reeth's inexcusable behavior. Maybe both, I don't know. Whatever method they used to attempt to justify this behavior, they failed to realize the human factor – a cop was paying money to a drug-addicted hooker for sex so she could get more drugs. Instead of helping a woman with a problem that was destroying her life, they were enabling this behavior; helping her destroy herself so they could have a good time.

The Sheriff was categorically furious. He wasn't pissed so much they were with a prostitute, but that they allowed a photo session and got caught. Bradshaw was on vacation in North Carolina at the time, and when news broke of the scandal, he drove his police vehicle back to Palm Beach County in record time so he could do damage control. He did the best he could; painted me as a disgruntled employee who released the records for revenge. He also stated that what Major Van Reeth did on his own private time was his own business and that the Sheriff's Office doesn't regulate the activities of off-duty employees.

They only regulate the off-duty behavior of anyone else who isn't a member of the inner circle, as per department policy.

Chapter 19 - The Sheriff tries Buying PBSOTalk with Taxpayer Money

In early April 2012, I came to my office and found a note slipped under my door. There was nothing on it but a phone number. I called, and it was a number for Rick Asnani, Sheriff Bradshaw's campaign manager.

According to Asnani, he and the Sheriff were interested in buying my website. They wanted to purchase it to shut it down because the site was doing severe damage to Sheriff Bradshaw and all of his many criminal cohorts. The site was exposing crime after crime committed by the Bradshaw administration, casting a light on their shady dealings and unethical practices, and he was up for reelection.

Out of curiosity, I met with Asnani, and I had him sign a confidentiality agreement. I did this to have proof of the meeting. Otherwise, he would be able to deny the meeting ever took place. I was almost positive he would suggest something illegal or unethical, which would nullify the agreement. At the meeting, Asnani said he wanted to buy PBSOTalk and have exclusive rights to any of the content of the site. I told him if the price was right, I would consider it, and I may have done just that.

A few days later, Asnani and I were on a telephone call, and he told me they would purchase the site for the sum of $80,000. It would have been tempting, except he informed me the money would come from the budget of the Palm Beach County Sheriff's Office. In other words, the taxpayers would pay for the flow of enlightening information to stop, leaving them in the dark. "Hell no. If you guys want to buy the site, the Sheriff himself is going to pay for it," I told Asnani. I wasn't about to let him squander taxpayer money on my site, because if I did, I would have been no better than the criminals running the Sheriff's Office.

When I declined to sell the site, Asnani called me back and asked if they came up with the money and bought the site, would I write any more bad stories about Bradshaw. I responded that if the sale included a notice of non-competition, then I would be legally bound not to write about the topic.

They were hoping I would say no, and they filed for a felony warrant for my arrest on the grounds of extortion. The only problem is, they have no idea what extortion means, or they were trying to bend the law enough to make it fit this situation. The prosecutor who reviewed Detective Kenneth Mark Lewis' warrant affidavit was smart enough to realize this. He determined that if this were "extortion" then any business transaction where a non-compete was signed would also be extortion. He denied their request for a warrant.

Bradshaw and Gauger were incredibly angry the prosecutor would not give them a warrant, but they were utterly wrong. They tried to trap me in a legal situation, call it illegal, and have me put in jail for it. I sent the details of the conversation to journalist Jose

Lambiet, who wrote an article that the Sheriff attempted to purchase my website with taxpayer money.

Chapter 20 - Vacationing in Russia

At a New Year's Eve party in 2011, my friends and I were playing a Driving in Russia video on YouTube. It was insane – some of the funniest video I had ever seen, and I knew I just had to go there and check the place out. While I was doing my research, I met a very cool woman on Facebook. It was my opinion she was what a woman should be. Not the most beautiful woman in the world, but smart as a whip. She told me I should come to Moscow to check out prospective business contacts. I flew to Moscow in February 2012 she was waiting for me at the airport.

I had a lunch meeting with a fascinating man named Pavel Borodin about bringing additional telecom technologies to Russia. It was fascinating to hear about his love of soccer (what the rest of the world calls football), and about his many orphanage charities.

In total, I spent one month in Russia on that first trip, sightseeing, getting to know people and falling in love with the charm and culture of the city. It's an immaculate metropolis with breathtaking architecture. Moscow is so different from my own city, but I felt so connected. All my Russian friends claim it's because I have a Russian soul, which may be true. One thing is sure- I loved the chaos and freedom afforded here in Russia.

People back home don't get this point about freedom, but it only takes me a moment to explain to them – America is a country with a vast number of federal criminal laws, and each state has a plethora number of state, local and municipal pages of their own laws. In essence, there is almost no activity you can do in America that isn't against the law. They say the average person in the United States commits three felonies per day, and I believe it.

A perfectly good example: Your best friend calls you on a Tuesday night and says he won two tickets to see your favorite baseball team play on Wednesday. The seats are incredible, and you know this opportunity won't come any time again soon, so you decide to call in sick to work on Wednesday morning. You figure that, after all, it's something everyone does now and then. You did not know, however, that you have just committed a "scheme or artifice to defraud" the company to their "intangible right to your "honest services" — a federal crime. This statute was so vague that a few years ago, the Supreme Court amended it to apply only to "bribes" or "kickbacks" that illegally influenced lawmakers. Regardless of Court's rewriting, Cato Institute policy analyst David Rittgers that "little has changed" in how ambiguous the statute is. As Justice Scalia stated, it still criminalizes "a salaried employee's phoning in sick to go to a ball game."

In another example, famous auto racer Bobby Unser was convicted of a federal crime and sentenced to six months in prison. Why? Because he got lost in a blizzard in Colorado for two days while snowmobiling, and was guilty of "unlawful operation of a snowmobile within a National Forest Wilderness Area."

And yet in another horrifying abuse of government power, James Rosen, a news reporter for Fox News, had several contacts with a State Department employee. The FBI, to obtain a search warrant for looking at Rosen's phone records and email, claimed that Rosen had violated espionage laws.

Judge Andrew Napolitano said, "This is the first time that the federal government has moved to this level of taking ordinary, reasonable, traditional, lawful reporter skills and claiming they constitute criminal behavior."

Most of the time, when people commit an innocent felony, no one notices, and everything is okay. However, when you have an abusive government who wants to put you in prison, all they have to do is examine your life and find a law you have broken. If there are 10,000 pages of laws to violate, the chances are, you are going to break many more than in a country like Russia, who only has 150 pages of common-sense laws to break.

So yes, I explain to my friends, Russia generally has much more freedom than the United States for the common citizen. There is a price to pay for that freedom, though. Don't like people riding their ATVs down the highway? Too bad. Live and let live.

I left Russia and enjoyed the trip so much, I returned for vacation five more times over the years. Each time, I enjoyed it more and more and found that Russia is entirely different than portrayed by the western media. Let's put it out there now: The media isn't just wrong about what Russia is like – they are patently dishonest about it.

To hear about Russia from the media in the United States, you would think you have to pay bribes for any service. Never have I been asked or even hinted to pay a bribe here. I'm not saying it doesn't happen, but it hasn't happened to me.

To hear about Russia from the news in the United States, You would think the people are crazy. They are indeed different with dissimilar values and a diverse culture that is wildly different from our own, but they aren't crazy. Well, maybe jumping in a cold river in the middle of winter is a bit crazy, but hey, don't knock it until you try it. It's great!

You would think everyone drinks vodka for breakfast, but it's not true. Vodka is like the national drink, and sure there are alcoholics, but there are alcoholics in the United States also. I know many people here that don't drink at all.

They think all of Russia has an arctic climate. If you imagined the United States being cut off anything south of Georgia, you would have an idea of the various climates of Russia. Moscow's environment is very similar to Asheville, North Carolina with the average temperatures being slightly lower. As I type this page, I am nursing a sunburn from falling asleep in the sun wearing a pair of shorts and a t-shirt. The first vacation ended, and it was back to Florida for me.

Chapter 21 - David Aronberg, State Attorney Scumbag

In April of 2012, I had received a copy of a check from a reporter at the Palm Beach Post, provided to them by David Aronberg. It was a check that Aronberg gave to the Palm Beach Post as proof that he paid for a flight provided by Martin O'Boyle. If he failed to pay for the flight, it would have been illegal, taking it as campaign contributions.

Using advanced image enhancement methods, I was able to extrapolate that it was initially a voided-out check, altered and given to the Post as fake evidence. I told my results to Rick Sessa. The significance of this was that David Aronberg had lied about taking illegal campaign contributions, and lied to the Palm Beach Post, providing them with false evidence. Aronberg and Sessa were on speaking terms, but I was not as I believed Aronberg to be pandering to whomever he could get votes, and was dishonest.

The next day, I was driving south on Military Trail, just south of PGA Blvd, when my phone rang. I answered it, and it was Rick Sessa.

"Hey Mark! I'm at Park Avenue BBQ. Dave Aronberg wants to meet with us. Can you come?"

I have known Rick for many years as he had a show called Cop Talk Radio and was keen on exposing corruption in law enforcement in Palm Beach County. Instead of being worried about scooping each other, we would freely exchange information with one another. At that time, our primary goal was to rid Palm Beach County of cancer that is the current Sheriff, Ric Bradshaw, who has engaged in too many crimes and cover-ups to count.

Sessa told me he was meeting David Aronberg at Park Avenue BBQ on Federal highway in North Palm Beach, and that Aronberg had requested I meet with them. Always willing to hear what people have to say, I agreed, "Sure Rick, be there in ten minutes."

When I arrived, they were sitting at a table on the north side of the building, in a booth against the east wall. Aronberg was sitting on the north side of the booth and Sessa was sitting on the south side (Aronberg was on the left, and Sessa was on the right of you were looking at the booth). He stood and extended his hand to shake, but I didn't give him mine in return. I just looked at him and said I was there to listen to what he had to say.

Aronberg had heard from Sessa that I had this check, and he begged me not to put it out on my website. He told me that if I didn't release it, he would give me the "A-list" of Democratic voters. He also told us that he would hold Sheriff Bradshaw accountable for the many criminal acts he has committed while in office. Because he was making the offer on his own accord, I agreed. The food came, and we began talking about strategy about how to keep Bradshaw out of office.

Aronberg was more concerned about getting himself elected. I wasn't against Aronberg getting into office if I knew he would draw a line in the sand against Bradshaw. So, I asked Aronberg what he wanted me to do to win the election. I started talking about mailers to the A-list he was going to provide, but Aronberg had other ideas. He mused about what would happen if his opponent, Dina Keever, was arrested for a crime.

If your opponent was arrested, I told him, it would be the end for your opponent's career. I asked if he had anything that could potentially get her arrested. It was then that Aronberg let out a bombshell request: Very skittishly and nervously, he said, "well, could you guys have cocaine planted in her car? Mark, she lives near you. You know people. Can you get it done? Then you could wait for her to leave, call 911 from a burner cell and say the person in the vehicle with their license plate was waving a gun. The cops would stop her, search her car and she would be finished."

I looked at Rick Sessa for a few moments, thinking it was some sort of joke. Aronberg was looking at us quietly and anxiously; I assume he was hoping for a positive response. Sessa said to Aronberg, "Are you fucking kidding me?" Aronberg realized we were shocked and then said, "oh, I was only kidding." Then he started talking about other methods that weren't so unsavory and illegal. Still, I am ashamed to say I kept sitting and listening to this clown. Sadly, meetings with Aronberg seemed like a plausible way to expose my enemies. Still, the filthy, unsavory ideas kept flowing from Aronberg's mouth.

Aronberg stated he could get the cash together to hire a very high-class prostitute to pose as a traveling sales manager, to seduce one of the top editors at the Palm Beach Post into going back to her hotel room with her. The idea was that there would be cameras hidden inside the room to get video. Aronberg stated the footage could be used to threaten to tell his wife, revenge-porning the poor sap if he published any more negative stories about Aronberg.

Aronberg promised files and information on the Bradshaw administration, as well as fair, impartial investigations in return for our help. Honestly, it was shady as fuck, and even entertaining the thought gives me serious pause as to my state of mind and what I was willing to do to get the help required to get Bradshaw and Gauger out of office.

The next day, Aronberg called me and told me to meet him. His gym was up inside some seemingly-abandoned building in downtown West Palm Beach, and he wanted to meet me in the stairwell to give me the list he promised. To his credit, he did. I received the A list of Democratic voters from David Aronberg to use in a mass mailing campaign against Sheriff Bradshaw. He asked me again if I had any ideas of how to deal with his opponent, Dina Keever, and how to get her from the race. And once again, he floated the planting drugs idea, but I told him I wouldn't do it.

He began talking about how to get the Palm Beach Post's editor's son (Randy Shultz) arrested because the Palm Beach Post had been very tough on Aronberg. According to Aronberg, the son of the editor was a law clerk for a federal judge, was illegally signing documents in the judges' name in his absence. He stated a whistleblower complaint coming from me would cause him a lot of problems. There was also another method discussed into bringing the Palm Beach Post over to Aronberg's side; that of blackmail.

He asked about the hooker blackmail idea again, and if I had any thoughts to engage in it, and I told him I hadn't given it much thought. On the way home, I was again questioning the depths that I would sink for Aronberg to expose my own enemies. It gave me severe pause to think I ever considered any of it, for which I was, and am deeply ashamed. But in the end, my conscience just wouldn't let me engage in wrecking the lives of the innocent to reach my goals. I called a contact from the Palm Beach Post, asked about Shultz' son and told him there was documentation that might be revealed to show dirt on Shultz' kid.

Another day passed, and a friend of mine, who we will only call Ashley - a world-class classical cellist, got her second DUI. She realized she had a problem with alcoholism, was extremely scared and asked me what she should do. I called Aronberg, who suggested we meet at the Duffy's in West Palm Beach, which we did. I brought Ashley, where we met Aronberg in one of the booths in the back. He talked to her and asked her some questions, and said he could help with the State Attorney in Martin County. He told me he would be in contact to give me details.

Aronberg called me a few days later saying he had the cash for the hookers and drugs that couldn't be traced back to him. He also stated he could have Ashley's charges dropped if I came through for him to get his opponent out of the race, but I told him I flat-out refused to do it. Aronberg was not very happy with that decision and told me I would not be getting any information on Bradshaw if he was elected.

When Aronberg stopped returning our calls, I decided I wanted to publish the story about the check after all. And so I did, with complete documentation and analysis about the check.

Chapter 22 - Burt Aaronson Email Hoax

After David Aronberg gave me the mailing list, I thought about the best way to wreak some havoc before the 2012 elections for the Sheriff, because I knew the fix was in. In Palm Beach County, which is primarily Democrat, the older voters vote for who they are told to vote for by the Democratic party. Joe Talley was running for Sheriff against Sheriff Bradshaw, and he was an excellent, honest candidate. So good, Bradshaw never, ever debated him. There were debates, but Bradshaw always bowed out and let Chief Deputy Gauger take the place of Sheriff Bradshaw. The fact the Palm Beach County Democratic Party would let that take place was shocking. Even more surprising, the questions asked of the candidates. The audience could submit questions, and the panel would ask them to the candidates.

I submitted some excellent questions. For instance, I asked why Sheriff Bradshaw thinks he should receive additional tax revenue when he was blowing millions on take-home cars. It was no small number, either. 135+ vehicles are handed out to civilian employees, like Christmas presents. I estimated it cost to the taxpayer to be over eight million dollars per year, when insurance, maintenance, and depreciation was factored in. I submitted another question about how the Sheriff was caught stealing a gun from the evidence room, purchasing lavish gifts for friends, and what the sheriff had to say about taking members of organized crime to dinner on the taxpayer's dime, in exchange for campaign contributions.

None of these questions ever made it into the debate though. Every time they would get one of those questions, they would shuffle it to the back of the question pile. The Democratic party of Palm Beach County had it rigged; they threw all friendly, straightforward questions to Chief Deputy Gauger, but with Joe Talley, they asked about more demanding and critical issues. Anyone who says the system isn't rigged… especially in the Democratic party, only needs to look at how they treated Sheriff Bradshaw while the same party demonized a candidate who was far superior.

I decided to attempt to even the score a bit. First, I hired an airplane to fly banners over West Palm Beach for high-profile events. At the Honda Classic, one of the banners displayed "Our Sheriff is a Thief – pbsotalk.com."

At the 4th of July celebration, I had another one that said, "Our Sheriff commits Felonies – pbsotalk.com."

Then I got very creative. One of the county commissioners, Burt Aaronson, who had all the condo commandos in his pocket, endorsed Sheriff Bradshaw. That means all the Palm Cards (little cards they give to each condo resident to tell them exactly how to vote) would have Sheriff Bradshaw's name on them.

I bought the domain name, "BurtAaronson.com," and the day before the election I sent out an email to the entire "A" list of Democratic voters in Palm Beach County (courtesy of David

Aronberg). The email had the subject line, "BurtAaronson.com no longer endorses the corrupt Sheriff Ric Bradshaw."

The body of the text contained a bullet list of everything known about Sheriff Bradshaw's criminal activities with links to supporting documents.

In fact, you can read the email for yourself:

From: BurtAaronson.com <info@BurtAaronson.com>
Sent: Tuesday, August 14, 2012 12:01 AM
To: 'mdougan@insurexecs.com'
Subject: BurtAaronson.com DOES NOT endorse the corrupt Ric Bradshaw for Sheriff

I have watched with great interest the race for Sheriff in Palm Beach County, and I am here to tell you that **we cannot** endorse the incumbent Sheriff Bradshaw. Instead, **we have chosen to endorse Joe Talley for Sheriff**.

Over the past year, I have learned of a vast amount of unethical, immoral and criminal activities being carried out by Sheriff Ric L. Bradshaw and his staff. These corrupt and illegal activities include, but are not limited to the following list, and for proof positive, I have included the links to the articles and documentation:

- Sheriff Ric Bradshaw was caught stealing a firearm from the evidence room (Click HERE to view the documentation).

- In the same sworn deposition, it was discovered Sheriff Bradshaw ordered detectives to falsify evidence against a black defendant to put him in jail. Sheriff Bradshaw has already been successfully sued for discrimination and is currently facing up to 31 lawsuits for discrimination. If victorious, the payouts for these suits come from the taxpayers.

- Sheriff Bradshaw's friend, Lt. Dan Burrows, was caught stealing the pain medication off the nightstand of a man who was dying of cancer. Sheriff Bradshaw refused to let Internal Affairs take any action and ordered them to hide his crimes (Click HERE to read the story). When PBSO SWAT Lieutenant Dan Burrows was caught stealing the pain medication off the nightstand of a dying deputy, he made that dying deputy to get out of his "deathbed" and open his safe to steal additional pain meds and firearms. Sheriff Bradshaw attempted to conceal this crime and arrested the disgusted IA investigator who leaked it to the media.

- Sheriff Ric Bradshaw was using his county credit card to treat campaign contributors to meals at lavish restaurants and bars. Some of these people have ties to the Colombo Crime Family (Click HERE to view the documentation). Sheriff Bradshaw was fully aware of these ties to organized crime, as it was pointed out by the Palm Beach Post in 2008 (Click HERE to read the Palm Beach Post article). The Florida Ethics Commission found that the purchases with taxpayer money were "not in the proper performance in his official duties."

- Sheriff Ric Bradshaw has been **extorting money** from seniors when raising their property taxes. He threatens they will become victims of violent gang-related crime because he will have to shut down their substations and cut police services. He then uses the money to buy off civilian employees who work for his campaign, to include about $6 Million per year in "company cars" the civilians drive to and from work and free gasoline, all funded by the taxpayer (Click HERE to view the documentation).

- Sheriff Bradshaw committed two felonies in May 2011 when he falsified an official document, alleging fraud, to receive a new county purchasing card in an attempt to hide his purchases from records request.

- Sheriff Bradshaw spent $12,313 to purchase silver-plated revolvers, complete with engraved name plaques, to present to each elected Sheriff in Florida. When public records requests were made, the Sheriff repeatedly lied (committing four misdemeanor counts of violating the sunshine law), however, a photograph from Sheriff Martin Crowder was obtained, as well as a confirmation that he was personally presented the firearm from Bradshaw. Also received was the invoice from the distributor which shows that they were purchased by the Sheriff's Office (Click HERE for the documentation). Note: the invoice has a typo, but it was made out to PBSO's address and the attention to PBSO Events Coordinator Carol Verdigi).

- Sheriff Ric Bradshaw spent $89,000 on three(3) massive BBQ grills to be used at reelection campaign events, and used for fundraising drives for the P.B.C. Police Benevolent Association. This does not include the three (3) diesel trucks in the amount of about $100,000. This information is known far and wide and even brought up in the candidate debate at the Pinellas County Sheriff's Office race. What an embarrassment to the citizens of Palm Beach County (to see the records, CLICK HERE).

- Sheriff Ric Bradshaw allowed a PBSO Lieutenant to commit felonies to include wiretapping and alleged rape, saying it wasn't the Sheriff's Office's place to become involved in one's personal life. There were credible allegations of rape, with evidence, though it was swept under the rug.

- Just last week, documents were posted on the site where the Sheriff, who owns a 1.1 Million dollar home in Ibis Country Club, was a defendant in a foreclosure where a judgment of $253,000 was awarded to the plaintiff. If this Sheriff Bradshaw can't manage his own finances for an investment property, how can the taxpayers trust him with a half-billion-dollar budget? CLICK HERE for the documentation.

- A website poll was conducted amongst people, primarily members of the Palm Beach County Sheriff's Office, where they were asked to nominate candidates for Sheriff and hold a vote against the incumbent, Sheriff Bradshaw. The question (written very fairly and impartially) was, "Who do you feel has the highest integrity and fairness to lead PBSO?" In a stunning defeat, the Sheriff received only 4% of the vote, the absolute lowest of all the nominees, while the highest ranked candidate received seven times that number at 28%. These are from people who are primarily deputies and know what Sheriff Bradshaw is about. I profess I am not in law enforcement, so I can't say if paying off civilian employees to work a campaign with tax dollars is legal or if the Sheriff needs to have BBQ grills values at $30,000 each.

Jim Donahue, however, **is in Law Enforcement**. In fact, Mr. Donahue is one of the most well-known authors on law enforcement topics with hundreds of articles to his credit. On a law-enforcement talk show, he stated:

"Ric Bradshaw is one of the ringleaders of one of the most corrupt public organizations in the country. I have seen what has gone on in Palm Beach County and recognize that in that county there is a level of corruption and dishonesty that puts the Chicago political machine to shame. In fact, it's the kind of people in power in Palm Beach County that are the kind of people my dad fought in WWII to defeat. They are threatening the very fabric of our republic."

You can hear the actual audio BY CLICKING HERE. I am sad to say I have discovered this level of corruption in Palm Beach County being committed by the highest law-enforcement official in the county. This has all been exposed by public documents that you can see for yourself (CLICK HERE TO VIEW). Luckily, however, the elections are just around the corner.

Legally, I can't tell you for whom to vote but I can tell you this – I will not be voting for Sheriff Bradshaw this election, or any other election. I feel voting for Sheriff Bradshaw is to give a nod of approval for corruption, waste, fraud and abuse against the taxpayers of this county.

I will be voting for Joe Talley, a man who I feel is the right person for the job, who has honor and morals. His website can be seen at www.joetalleyforsheriff.com

It is _imperative_ you review these documents and VOTE for the ethical candidate!

This is not an advertisement. This is only an informational message to let you know who BurtAaronson.com endorses for Sheriff of Palm Beach County. If you do not wish to receive any further communications from BurtAaronson.com, please email to opt out of any further messages. You can also write us at 120 South Olive Ave, West Palm Beach, FL 33401

BadVolf | by: John Mark Dougan
The True Story of an American cop avenging a corrupt system

To unsubscribe from receiving similar emails in the future, please .

Everyone was talking about the email - Politicians, cops, and reporters. I had dozens of calls from people laughing about it or asking if I was the culprit behind the prank. The Palm Beach Post reported this under the title:

"Aaronson seeks Investigation into faux email blasting Bradshaw in sheriff's race"

The article starts out saying:

"In a digital election-day dirty trick, an email began hitting computer mailboxes late Monday and continued spreading Tuesday, urging voters to reject Sheriff Ric Bradshaw's bid for a third term because of a series of serious, but mostly unsubstantiated, ethical breaches."

What the writer, Jane Musgrave, failed to tell the people in the article is that all of the documentation was right on the website. Unsubstantiated by who? Yeah, of course, the cops were looking the other way, and the Palm Beach Post was too busy sucking up to the Sheriff (whose campaign paid them tens of thousands of dollars for advertising and endorsements) to bother substantiating any of it for themselves. Ms. Musgrave continued to write:

"The key to the power of the email is that it was purportedly written by Democratic powerhouse Palm Beach County Commissioner Burt Aaronson."

But actually, Jane Musgrave was wrong, misleading her readers. The email was sent by BurtAaronson.com with no mention of the actual author. Just because people were confused, assuming Burt

Aaronson wrote it doesn't mean he purportedly wrote it. According to Ms. Musgrave:

> "An angry Aaronson denounced the email Tuesday, saying he was '1 million percent' behind Bradshaw."

Overall, however, I liked the article, especially when she wrote:

> "The website, BurtAaronson.com, is owned by Bradshaw's nemesis, computer whiz John Mark Dougan. For months, the former sheriff's deputy has featured many of the same allegations made in the email on his various websites — including pbsotalk.com."

Ms. Musgrave goes into detail on how Aaronson acted like a humorless, petulant child, demanding an investigation from the Palm Beach County State Attorney's office. According to Musgrave, Aaronson told her "I'm just absolutely livid that someone would steal my name and use it this way. I'm looking into whether this guy has stepped over the line."

Rick Asnani, Bradshaw's campaign consultant, the guy who tried, and failed to buy my website also told Ms. Musgrave, "I think this time Mr. Dougan has gone too far."

When Ms. Musgrave called me, I remained noncommittal about my involvement in the email campaign, saying, "Why does everyone blame me?" I indicated to Ms. Musgrave that anyone could have posted the email on BurtAaronson.com and emailed it to what some claimed was an A-list of Democratic voters.

In her article, Musgrave continued:

> "Antonacci called the phony email 'outrageous conduct.' But, he said, it doesn't appear to violate any laws.

"It's something Congress needs to deal with," he said, adding that laws have not kept up with mischief that can be wreaked on the Internet."

I'm glad Antonacci was objective about this prank. To me, that shows he would make a great State Attorney, but really… how is Congress going to deal with this? Even if they could, they work so slowly. Still, they were out for blood, and Rick Asnani tried to have me investigated for violating federal election laws – by using fake news to try to influence an election. Hmmm, phony news to influence an election? Where have I heard that recently?

The most troubling part of the article was claiming "… a series of serious, but mostly unsubstantiated, ethical breaches…" I had the documentation all laid out for anyone to view. Had the Palm Beach Post done its job for the citizens they are supposed to inform, they would have investigated the allegations and corresponding documents for themselves and verified the ethical breaches instead of looking the other way to curry favor with corrupt politicians.

As you might guess, people were pissed, calling the State Attorney's office in an attempt to have me arrested for identity theft. The elected State Attorney, Michael McCaulife, was embroiled in various scandals and quit before his term was over. David Aaronberg hadn't been elected to be the State Attorney yet; the Florida Governor had appointed an interim State Attorney named Peter Antonucci who reviewed the case.

Gauger was thrilled, confident that I was going to be arrested for a crime. He called local-area reporters to inform them that John Mark Dougan would soon be incarcerated. Disappointment bitch slapped him in the face when the State Attorney who was reviewing the case realized the email was sent out saying BurtAaronson.com, and not purporting to be Burt Aaronson. And for that reason, the person who owned the domain BurtAaronson.com couldn't be charged with a crime.

My source inside Mahogany Row (that's what they call the administrative section) at Headquarters called me up laughing hysterically. He told me Gauger was so angry; he was stomping around, swearing, slamming doors and sulking a brat having a tantrum for not getting the Barbie doll she wanted for Christmas.

I was laughing, too, because of the absolute stupidity of these people. How could anyone expect to arrest the legitimate owner of a domain for using the domain's name in advertising, marketing or mailing? Whatever, it was a cause for celebration. I went out that night and had some drinks.

> *"If an injury has to be done to a man it should be so severe that his vengeance need not be feared." - Niccolo Machiavelli*

Chapter 23 - Other Websites around the United States

RentonTalk

In December of 2012, while listening to Cop Talk Radio, I heard the story of "Mr. Fuddlesticks," in Renton, Washington. Mr. Fuddlesticks was a cartoon character created by an anonymous Renton, Washington character that would reenact parodied accounts about cover-ups that were happening in the Renton Police Department. The cartoons were wide-ranging, talking about things from female Renton cops having sex with suspects, sexual misconduct, drugs, bad arrests… and many other incidents, hidden from the public.

On Cop Talk Radio revealed that the Renton Police Department ignored what should have been free speech and instead called it "cyberstalking." With that frivolous charge, Renton Police Department was trying to obtain warrants to serve to YouTube for the IP address of the person that was posting the cartoons. This major assault of free speech showed how low police departments go to suppress dissidents. I decided to step in.

I modeled the forum RentonTalk after PBSOTalk and provided a way for the Renton cops to post anonymously. It was a major scandal. You had cops fighting anonymously, accusing others of serious allegations, and I provided the person behind "Mr. Fuddlesticks" with an email address under the name of Steven Schwartz so that he could make public records requests to the City of Renton without being caught. I ran my own email server and hosted RentonTalk on the same one, so there was no danger for the identity of Mr. Fuddlesticks to be discovered.

You may wonder why I still refer to the person as Mr. Fuddlesticks; it's not to protect him, it's because I never asked him for his name. It wasn't my business, and frankly, I didn't want to know. If I didn't have that knowledge, then no one could ever compel me to divulge that information. For me, that benefit far outweighed any need to satisfy my curiosity.

Predictably, the Palm Beach County Sheriff's Office and Renton Police Department joined together to share notes and start a joint criminal investigation into me and my site. Detective Kenneth Mark Lewis even flew out to Renton, the other side of the country, to discuss ways they could arrest me and get the site shut down. Truthfully, the site was doing an incredible amount of damage to the reputation of Renton's leadership because so many terrible things were exposed to the public. Not only that, but it was pitting different divisions of the city administration against each other. The City Manager was fuming when RentonTalk revealed he was running around with police lights in his personal car. The citizens wanted answers, and the mayor took it out on the Chief and Asst. Chief.

A few months later, I received an encrypted message from Mr. Fuddlesticks, saying someone had posted a list of all of the police officers' social security numbers, and that the Secret Service was now involved. He told me that he was going underground, and asked me if I could take down the site. And so, I did. I never heard from Mr. Fuddlesticks again, and I have no idea whatever happened to him. I can only hope he made it unscathed, without getting caught.

HuronTalk

RentonTalk was such a hit, an employee of the Huron, California police department contacted me asking for a site. Huron was quite the criminal enterprise, and when all was said and done, several members of the police department and town council were fired or arrested, all due to the information that came out on my site.

With HuronTalk, there was anonymous information about all manner of scandals, including a Huron police officer who was giving information to gang members, a Huron police officer having a sexual relationship with a 14-year-old girl and city council members embezzling hundreds of thousands of dollars.

Again, the Palm Beach County Sheriff's Office paid Detective Kenneth Mark Lewis to fly there and aid them in an investigation in an attempt to have the site shut down and have me arrested.

Chapter 24 - Homicide Coverup of Two Black Deputies

On November 28, 2007, 23-year-old deputy Jonathan Wallace and 33-year-old Donta Manuel were killed in the line of duty. Not by a suspect, but by fellow deputy Gregorio Fernandez.

Several Palm Beach County deputies were chasing a kid who stole a crappy old Honda. Wallace and Manuel were standing in the road, fixing a set of stop stick designed to puncture the tires on cars that won't stop for the police. It was incredibly dark at the high rate of speed Fernandes was driving, it was impossible to avoid hitting the two deputies.

Fernandez was driving at over twice the speed limit, such a high rate of speed that it was deemed to be criminal by THI (Traffic Homicide Investigator) Troy Snelgrove. Fernandez struck Wallace and Manuel while going 111 miles per hour (179 km/h), impacting them so hard, their arms, legs, heads and other body parts were ripped off and flew hundreds of feet. PBSO put out a search party to find all the body parts of the deputies, but they missed several – like a leg. An arm. A head. Things of that nature. A few days later at a vigil to remember the fallen deputies, someone spotted one of their legs floating in the canal.

THI Snelgrove wrote in his report that "Fernandez drove his vehicle in a willful and wanton reckless manner with disregard for the safety of persons on the roadway. This reckless driving resulted in the death of Jonathan Wallace and Donta Manuel." He forwarded the investigative report to the Palm Beach County State Attorney's office.

At this point, you may guess that the State Attorney's office prosecuted Deputy Fernandez for vehicular manslaughter, but you would be wrong. The Sheriff had ordered the alteration of the report, so the blame fell squarely on the two dead black deputies.

Sheriff Bradshaw thought it was much easier to cover up the death of two black deputies with families so poor that it would be hard to bring forth any legal action. The State Attorney's office was complicit in the cover-up, and the entire story went away until tips started coming in regarding the report that had been covered up.

The report was sent anonymously in 2014 and that information was given to a reporter, Katie Lagrone at Channel WPTV 5 who started poking around. Eventually, Lagrone was able to obtain the original and did a big story on the incident.

Chapter 25 - Seth Adams

Background of the Scandal

One of the biggest scandals of the Palm Beach County Sheriff's Office came in 2012, when a friend of mine, Sgt. Michael Custer, shot an unarmed young white male on the property where the victim lived, late at night. The man, Seth Adams, was known throughout the community as a kind, upstanding citizen. Adams was killed when he and Custer argued over Custer's presence in an unmarked service car on the parking lot of Adams' landscaping business/home. Custer said he thought Adams was going for a gun when he fired his Glock, killing Adams.

Just an hour and a half after the shooting, Sheriff Ric Bradshaw immediately justified the shooting, saying Sgt. Custer was attacked and feared for his life. After that, however, details of the shooting began to leak out, and there was public outrage.

The details that were leaking out were things like:

- A neighbor heard gunshots and then tires squealing like someone was fleeing the scene.
- A wet spot in the crime scene photographs, like another car was parked at the scene.
- The man shot dragged himself over 100 meters to get his brother's attention, leaving a trail of blood.
- The ballistic evidence didn't match the statements of Sgt. Custer. Custer said he fired from the side of the truck as Seth Adams reached inside his vehicle, however, it was clear Sgt. Custer was standing at the back of the vehicle when the shooting happened.

But the most scandalous detail to emerge is that when crime scene investigators tested Custer's clothing for Seth Adams' DNA in an attempt to claim Adams attacked Custer. Instead, they found a third, unknown set of DNA on the crotch of Michael Custers' pants, around the zipper area.

The Coverup of Sgt. Custer's Crime

There had been numerous postings on PBSOTalk about Custer's affair with a female detective named Victoria Miller dating back to 2010. Custer himself called me in 2010 and asked me to remove the postings. As a friend, we chatted, and he told me the affair was no one's business. I agreed, and I deleted the posts for him.

The day after the shooting, before all of the details came to light, I called Custer to check on him. As far as I knew, he was a friend and a victim who was attacked by a maniac. Custer told me he was okay and revealed to me that he was having a rendezvous with his mistress, Det. Miller. With its seclusion from public view and that fact it was just two blocks from Custer's home, the Seth Adams property would have been a very convenient place for an affair; it was a large, dark parcel of land obscured from sight and was just a few blocks from his home.

I didn't go into detail about the meeting with Det. Miller because I was concerned for my friend and the emotional stress he was facing. But after the details of the second car came to light and the investigation revealed unknown DNA on Custers' crotch, I began to believe that something sinister had happened. It was a certainty that the attorneys for the parents of Seth Adams were going to reveal the truth.

The shooting incident became a massive coverup on an enormous scale rarely seen in law enforcement. Sgt. Custer and Det. Miller both signed sworn affidavits that the two were not romantically involved, and claimed they never were involved in any type of relationship. I knew this to be an outright lie. I took the responsibility to contact the Adams' attorneys, telling them I had personal knowledge of the affair because the Sheriff's Office was lying to them.

The attorneys demanded to examine Sgt. Custer's mobile phone for text messages between him and Victoria Miller. That phone, however, was suspiciously "Lost" by the PBSO detectives investigating the case, despite incredibly stringent policies regarding the handling of evidence and chain of custody. To make proving their case more difficult, Sgt. Custer's laptop was "routinely" destroyed by the Sheriff's Office so that no evidence from it was also unavailable.

Custer's past performance evaluations were hidden from the Adams' attorneys. The records were uncovered, thanks to a whistleblower's tip, and the results were positively shocking.

Custer's performance evaluation by his Captain just the year before stated:

"Sergeant Custer has difficulty assessing critical incidents and making sound decisions under pressure." The supervisor also described Custer as "indecisive in critical situations" and needing "to improve his decision-making ability."

After the finding, tempers flared at a hearing in the Seth Adams lawsuit when a federal magistrate pronounced himself "shocked" at the behavior of Palm Beach County Sheriff's Office brass. The angry exchange, according to a transcript obtained by journalist Jose Lambiet at Gossip Extra, came as lawyers for the family of Adams told the judge PBSO didn't give them proper personnel files for Sgt. Michael Custer, and instead were hiding the records.

The judge assigned to the civil rights lawsuit filed in West Palm Beach by Adams' family, Federal Magistrate James Hopkins, admonished PBSO by exclaiming, "It's really quite shocking. The Sheriff's office performance appears to be shocking."

The outburst came as Richard Guiffreda, PBSO's contracted lawyer, tried to play semantics with the words "personnel file."

"If the Sheriff's office is hiding behind the fact that this is not a personnel file, this is shocking," Hopkins insisted. At the hearing, attorney Wallace McCall, who represented the Adams' family, asked Hopkins for help dealing with PBSO's release of paperwork. A whopping two years after the shooting, McCall told Hopkins he had yet to receive some of Custer's evaluations. At one point, PBSO erroneously claimed that the papers didn't exist because the agency had quit doing certain types of evaluations.

"I think there's a disconnect in terms of what type of performance evaluation we're talking about," Giuffrida told Hopkins.

"What's the difference between a personnel record and a personnel file," Hopkins finally wondered.

"There's no distinction." Though Custer was a sergeant and the leader of one of PBSO's elite tactical units for over a year before the evaluation, his supervisor wrote: "He has not learned the necessary job skills to be effective at this assignment."

According to the Hopkins transcript, PBSO was also dragging its collective feet in providing emails between the PBSO employees who investigated and deemed the Adams shooting justifiable. Last month, a whistleblower made available to Gossip Extra emails between one investigator and his bosses. PBSO has yet to provide them to Adams' lawyers.

Jose reached out to the sheriff's office for comment, but Bradshaw's policy is to not cooperate with media organizations that he thinks are against him.

At every turn, the Palm Beach County Sheriff's Office hid, destroyed, covered up, and concealed evidence vital to revealing the truth about what happened that night. And that's not all. Just a year after the shooting, Detective Victoria Miller had given birth to a little boy who looked suspiciously like Sgt. Michael Custer. When asked who the father was, Det. Miller claimed she was artificially inseminated, though never provided any documentation regarding the procedure. What's even more suspicious, the baby's godmother was none other than the wife of Major Van Reeth, the head of the guy in charge of investigating immoral or illegal conduct by deputies.

There's been a lot of speculation on the site. Most people, including me, believe Victoria Miller was present when Custer shot Adams, and then fled the scene. Others take it one step further, thinking that Custer and Adams were, in fact, having an altercation, and that Miller was the one that shot and killed Adams – and that Custer was taking the rap to save her reputation. I'm not one for conspiracy theories, but it seems entirely plausible to me.

Law Enforcement Intimidation of a Hostile Witness

In April 2015, after I had submitted my own affidavit to the courts concerning Sgt. Michael Custer's admitted involvement with Detective Victoria Miller, the Palm Beach County Sheriff's Office started a brutal campaign of harassment against my family as retaliation. My father was diagnosed with Mantle Cell Lymphoma that was likely to be terminal; PBSO hired people to knock on my father's door and call his phone at all hours of the day and night. People would go to his home acting confrontational.

My wife, Kelly, with whom I was separated from at this point, was also harassed severely. PBSO hired people to knock on the surrounding neighbor's doors, showing my photograph, telling them I was a danger to the community. They were also knocking on Kelly's door and harassing her.

On Easter day, 2015, one of the hired goons ran her car in front of Kelly's car, with my two children in the back seat. Kelly was distraught when a woman who had harassed her earlier jumped out of the car. That lady began chasing Kelly's car with the kids in the back seat through the neighborhood, causing a real risk of a crash. I contacted the attorneys for PBSO at their homes, demanding they knock off the harassment. In one case, I got into a heated exchange with one of the attorneys, and he recorded the conversation. The recording was edited and provided to the judge in their attempt to have me disqualified as a witness, but I wrote my responses, ordering them to preserve their electronic devices for my defense of their claim. Providing altered evidence to a judge in a hearing is a felony.

 I wrote a letter to the courts telling them my family was facing severe retaliation because I was a witness against a law enforcement agency. I have included that letter on the appendix n my website, www.badvolf.com

Chapter 26 - "False News" Evidence Compels Testimony

One of the things that infuriated me off about the Seth Adams case was the fact that Sheriff Ric Bradshaw, Chief Deputy Michael Gauger, and Victoria Miller were all exempt by the courts from testifying about what they knew. The American court system has raped lady justice so hard, she's petrified, constantly looking out of her blindfold with one eye. These people damned sure knew what happened, and they systematically assisted and sanctioned the coverup. The judge was a bit of a coward in calling the Sheriff's Office out, so he exempted the orchestrators of the coverup. Hurley wouldn't overturn the exemption unless additional information came to light. I took this as a sign to "provide" the evidence needed to compel the three complicit, crooked law enforcement officers to testify.

On March 26th, someone anonymously sent a PDF file showing a possibly-incriminating email chain to a journalist covering the Seth Adams shooting. They contacted the Sheriff's Office, who gave him a "No Comment." The publication broke the story fueling outrage and speculation. The rest of the media, quick not to be left in the dust from such salacious news, jumped on the story – how predictable. The judge, knowing that the Palm Beach County Sheriff's Office had been hiding other documentary evidence, granted the motion by the Adams' attorney to compel a total of five additional people to testify about what they knew about the Seth Adams killing. The results were positively shocking; all five of them refused to answer questions, invoking their right to remain silent on the answers. The founders created the 5th Amendment for cases where answering a question would result in self-incrimination and prosecution for a crime. When people refuse to answer questions on the record, it's pretty much a sign they've done something wrong. The Sheriff himself invoked this right over <u>one hundred</u> times during his deposition.

The email that caused such a controversy? It was nothing more than a work of my fiction, made in just a few minutes with a combination of Microsoft Word, Adobe Photoshop, and Adobe Acrobat. Was it the right thing to do? I think yes. The American justice system doesn't protect the innocent, the victims, or the righteous. It had been systematically perverted by lawmakers and lawyers to protect the guilty, the abusers of power, and is crafted in such a way to help people in the government commit crimes without being caught.

For further proof of this, look no further than the recordings of Detective Kenneth Mark Lewis, coming up in a few chapters.

Chapter 27 - Fake News! So easy to do…

"Vengeance is sweet. Vengeance taken when the vengee isn't sure who the venger is, is sweeter still." - Gary D. Schmidt

After the incident with Seth Adams, I decided to get a bit of revenge on my own. I created a few fake news sites and got the stories blasted all over the country by other sources. There is a psychological component to fake news. A set of rules to make a fake news site believable.

First, the domain name. When buying a domain name, it has got to be kept short and official sounding. No one is going to believe a domain with an obnoxiously-long domain name. The domain extensions are flexible; in fact, more people believe truth from a .org domain than a .com domain, because .org domains tend to be owned by more legitimate, official companies, agencies, and charities.

A fake-news site is nothing without real news. There must be real news with actual photos on the front of the site, so the fake story blends in and becomes believable. If someone goes to a news site with just one story, the fictitious one you are trying to sell, they are going to know it's a sham.

Populating a site with real stories is not very difficult to accomplish. The easiest way is to search for other news sites that have full-text RSS feeds. Russia Today (RT) used to have a full-text feed, but it changed to short RSS snippets in 2015. Many news sites have the RSS logo on them. Just give the logos a click and see what the result happens to be. If you see an entire story encoded in the XML format, it's full text. If you see just a short portion, then it's not.

Once you find sites with full-text RSS feeds, you need to bring them into the website with an RSS feed aggregator. Some aggregators will even bring in the featured photo, so you don't have to spend time finding pictures for the stories. Then you just need a bit of software (or to write your own code) that sets the imported photo as the featured photo in your fake news site. Just like magic, when you do these steps, you have a working fake-news site. If you manage your own server, it takes an hour to set up from the time you buy your domain name to the time it's ready to start giving fake news. Right now, take a look at DC Weekly. A reporter doing a story on me told me it's the best fake news site he's ever seen, and I don't think I spent more than an hour and a half on it before getting the news to start populating with a nice logo at the top.

There is one more critical component to a fake news site, and that's the story itself. If you want a story to go viral, it must include hot-button topics that generate outrage. The topic you choose should be relevant to current events. Once you write the story, then you have to get the word out by any means necessary. Reddit is a great way, but there are also news outlets that allow you to submit stories before they make national headlines.

I bought several web domains, one of them being DCPost.org. I set it up to look like a legitimate news site as described above. I sucked stories from RT news to populate the DCPost with genuine stories of significant events from around the world. The site would update automatically so that there was a good history for people to see. I would throw in stories that were so outrageous and heinous, that people would believe them. I would pick hot-button topics that I knew were sure to give the loud and obnoxious protesters a reason to scream.

In 2015, everything was about the Occupy movement. These assholes would block the roads, pissing all of the hard-working citizens off, and I wanted to leverage that hate and anger to mess with the Sheriff. I wrote a fictitious story about how Sheriff Bradshaw told a group of elderly white people to run over black people protesting in the roads. I filled the article with real facts about the Sheriff's treatment of minorities and illegal deeds at the Sheriff's Office with links to other news outlets that reported on those other past deeds. It made the story much more believable, and people were pissed off at the Sheriff all over the country. Hundreds of news outlets fell for it, including publications in Europe that wrote about the story.

When you think about it, it's no different than what the Sheriff himself has sanctioned by allowing and encouraging his officers to falsify their police reports. When a cop writes an affidavit, report or warrant indicating facts that are not true, it can cause irreparable damage to the lives of the innocent. Think of that before you become outraged at me for returning the favor to a bunch of crooks.

Chapter 28 - PBSO Enlists a mob snitch to investigate me

PBSO secretly had arranged a few meetings with a weasel who turned into a confidential informant for Chief Deputy Gauger in exchange for having theft charges dropped. This guy, an angry little criminal, used to be an accountant for mafia boss John Gotti but flipped into a confidential informant to save himself from going to jail. He was put in the Witness Protection Program and relocated to South Florida, so I knew what kind of weasel he was.

A few years later, the FBI dumped him like a turd in the toilet; apparently, they recognized his value and worth to society. His wife also realized she was with a complete loser so she, too, flushed the bowels of her life and got rid of that piece of crap. He was arrested in January 2015 after stealing a check from an attorney's desk and depositing it into his account.

That same month, he called me. Hey Mark, can you meet me? I have some information for you, and I want to see if you can help me with a problem. I will pick up the tab for lunch."

The thing is, I knew what kind of person this weasel happened to be; a nasty little piece of garbage who would do anything to save his ass. I had told Jose Lambiet as much as I was driving to the rendezvous. Jose told me to be careful and not to trust this guy. I already knew it.

We met at the Yard House in Palm Beach Gardens. At the meeting, he ordered a soda and asked me if I wanted one; I ordered a beer and an appetizer, which made the cheap little bastard grimace. He started asking me questions about giving information to Jose Lambiet and asked if I had contacts in the Sheriff's Office who could help him with his charges.

He had set his phone on the table with the microphone facing me, and my suspicions of the obvious told me he was recording me. I told that guy all sorts of garbage, mostly, anything that wasn't true but sounded true enough.

After the meeting, he paid the bill, and that piece of trash didn't even leave a tip to the waitress. I said to him, "Aren't you going to leave a tip?" to which he replied, "Nah, she's young. She has plenty of time to make money when she's older." When he turned to walk away, I threw down about five bucks for the tip, walked back to my car and went home. Probably to take a shower to wash off the guy's vile slime.

Chapter 29 - Catfishing Detective Kenneth Mark Lewis

In July of 2015, I was told by one of my sources that the Sheriff's Office was actively looking for a reason to throw me in jail to prevent me from testifying in the Seth Adams case. They had been looking for ideas for years, but now this case was about to explode in their faces. The judge had already accused the Palm Beach County Sheriff's Office of outrageous conduct in hiding evidence and documents for the case, and my testimony was going to be the final piece to ignite the fuse.

Just a little background information on this subject, the first time I had ever heard of Detective Kenneth Mark Lewis, was in 2012 when Internal Affairs Detective Lieutenant Dean Johnson told me that he was investigating me after Johnson was arrested. I wanted to find out about this guy, so I posted on PBSOTalk, asking if anyone knew him. Some user had posted that he was bitterly divorced because his wife was having sex with all the migrant workers in Belle Glade.

I received the following email that referred to Det. Lewis in the 3rd person. First, part of the email header that assured me it was sent from Detective Lewis (I am removing some of the stuff that doesn't matter, but you can find it on the site):

```
Received: from fire1.pbso.org (HELO MAILHTS01.pbso.org)
([209.149.216.2])
by p3pismtp01-028.prod.phx3.secureserver.net with
ESMTP; 11 May 2012 05:21:25
-0700
Received: from MAILMS05.pbso.org
From: "Lewis, Kenneth M" <LewisK@pbso.org>
To: "'info@pbsotalk.com'" <info@pbsotalk.com>
Subject: Info
Thread-Topic: Info
Thread-Index: Ac0vZXDPXQe46Y3bTqadtJYx1UqSOA==
Date: Fri, 11 May 2012 12:21:22 +0000
Message-ID:
<0A3C69F0F357244DB775B17A9088215008B831@MAILMS05.pbso.org>
x-originating-ip: [172.22.166.152]
```

And then the message:

"Mark,
Just want to give you a heads up on a few things. First I encourage you to look closely @ what information you are getting from Mr. James Donahue. The warrant for him was filed before he went to pick up his filing packet for sheriff and he had already moved to Daytona and applied for a job at a cop shop there. You should read the PC and the report. It's not rocket science, Mr. Donahue said he was a Federal Agent in order to enter the academy, and he wasn't. That investigation was pushed by FDLE, not the sheriff. He has a lengthy history of fabricating stories and has been arrested in Michigan for impersonating a police officer, all public record. As far as Lewis, he is a careful meticulous investigator. He has no agenda and will not be swayed by Bradshaw or Gauger, he is a straight shooter and well respected in the community. He has been donating time and money to HOMESAFE and several other charities. I know his family did own one of the largest law firms in Washington, Baltimore and I think had offices in California and Europe? Not sure about Europe. I also know for a fact he is not a close personal friend of Gauger. Lewis was asked to look at you by the State Attorney. As far as investigating you, I would

imagine if he had something on you the warrant would have already been filed, if nothing is there he will not file or put his name on it. ask some of your insiders... Also your post about his ex-wife, the information about her running around was pretty close but you got her name wrong. Only someone very close to her would know her middle name was sue, she does not go by that. She is still in the area and works for a large chemical company in BG. Check it out............
I have more, will type you later"

If you are reading my book, you are probably a smart person. And it doesn't exactly take a rocket scientist or nuclear physicist to notice this buffoon sent me an email pretending to be some anonymous person, complimenting himself, but accidentally did so from his work account.

"Holy Hell!," I thought. It HAD to be a joke because no one could possibly be that stupid, right? But no, I opened the header of the email (as shown above)

and the sending server was listed as fire.pbso.org with an IP address of 209.149.216.2. If you are a tech nerd like me, you know it makes it definitive that it came from PBSO's mail server. If you aren't a tech nerd like me, well, you just learned something new. You can see the rest of the email exchange in the appendix, it's a hell of a funny read. Now that the background is out of the way, let's continue with our story.

Naturally, I wanted to find out what they were up to, so I devised a plan to do just that. Having spoken to Detective Kenneth Mark Lewis in the past, I knew he was of weak mind, a borderline imbecile, so I didn't think it would be tough to fool him.

I put together a plan to "catfish" him. To do this, I rented a server overseas so it would be difficult to trace, then I set up PBX software on it. PBX software is software that allows a company to route SIP trunks to various locations, and it gives you lots of functionality regarding call routing, bridging, and in my case, spoofing telephone calls.

I was able to get a SIP trunk with a Manhattan (New York City) DID telephone number and had the calls from the PBX system routed through that. I know what you are thinking… wouldn't Detective Lewis recognize my voice? I thought that, too. Which is why before going to the PBX system, I routed my outgoing voice through a digital voice changer. I set up the sound output to change my voice to that of a woman. I tried the call on several different people before I called Detective Lewis, and they were all completely fooled. I knew I was set to make the calls, as long as I had a story set up.

I thought about it and decided that no matter what I did, Sheriff Bradshaw, Chief Deputy Michael Gauger, and Detective Lewis would get together and come up with some kind of lie about how they knew I was behind the call. They would say they were leading me along to get information, telling me what I wanted to hear. After thinking of a way to give proof positive that Lewis has no knowledge, I came up with the idea that if I were to have Detective Lewis do something he thought was a criminal act that could be proven, that he would not have the ability to say he was merely telling me what I wanted to hear. Because if he knew it was me, why on earth would he commit a crime?

Detective Lewis has a small construction and renovation contracting service that I found online. It was the perfect opening. I decided that I would call Detective Lewis and tell him my boyfriend and I (he thought I was a woman, remember?) were moving to his city and wanted to know about remodeling a house for us to reside. That's the exact opening I used, and at no time did I ever mention his job as a detective. I thought if I gave him a reason to believe he was about to fuck some young hottie, he would bring that up on his own.

I made the first call as "Jessica," and told Detective Lewis about the plan to move down with my boyfriend, hired by a chemical company in Belle Glade. I informed Lewis we were considering a few different houses, all needing the appropriate renovations. Detective Lewis was thrilled that someone would seek him out and give him business. That person's name was "Jessica."

In the first few hours of talking to him, I told him my father owned one of Wall Street's largest consulting firms for the mergers and acquisitions of brokerage companies. He learned that my (Jessica's) family owned many homes and a private jet. He bought that shit, hook, line, and sinker. Such a gullible fool. He sent me a photo of his house, as well as a photo of himself, from the late 1980's. It was so pathetic, so laughable; it was almost hard not to cry in hysteria. I sent him a photo of "Jessica" back, who wasn't Jessica at all. Rather, it was a photo of a Russian woman who happened to be on my VKontakt friend's list. Vkontakte is the Russian equivalent of Facebook. In researching information for this book to refresh my memory of the dates, names and such, I discovered the photo used to lure him in is of a Russian actress, Ekaterina Klimova. In hindsight, I should have picked something a little less high profile. But hey, a shout out to Ms. Klimova, thanks for inadvertently helping me take down a dirty cop!

A few days after the first phone call, I (Jessica) sent him a text message saying that I was deeply upset because I broke up with my boyfriend. I told him I needed to get out of town and that I was going to hop on the plane and come to Florida to see him, needing someone to console me in my time of despair. He was completely on board and offered to pick me up at the airport. I told him it would be fantastic, and I was really looking forward to meeting such a sexy, older man.

No doubt, Detective Lewis spent the next few hours jerking off in his desperate anticipation.

Later that night, I sent him another text, saying I had calmed down and needed to pause and think about my options. He was very kind, very understanding. The poor bastard was probably very sexually frustrated to the point he humped his dog.

Still, it was a grand opening to start talking about our future together. And Detective Lewis was only too happy to talk about our future. That's also when he told me he was a part-time Detective for the Palm Beach County Sheriff's office. He requested I google him to see some of the cases on which he had worked.

Now, when I take on a role, even the part of Jessica, I get totally into it. So I did just what he asked, I googled his name and saw the incident where he posted on PBSOTalk about his wife was at the top of the page. I felt this was an excellent opportunity to pull away and let him engage in a chase. For some reason, guys are suckers like that; we love the "hard to get." So I decided to play that guy like a fiddle. I sent him a text message saying I googled his name and was shocked he would say such nasty stuff about his ex-wife. I told him I didn't want to be with a man who would do such a thing.

Poor Detective Lewis, he was so desperate to explain the situation, he said, "Remember I was telling you I am a detective? Those posts are because of a guy named John Mark Dougan." Detective Lewis continued to tell his story about how he was pursuing this elusive guy, and how he and Sheriff Bradshaw were trying to have me locked up for anything they could find.

In the course of his explanation, he went into great detail about how they had illegally been hacking into my Social Media accounts and investigating every aspect of my life. He stated they even obtained my FAA medical exam and were trying to have me prosecuted for lying to get my pilot's license.

On a side note, what they call a lie wasn't at all. I have a mild case of Tourettes that sometimes makes me blink a bit more than average. But it's absolutely never affected anything in my life. I was in the Marine Corps and participated on the Rifle and Pistol team, ranking in the top ten in the nation. I was the squad leader in my police academy and had the best score by far on the pistol range.

My skills were so excellent that one day, after the instructors at the Palm Beach County Sheriff's Office got bored with me eliminating other deputies in the tactical maze, Corporal Gavin Phiffle decided to put me against three deputies. In the tactical maze, which is about 100 yards long, one person starts at one side, and another (or in this case, three) begins at the other end. There are objects to take cover behind to prevent being shot by your opponent. I entered the maze and saw the three adversaries on the opposite side. I went to the right as far as I could go to have a straight shot, and I took all three of them out in a matter of seconds, one after the other, with a Glock pistol shooting Simunition rounds.

After I eliminated the three challengers, Cpl. Phiffle came up and put his fingers on my neck to feel my pulse, and he stated my heart wasn't even beating fast. He said he had never seen anything like it.

Which brings me back to the original point regarding the medical exam. When the doctor asks you questions, he asks if you have any neurological conditions that would interfere with the operation of an aircraft. I told him I had a mild case of Tourette's, but that if anything, it sharpened my focus and coordination. He agreed with me and said that didn't count – they were looking for things like epilepsy, seizures, etc. And so the "No" box was checked.

If I were going to lie about my medical condition, I wouldn't have disclosed that I have had kidney stones, which required me to get additional tests done to make sure there were no more in my system.

Really though, my FAA medical form was no business of the Palm Beach County Sheriff's Office – that is federal, and they are a county law enforcement agency. Not even remotely in their jurisdiction. Still, they combed through my entire life, looking for something they could try and hang me on. And they worked hard to do it. Detective Lewis stated they decided to bring their case to the FBI, but then they saw I was traveling to Russia, so they wanted to find out "what I was up to."

When I was taking photos in Russia, the Palm Beach County Sheriff's Office and the FBI were watching my every move. They were examining my metadata and reading all of my emails. Detective Lewis? He spilled the beans about their criminal activity, using the power of Law Enforcement to target not only me but any dissident who didn't agree with them or their tactics.

One of the things that caught my attention during our conversations, he brought up a meeting I had with Pavel Borodin. As mentioned earlier, it was a discussion I had about bring telecom technologies to Russia. The Palm Beach County Sheriff's Office had a photo of us eating at the Bison Steak House, taken with my phone.

The investigators made up some nonsense garbage that Borodin's son was the ringleader of a criminal organization in Russia that dealt with identity theft and child pornography and that I was involved. It was shocking to hear, not only because it wasn't true, and I don't even think Borodin has a son, but the blatant, outright violation of my rights and outright lying the government will use to "generate suspicion" for warrants and other things to violate the rights of citizens.

Then, there's the hypocrisy of the entire situation. To my knowledge, Borodin is a good man that loves soccer and donates a significant amount of his money sponsoring orphanages. The only way the greedy assholes at the Sheriff's office would ever give to the needy is if they could do it with county money and get paid in the process.

I would later use this lie that they created to fuck with them and get the media interested in exposing what was going on. More on that later, though.

Detective Lewis said he spent years on the taxpayer's dole, authorized by Sheriff Bradshaw and Chief Deputy Michael Gauger, traveling all over the country and using county resources to "tear into the lives, families, and businesses of anyone" who politically went after the Sheriff or others. Besides me, he specifically named two other people: Jim Donahue and Rick Curtis. But after Lewis made these admissions, I found out they were just part of the many people they tried to have thrown in jail for being political dissidents.

After they admitted to illegally accessing my social media accounts, I decided to see how far they would go. I found a woman on Facebook and claimed to Mark Lewis she was my wealthy father's wife. I told Lewis she had been acting suspicious, and I caught her with a laptop in the laundry room with the door closed in the dead of night. I told Lewis I was worried she was orchestrating a plot to steal my father's money and asked if he could help.

Lewis eagerly said he could help, and I asked if he could find out what she was writing; he assured me he could. I told him, "Well don't you need a warrant or something?" The response was bone chilling to anyone who believes the American Constitution holds any weight in our society, or anyone who believes that law enforcement cannot abuse their limitless powers. He said, "We don't need warrants, I can use the Sheriff's Office and go in the back door."

I told him I was willing to pay him for investigating her, and said, well what if we find that she's up to something? Is there something we can do?" Just when you thought the conversation couldn't turn any darker, there was a discussion about how he could log into her profile as her and post a public comment on her Facebook page that would rise to a criminal level, making it look like she did it by mistake. Detective Lewis would then make an anonymous tip to the local police in her jurisdiction and have her arrested. "Holy Hell!" was the only thing I could think at that point. And if you don't believe it, listen to the recordings for yourself on the PBSOTalk website.

In the end, no one did a damned thing. Not the media, not the FBI, not the SEC… however, I made him, the Sheriff and Chief Deputy Gauger look like the complete corrupt fools that they are.

Chapter 30 - The Rise of BadVolf

Since the government was now blaming me for being in cahoots with Russian hackers, I decided to create my own persona; I became the Russian hacker named БадВолф (pronounced BadVolf). I posted the audio recordings, text messages and everything else I had from the conversations under the username of БадВолф on the PBSOTalk website.

I sent everything to the media; in a little bit of disinformation, I opened the metadata of the text message files with Adobe Lightroom, changed the GPS coordinates to the center of Moscow, which happens to be the Kremlin, and then I dropped a subtle hint to the journalists to examine the photo data closely. Text messages don't contain lots of metadata like GPS coordinates, but they didn't know that. I chose a corner of the Kremlin facing the Moscow River and Gorky Park, because I thought having the best view, it was most likely to hold the most high-level leaders. No doubt the US government knows who is where in the Kremlin, so it was information that probably drove them nuts.

My favorite article about the catfishing was written by PINAC journalist Carlos Miller. With his permission, here is the article:

Article: Florida Sheriff's Internal Affairs Investigator Duped Into Revealing All on Secretly Recorded Conversations With Random Woman He'd Never Met

```
A Florida sheriff's internal affairs investigator who
was trying to woo a woman he had never met by
exchanging phone and text messages with her, ended up
revealing confidential information to her as well as
seek inside trading information from her, thinking she
was a wealthy Wall Street heiress who travels the
country by private plane.

Instead, "Jessica" turned out to be an investigator
herself, recording every one of their calls as well as
make screenshots of every one of their conversations.
```

Everything.

All of it.

Every piece of damning and embarrassing evidence is now posted online, including on PINAC.

As a result, Kenneth "Mark" Lewis, a 30-year veteran with the Palm Beach sheriff's office, has drawn the attention of the FBI, who have already been investigating the beleaguered department for months.

And Jessica? The sexy, smart and sophisticated woman he had been chatting up for days?

She doesn't exist. At least not in the way she presented herself to Lewis.

The woman in the photo she sent him is actually a Russian woman named Ekaterina. And the woman on the phone did not sound remotely Russian.

However, the EXIF data on the text messages posted online traces back to Moscow. A stone's throw from the Kremlin.

Perhaps even inside the Kremlin.

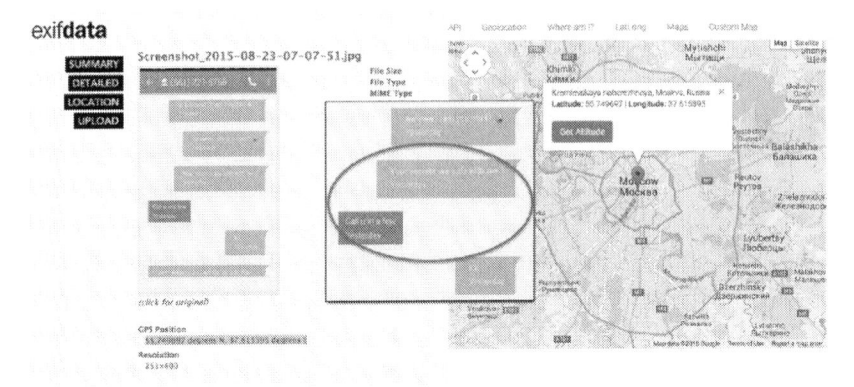

More than 4,000 miles from Wall Street in Manhattan where the woman was claiming to be.

Lewis' Response

However, Lewis claims he knew it along, telling Jose Lambiet of Gossip Extra that he didn't even believe Jessica was a woman, but a man using a voice changer.

But it's obvious he was completely fooled by the sultry Jessica, thinking he was on his way to getting laid and maybe even getting rich.

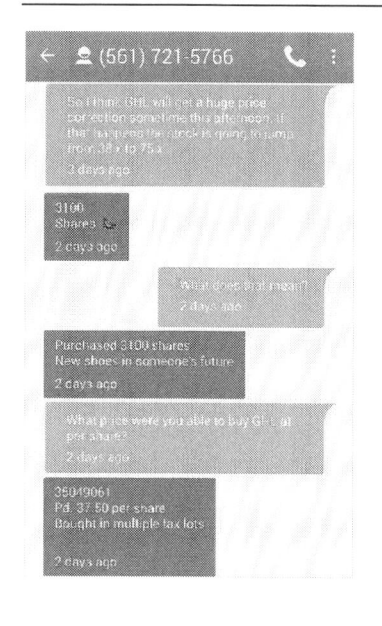

After all, he ended up spending $119,850 on what he thought was an insider stock tip about an upcoming merger that she told him would double his money.

But there was no merger.

And there has been no profit.

And there is no shame as Lewis tried to explain himself.

According to "Bradshaw, who's up for reelection, does not comment on stories published in media organizations that he sees as hostile to PBSO. So we reached out to Lewis himself.

"We suspected she was a faker caller!"

"I know why you're calling," Lewis said, "and to be frank, I don't care what's on those tapes.

"I was onto that person and I figured she wasn't who she claimed to be."

Lewis says he now believes the caller was Dougan, who managed to turn the tables on PBSO thanks to a digital voice changer.

Not so romantic now, is it?

"We started suspecting this was a fake caller a couple days into it," Lewis said. "I've been around the block a few times, so gimme some credit here. If a chick who claims to be rich calls you out of the blue and sends sexy pictures of herself, it's likely to be too good to be true."

Actually, Lewis' demeanor on the tapes changed Friday, after he realized he didn't even know his telephone pal's last name after hours of chatting."

FROM RUSSIA WITH SCORN

The mastermind behind this intriguing plot appears to be Mark Dougan, a whistleblower, and former Palm Beach County deputy who resigned in 2009 after blowing the whistle on other deputies before launching a site called PBSOtalk.com, encouraging deputies to post anonymous criticism against Palm Beach County Sheriff Ric Bradshaw.

But Dougan told PINAC he had nothing to do with the recordings.

"I had advance knowledge of the conversation but did not realize they were being recorded," Dougan said in a telephone interview with PINAC Monday night.

"I was trying to get information for my civil suit. They've been suing me for defamation for three years."

He said the department has spent more than $1.5 million in taxpayer's dollars to investigate him over the last four years.

He also said it was his friends who did the recording without his knowledge as a way to help him in his ongoing battle against the Palm Beach County Sheriff's Office.

Dougan frequently travels to Russia and has many friends there. He said the recordings were not made in the United States, so there is no violation of wiretapping laws.

Besides, nothing they did was worse than what Lewis has done. Or at least what he bragged to have done in an attempt to sweep Jessica off her feet.

Hacking. Stalking. Spying. Spending years investigating Sheriff Bradshaw's political foes, bragging about how he had sheriff candidate Jim Donahue arrested in 2011 after two years of investigating him, forcing the nationally renowned law enforcement consultant to drop out of the race.

LEWIS' CLAIMS

Donahue's charges, according to Lambiet, who is based out of Palm Beach County, were mysteriously dropped before his trial.

Lewis bragged of traveling to Michigan and Canada and searching public records for two years to find dirt on then-Sheriff candidate Jim Donahue, who got arrested in March 2011. A nationally renowned law enforcement consultant with no criminal record, the 67-year-old Donahue ran against Bradshaw after he discovered what he claims was PBSO's mismanagement of $15 million earmarked for new technology. Six weeks after Donahue filed his candidacy, he was charged with five counts of altering public documents and arrested during a police symposium in Fort Lauderdale. Donahue abruptly left the campaign trail but days before his trial in 2012, prosecutors mysteriously dropped the charges:

This is what Donahue had to say about Sheriff Bradshaw earlier this year, according to DC Post:

> "Ric Bradshaw is one of the ringleaders of one of the most corrupt public organizations in the country. I have seen what has gone on in Palm Beach County and recognize that in that county there is a level of corruption and dishonesty that puts the Chicago political machine to shame. In fact, it's the kind of people in power in Palm Beach County that are the kind of people my dad fought in WWII to defeat. They are threatening the very fabric of our republic."

In one of the conversations with Jennifer, Lewis says he has been investigating Dougan for four years but has been unsuccessful at arresting him because of that pesky First Amendment.

"Believe it or not, so much of what he does is freedom of speech," he said before admitting that they went to the FCC, the FBI and the Secret Service to try to get Dougan to stop writing about them.

He also tells Jennifer that Anthony Rodriguez, the department's social media guru, was able to hack into Dougan's computer while he was in Russia, enabling them to view his photos before he even posted them online.

"I could even tell you what f-stop he used and what the lighting was," Dougan bragged.

They also hacked into his Google Analytics, which he said enabled them to investigate who has been reading Dougan's site.

"We hacked into his analytics, so know exactly where it's coming from, how many people are on there, we got the whole scoop on it," he said.

He also made a chilling statement about being amazed Dougan is still alive, considering he has pissed so many "powerful people" off.

"Some of the things he's done would make you so mad, when I have meetings with some of these government agencies, trying to decide what they're going to do with him, we are amazed that he is still alive. He has really made some powerful people extremely angry. Some very wealthy powerful people."

And he said that along with hacker Rodriguez, they created "soft communities" of fake Facebook profiles, specifically of "young girls" who friended Dougan's sister, which led to Dougan friending them.

And he said they go into people's neighborhoods with "special software" to investigate people inside homes.

"We can tell exactly what your signal is, we can tell the type of server you're using, we can tell you the size of it and we can tell you where it's located in your house," he said.

OUTSMARTED BY THE ENEMY

Despite Lewis' claims to having extraordinary skills in investigating people, he fell for the oldest trick in the book. The lure of a beautiful woman. At 56 years of age, you would think he would have learned by now.

But she did a genius job of flying underneath his radar and getting him to talk about his investigative techniques on Bradshaw's political foes.

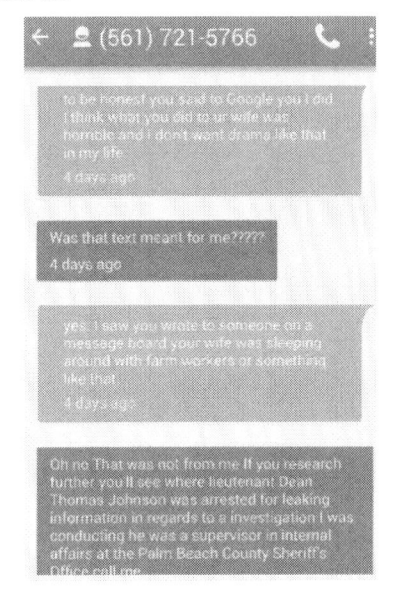

It started in July when Jessica called Lewis out of the blue because he had a contractor's license. She told him she was moving down to Florida with her boyfriend and needed a contractor.

Then she told him she had broken up with the boyfriend and acted as if she needed a shoulder to cry on. And then she gave him the classic push-pull courtship to reel him in, telling him she was flying down to meet him, then changing her mind at the last minute.

And then she skillfully got him to talk about Dougan by telling him she had Googled him and learned something he had done to his wife when it was allegations against Dougan, which naturally got him to start talking about Dougan, whom he has obsessed about for four years.

As much as Lewis tried to impress Jennifer with his investigative techniques, it is obvious he can learn a thing or two from her.

As you can probably imagine, the fallout from the recordings was intense. Even the comments from the articles were classic, with posts like:

> *"Isn't it incredible, when a cop openly admits to destroying lives and compromising the integrity (if there is any left) of his entire department, just to increase his chances of getting laid!"*

> *"Two Tapes++Two Tapes is all I've listened to, and they are down to the bone-chilling. This country is worse than East Germany, and the Stassi ever dreamed of being. Hitler, Himmler, Stalin, Mao and especially Pol Pot would be so proud of how this country is an absolute Police State."*

> *"Oh, this is just too good. First I've seen of it. Even as far away as Oregon, we've heard of what a corrupt and despicable man is big sheriff Bradshaw. That one of his goons would be so stupid as to be conned in such a manner is very telling. Esp. one with*

30 years of 'experience.' What a freak show that sheriff department is..."

"This is Organized Crime, not just a bad Cop. If you bother to listen to all the tapes and go over the detailed info, he gave himself up incriminating his other gang members, using every Illegal Electronic Devices the PD owns for personal gain even... Notice: This is a wake-up call ANYTHING you do online is monitored and will be used to convict you, smear you; just whatever it takes. Did you hear Homeland Security Access in their pocket?"

Still, the local media, being terrified of Sheriff Bradshaw, pretty much looked the other way. Sure, the Palm Beach Post and Channel five wrote soft about the story but gave them ridiculously easy interviews.

When channel 5 interviewed Detective Lewis, they let him say he knew it was a setup, but they were too chickenshit to ask about the $119,850 illegal stock trade he made near the end of the conversations; definitive evidence he had no idea it was a setup but was also a federal crime for which he should have gone to prison. Nevertheless, useful information was garnered from the recordings.

You may wonder if the anyone ever bothered to investigate the entire thing. From the federal crime of insider trading, offering to hack the accounts, using law enforcement resources to plant digital evidence on an innocent civilian, admission of the targeting of black people, admission of conspiracy to destroy evidence and the disclosures of using law enforcement resources to go after political enemies, surely some law enforcement agency investigated. Maybe the FBI. The SEC? The State Attorney's Office or FDLE? The answer is "No!" That's right; they all walked, scot-free. Well, almost.

Detective Lewis wasn't charged with any crimes, but Internal Affairs investigated him for giving up confidential information. He was forced to retire permanently.

The PBSO brass was exceptionally pissed off at Lewis for being so stupid, but come on; it would be hard to find a smart cop that would do the illegal things Lewis admitted to doing.

Well, I guess it's something; getting a monkey off my back and getting a dirty cop off the streets. No doubt, however, that Sheriff Bradshaw and Chief Deputy Gauger found someone to replace him in doing their dirty deeds.

The End Result of the Lewis Recordings

A few chapters ago, I told you how the laws in the United States were created to help government employees break the laws without getting caught. This incident is a prime example. Despite the numerous admissions that Det. Lewis made, he wasn't found guilty of a single ethics violation. There are a few reasons for it. First, to implicate Detective Lewis, the Florida Ethics Commission would have had to incriminate the Sheriff.

More importantly, though, Florida law states that recording others admitting to crimes without their knowledge is illegal, and any recordings, as a result, cannot be used against the person confessing to those crimes. The person who records the conversation, however, can be punished by up to five years in prison for each recording.

Chapter 31 - People Targeted by the Sheriff's Investigations

Author Jim Donahue, Candidate for Sheriff

Jim Donahue is a renown law-enforcement officer with hundreds of works to his credit. He discovered an $18+ million dollar discrepancy in Sheriff Bradshaw's technology budget, and he had suspicions of embezzlement. When Mr. Donahue decided to run for Sheriff and to use that as part of his platform, the Sheriff didn't want any of that.

The Sheriff and Chief Deputy Gauger sent Detective Lewis flying around the country, investigating Jim Donahue's past. They never really came up with much, except some wild speculation that Donahue had forged some reference letters from his friends. And with that accusation, Detective Lewis fabricated enough probable cause to arrest Jim Donahue while he was on a stage giving a class about law enforcement.

Prosecutors offered Donahue a plea deal. What dishonest prosecutors do with a nasty, fraudulent case, is use the threat of spending half a life behind bars for a felony conviction to get them to agree to plead guilty to one misdemeanor, time served, and everything else dropped. The benefit is that in agreeing, there is no chance you will lose 20 years of your life and the prosecutors and people like the scumbag Chief Deputy can tell people, "See? That guy is a criminal, and he even pleaded guilty. Innocent men don't plead guilty." Which is such crap when you weigh the risk of spending the next 20 years in prison on some made up bullshit. It's a tactic used by prosecutors that should be banned.

Donahue, however, he told the State Attorney's Office to stick the plea deal up their asses as he never did anything remotely close to what Detective Lewis alleged. Donahue provided them with affidavits from the friends whose letters Lewis had claimed Donahue had forged. Those affidavits stated that the letters were not forged; they had written them.

The State Attorney's Office dropped all charges against Donahue four days before the trial, because they knew the case was a basket of lies that they would have an impossible time proving. An insider at the State Attorney's Office told me the Assistant State Attorneys on the case were pissed that Detective Lewis included so much supposition and false claims as factual. While they wanted to drop the case immediately, the current State Attorney, Michael McAuliffe, a close friend of Bradshaw, ordered them to pursue it for as long as they could, just to see if they could get a guilty plea.

When Cop Talk radio interviewed Donahue and asked about Palm Beach County, he stated:

"Ric Bradshaw is one of the ringleaders of one of the most corrupt public organizations in the country. I have seen what has gone on in Palm Beach County and recognize that in that county there is a level of corruption and dishonesty that puts the Chicago political machine to shame. In fact, it's the kind of people in power in Palm Beach County that are the kind of people my dad fought in WWII to defeat. They are threatening the very fabric of our republic."

Former West Palm Beach Fire Captain Rick Curtis

Another one of the poor saps that Detective Lewis admitted to investigating out of political retaliation was Rick Curtis. Detective Lewis said he was targeting Curtis on the orders of Chief Deputy Michael Gauger as a favor to judge Marni Bryson because Curtis embarrassed her. Rick Curtis was a Captain with the West Palm Beach Fire Department arrested on suspicion of driving under the Influence. Did he? Perhaps. Probably, but the DUI arrest isn't the troubling part.

> *"This judge owes me big time. So if some point in the future he even needs it, he can call up the judge and say, 'Hey, remember when I took care of this for you?' There's nothing better than having a fucking judge if your fucking back pocket." – Bobby Anderson, former K9 Lieutenant with the Palm Beach County Sheriff's Office*

You see after Judge Marni Bryson sentenced Rick Curtis to three days in jail, he appealed it, saying Bryson handed down such a harsh sentence because she was having an affair with his union rival, another captain in the Fire Department. He argued, rightly, that Ms. Bryson should have recused herself from the case. Still, Bryson failed her judicial duties to prevent a conflict of interest or appearance of any improprieties, so Curtis was granted his appeal. The ensuing media coverage was incredibly embarrassing to Judge Bryson, and she wanted revenge.

She enlisted the help of scumbag Chief Deputy Gauger and his co-scumbag henchman, Detective Lewis. Chief Deputy Gauger assured Ms. Bryson they would find a reason to lock up Rick Curtis for embarrassing her. So, Detective Lewis set on a two-year witch hunt, investigating Curtis. During the recordings, Lewis stated he was picking up one of Curtis' depositions from Chief Deputy Gauger so they would be able to arrest him for perjury. And the reason Detective Lewis gave that they could make such an arrest? He stated Rick Curtis had claimed in the deposition that it was a conflict of interest that Judge Bryson was having an affair with his union rival, but he lied because the relationship ended in the past.

What Detective Lewis had done was mince words to have a reason to arrest Mr. Curtis and drag him back to jail. Detective Lewis stated about this type of retaliation, "Does it mean anything in the long run? Probably not, but I'm going to make his life miserable."

You may be asking yourself what the connection between Judge Bryson and Michael Gauger happens to be. Good question, and it was answered by a long-time friend of Gauger, Lt. Bobby Anderson. He said, "Gauger's kid has been in a lot of trouble. Now Gauger can say, 'This judge owes me big time. So if some point in the future he even needs it, he can call up the judge and say, 'Hey, remember when I took care of this for you?' There's nothing better than having a fucking judge in your fucking back pocket."

Corrections Deputy Paul Smith

Paul Smith was another one to get on the wrong side of Bradshaw and Gauger. Except this person happened to be a corrections officer at the Palm Beach County Jail. Smith had come forward, blowing the whistle on a lieutenant who was sleeping on duty. Detective Lewis filed perjury charges against Smith with the hopes of getting a warrant for his arrest. Sources tell me that after Detective Lewis' debacle in arresting Jim Donahue and putting the State Attorney's Office in such a shitty position, they demanded Lewis file for criminal warrants in the future. This was another case that would have been a clusterfuck for the State Attorney's office; another one of Detective Lewis' "perjury" cases.

What did Deputy Paul Smith say that Detective Lewis claimed was perjury? Smith said the lieutenant sleeping on duty was causing hazardous conditions, and Detective Lewis felt it was not creating a dangerous work environment. Notice that Lewis couldn't attack the allegation that the Lieutenant was sleeping on duty; no, once again, he manipulated and twisted statements into a case of Perjury.

Investigative Reporter Katie Lagrone

Katie Lagrone was an investigative reporter with WPTV Channel 5 in West Palm Beach. She was one of the few people in Palm Beach County with the spine and the guts to report on things happening in the Palm Beach County Sheriff's Office. One of her big stories was the disproportionate number of unarmed citizens in Palm Beach County that were shot and killed. If her story, she reported that 25% of all white people that were shot and killed were unarmed and a whopping 33% of black citizens had no weapons. Lagrone pointed to several cases where what Sheriff Bradshaw and the reports told the media were utterly contradicted by evidence.

She proceeded to show a video of a black man running away from a deputy named Lin. Lin went to stop the guy, Dontrell Stephen, on his bike and exited his patrol car. The Stephens jumped off his bike and began to run, and Lin shot him four times in the back. Stephens lived, however, he is now a paraplegic confined to a wheelchair for the rest of his life. When the jury heard the facts and saw the video, they awarded Stephens a whopping 23 million dollars. The Sheriff had the nerve to call the verdict "shocking." It's not surprising, coming from a man so morally bankrupt that he thinks lying on reports and hiding evidence is okay.

Lagrone also showed a video of a cop who shot into a car, killing the mentally-handicapped driver. The deputy who did the shooting said the vehicle was accelerating towards him, and he shot the driver to stop the threat. Video from the camera at the intersection told an entirely different story.

In short, Lagrone was showing the public just what types of lying criminals were running the Palm Beach County Sheriff's Office, and she had to be stopped. In the wise words of Gauger's good friend retired Lt. Bobby Anderson,

> *"Anyone who fucking goes after Ric, he puts Detective Lewis on them to get any shit they can find."*

What happened to Katie Lagrone was stooping to a new low of despicable retaliation. Detective Lewis and his henchmen watched Lagrone's house for a while, and they called Department of Children and Families claiming she and her husband were neglecting their kids.

Chapter 32 - Hacking Mark Lewis in Retaliation

After the revelations of how Detective Kenneth Mark Lewis was hacking me and my social media accounts, I contacted the Palm Beach Gardens Police Department and the Federal Bureau of Investigation. Both of them refused to do anything about it, citing some blatant lie why they were unable to investigate, but the secret reason was apparent: "We don't investigate cops for abusing their authority."

As you could imagine, I was outraged. I spoke to some of my friends about it, and I decided if I was not entitled to my privacy and they were free to breach their oaths for retaliatory purposes, then no one in law enforcement deserves to have their privacy. I mean really, why should they be able to trample the laws that they rigorously enforce for themselves?

I started a website called Stop Cop Spying, to help citizens safeguard themselves from abuses of power as I sustained. Stop Cop Spying gave videos and tutorials on how someone could safeguard their computers, phones, and tablets from law enforcement officers that act with criminal intent, like Sheriff Bradshaw, Chief Deputy, Michael Gauger, and Detective Lewis.

The downside of the website is that that information could be used by criminals to cover their crimes. But the way I see it, if the bad actors in government are going to abuse their law-enforcement authority and violate the privacy of citizens, and other law-enforcement agencies will let them get away with it, the government should not be able to access anyone's data.

Had they acted with responsibility, I would feel differently. But I still wasn't satisfied. I was, frankly, furious the criminals at PBSO were able to get away with it, so I decided to even things out a bit.

The first step was to directly respond to Detective Kenneth Mark Lewis by hacking his email account. He admitted to illegally accessing my accounts, and the FBI did absolutely nothing. The FBI was sending a clear message that this behavior is allowed, so I took advantage of their decision on the matter. After hacking his account, I changed his username and password and sent the information to the media, along with documents he had emailed to himself in his campaign against dissidents.

I also sent a letter from Lewis' email account as "BadVolf" to the top administrators of the Palm Beach County Sheriff's Office and journalists, BadVolf informing them he hacked Lewis' account in retaliation for them hacking Dougan's account. BadVolf told them they would all be facing similar retaliation.

To be honest, "hacking" implies a breach of security protocols using clever code or security vulnerabilities, allowing access to an account. This wasn't the case at all. It was done using social engineering, using Yahoo's password reset function. When going to the "Forgot your Password?" prompt, Detective Kenneth Mark Lewis had set up some security questions. The first question asked where he was born and the second was where he spent his honeymoon.

I elicited the answers to these questions from Lewis while talking to me as "Jessica." I asked Detective Lewis in my sweetest Jessica voice where he was born, and he said at Bethesda naval hospital. In another conversation, we discussed the topic of marriage. I asked him where he took his wife for their honeymoon, and he told me they went to Vegas. After that, accessing his account was super easy by using the password reset. I learned a lot from breaching his account. Lewis spent years drafting anonymous documents to various government agencies asking them to investigate me. He also had a profile on Plenty of Fish, a free dating website. Incidentally, to read his profile was like going to a comedy show. I wasn't able to stop laughing, and I will bet neither could the women that clicked on him.

Still, that wasn't nearly enough. Suing the government doesn't do anything – the taxpayers foot the bill for the wrongdoing of bad actors in the government. Someone had to effectively show others in Law Enforcement they need to hold their brothers accountable for violating the constitutional rights of Americans.

Chapter 33 - Doxing 14,000 Police, Federal Law Enforcement, and Federal Judges

In 2014, I created a company called Legalstork, and created a nifty little search tool that was free to my customers. It would let process servers find people by any number of criteria. It was all public record, harvested from the Voter Registration databases from several states. I found a fundamental flaw with the records that were supposed to be confidential. Florida, for instance, when you renew your driver's license and register to vote, you sign a form claiming you are a confidential record. A person who is confidential is exempt from their data being listed in public record. Law enforcement, judges, FBI and CIA agents – all confidential records.

The problem was created by two very important components. The first, the department that handles voter registrations didn't know initially these people were exempt from public record; it would take some time for the exemption to make it to them and to redact the information from the database.

The second problem was that the Voter Registration roles were released every month, meaning a voter's information would be released one month but in the next month, it would have an asterisk in the name, address and other fields. For example, in March 2012, police officer John Doe might get a driver's license and register to vote. The voter's database might assign him voter ID number 012345678. The information in the initial month would look like:

012345678|John Doe|123 Main Street|(561)555-1212

But in the next database dump, it would appear as:

012345678 | * | * | *

From this information, I realized you would be able to dump every record, month after month, into a database and search for unique values. If you wrote a query to search for Voter ID values with a matching Voter ID value with an asterisk, you know that person is a confidential record.

And so, that's what I did. I downloaded every month of voter registration databases and wrote code to evaluate hundreds of millions of rows of data. If you are curious or want to do it yourself, I will put the code I wrote on my website, BadVolf.com

I made sure to include that information in my search program for the process servers. If there was a confidential record detected, it would show the information, but it would list the record as a suspected confidential record. After a while, I opened the search function to the public and blasted out the link on my website, PBSOTalk.com, telling people something to the effect, "Oh no! Our information is exposed but I was able to remove it with the removal link."

And yes, I had a removal link. I wrote that we value the privacy of civil servants, and if they were a civil servant, they could request to have their information to be removed as long as we could verify they were a civil servant. The people had to list their department names, mobile phone and email address. It also logged their IP addresses, and I was able to match that data with all the searches they conducted. I didn't do anything with that information, but I held it, just in case. I admit it was a bit sinister.

Later, I owned a company that did geospatial marketing; taking datasets and matching them with other criteria to target people for advertising campaigns. For instance, a hair salon might want to know the married women living in houses worth over $400,000 within two miles of their location. I would spend more money targeting less people, but ideal candidates to be customers, for these businesses. I could even target the husbands, sending them gift cards that needed to be paid for and activated before their wives' birthdays. It took the effort out of gift shopping for the guys that didn't have the time to focus on their loves. It also saved my clients about 20% of their advertising budget while increasing their business significantly.

A few months prior, I discovered an oversight in the data releases for the county GIS department. In one dataset, they had the property ID number and all the details on the house, including the owners. If the owner was a law enforcement officer, their addresses were marked with an asterisk.

In a different dataset released by the country GIS department, they showed only property ID and details without owner information, so they didn't bother with redacting addresses. The problem with that is clear; anyone with knowledge of GIS databases could join the two tables together using the property ID as the primary key and create their own list of confidential names and addresses of Floridians, such as law enforcement officers, FBI and CIA agents, federal judges, etc.

It would also compromise safe houses owned by the government. I harvested all of this data.

After I found out PBSO was illegally accessing all of my stuff and the FBI refused to take any action, I combined all of this data, turning it into a searchable table, and posting it all online.

I am sure this was some of the information that broke the straw that broke the camel's back; hypocrisy in action, and the agents with the FBI, State of Florida, and Palm Beach County Sheriff's Office decided that they deserved the privacy of which they were so willing to rob others whenever they wanted. I was watching as thousands of search requests were coming from Langley, Quantico, Ft. Meade and Washington D.C. I think anyone reading this book knows what government entities are located in those places. If not, take a moment to google it.

Chapter 34 - Media's Willingness to Blame Russian Hackers

The story about the leaked confidential names, hacked emails, and Russian involvement was blasted everywhere by the press. With the disinformation I put out and just a little bit of help from my Russian friend Alexey, the media coverage was sensational. Brilliant. The news media was so excited to report on Russian hackers engaged in a cyber-warfare campaign in my defense. Publications all over the country covered it. All it took to get the media on the bandwagon was to give them a face they wanted to hate. It didn't matter there was absolutely no proof of Russian involvement – it merely made for salacious headlines. Gawker Magazine was in communication with me and the "Russian hacker." The author wrote:

```
Why does this Russian guy care about what goes on at a
sheriff's department halfway across the world? Are
deputies in Florida really spying on journalists? Does
BadWolf even exist?
```

BADVOLF | BY: JOHN MARK DOUGAN
THE TRUE STORY OF AN AMERICAN COP AVENGING A CORRUPT SYSTEM

```
It was easy to imagine Dougan or some other local PBSO
critic fabricating a "Russian hacker" persona to avoid
being prosecuted for breaking into a government
computer. A Russian-American colleague and I even tried
to devise a way to subtly test BadWolf's Russianness
during my first chat with him, until he slipped into
his native tongue and called someone a крутой—a slang
word roughly meaning "badass" or "tough guy"—and
allayed our skepticism. Over weeks of subsequent
correspondence with BadWolf, it became clear that he,
at least, was the real deal.
```

Of course, I was able to fake it – I had spent a lot of time in Russia at that point, and I knew a few words. I also had a Russian friend nearby to help with the more delicate aspects of the conversation. That aside, the content of the article is pretty much sound. Andy, if you are reading this, I am really sorry for the deception. There's no way you could have ever known.

The FBI and the Sheriff's office were not exactly happy with the names, addresses and phone numbers posted online. Some of the confidential properties were safe houses. They concocted a story about the Russians and me hacking government computers based on no evidence whatsoever, and they knowingly used the lies of Lewis Kasman, the mafia informant, to obtain the search warrant on my house.

Chapter 35 - The Final Email Blast

On March 8th, 2016, election time was rolling around again. I owned the domain name SheriffBradshaw.com, so I decided to give a little hand to former Riviera Beach Police Commander Rick Sessa, who was running against the Sheriff. I wrote some code that evaluated the Florida Voter Registration database and would tailor a parody email for each person based on their race, sex, and age. The email for me looked like this:

From:
Sent: Thursday, March 10, 2016 5:21PM
To: J.M. Dougan
Subject: Sheriff Bradshaw Needs your Help!

Hey Mark!

As a Palm Beach County resident, I know you support corruption at the highest levels. This is why I need your support, to make sure I keep power in office and to sustain the culture of corruption I have put into place in Palm Beach County. This election season is more important than ever because I, Sheriff Bradshaw, am being challenged by candidates running on platforms of "integrity" and "Reform" and we can't have that. Just speak to my employees, and you will see they simply love me. Why?

Major Robert Van Reeth (left), is my personal pick to lead Internal Affairs, to be the compass for agency morality. Also in the photograph is Jeffrey Van Reeth (his underage son), a few guys from the PBA... oh, and ignore the naked prostitute who was high on blow. We fully support the exploitation of desperate women and girls, just ask all the deputies that fly to Costa Rica to have sex with juvelines!

Freedom!

And isn't that what this country is built upon? I put the best people in power to get as much freedom as we (PBSO, not you people) possibly can. With that freedom, we engage in all manner of crime and corruption to make our occupation the best it can be!

Not only is my Chief Deputy Michael Gauger a very shady character making back-door deals with corrupt judges to illegally target and investigate citizens for our personal benefit, but my personal choice for Internal Affairs was free to pose on a public golf course with his juvenile son and a naked prostitute who was snorting cocaine at the event. What could be freer than that?

Murder, of course! In 2012, one of my deputies was allegedly having an affair with another detective in a private parking lot. When caught by the owner/resident that lived there, he shot the unarmed kid (Seth Adams). We have destroyed evidence and spent hundreds of thousands of taxpayer dollars so far in an attempt to cover it up, and although it seems to be failing, our deputy will not face criminal charges, free to lead his free life in the future. See the Palm Beach Post article entitled, "Federal judge blasts PBSO for destroying evidence in shooting death."

BadVolf | by: John Mark Dougan
The True Story of an American Cop Avenging a Corrupt System

Chance
THIS CARD MAY BE KEPT UNTIL NEEDED OR SOLD
GET OUT OF JAIL FREE

As Sheriff, I have created a culture of corruption unseen in any other jurisdiction in the United States. It's not only for the wealthy or politicians, either. It's for anyone who supports or votes for me, or can do me favors. Just ask Judge Marni Bryson, who was embarrassed by a defendant. I had that defendant investigated for years in an attempt to incarcerate him for his free speech.

Please keep your voter receipt and this "Get Out of Jail Free" card in your wallet and if you get pulled over by a Palm Beach County Sheriff's Deputy, just show him this information.

You will be celebrated like a hero, joining the likes of Sgt. Hightower, who committed a felony, Lt. Burrows, who got stealing narcotics from a man dying of cancer and is still working in the ranks, and many others I recognize as my supporters.

> Jim Donahue, a prominent author in the law enforcement community, wrote, "Ric Bradshaw is one of the ringleaders of one of the most corrupt public organizations in the country. I have seen what has gone on in Palm Beach County and recognize that in that county there is a level of corruption and dishonesty that puts the Chicago political machine to shame. In fact, it's the kind of people in power in Palm Beach County that are the kind of people my dad fought in WWII to defeat. They are threatening the very fabric of our republic."

Oh, and don't even get me started on that mentally challenged Hutton boy that tried to drive off from our deputy Franqui. Luckily, deputy Franqui shot him and yes, fortunately, my agency covered it up, lying and suppressing evidence so Deputy Franqui could keep "protecting" the other citizens. The ones that aren't mentally challenged. We even covered up my secretary's son shooting his neighbor after covering up and manipulating evidence. It could have been a devastating lawsuit because we waived his psychological testing, but luckily, that case just settled for $600,000. The taxpayers should be happy because we don't care. It's not our money.

We got the black population covered, too. When Deputy Lin shot that unarmed kid in the back four times and the deputies got caught lying by their car cam, conspiring to cover it up, we cleared Deputy Lin by hiding the tape and fighting to keep it out of court. Sadly it was discovered, and we wound up spending 23 MILLION dollars. Yes, that's almost as much money as we spend giving take-home "company" cars and free gasoline to civilian employees that work on my election campaign, but who's counting? Not us... it's not our money, remember?

Mark, Our goal is to keep blacks in their place and out of your community. Being in a Christian religious organization and having ties to the Ku Klux Klan really helps me in my task. People say I look just like Hitler, but it's more about looks. I do everything in my power to act like him also. It's why we hunted so hard for the Black Lives Matter protester who was using tape to post signs. We launched a full-scale investigation to stop this man on the grounds of "vandalism" while we left the "lost dog" sign hangers alone. It's why I have been sued for discrimination so many times. It's why I have ordered detectives to falsify reports to put blacks in jail where they belong. The ability to frame, convict and kill blacks is the reason the old Jewish population and condo heads love me and Chief Deputy Mike Gauger and I. Our new inside joke among the administration at PBSO is that "I MADE THE JEWS LOVE HITLER AGAIN!"

A few may say these things seem like massive civil rights violations, but they are just us getting around some pesky rules no one cares about anymore. My investigator, Detective Kenneth Mark Lewis, has been illegally investigating journalists that write about corruption and crime at PBSO. Not only just investigating them, but Det. Lewis has been hacking into their computer systems and finding ways to incarcerate them to discredit them. It's why we can't release the investigation to the public!

A few years ago, a man named Jim Donahue ran found $18 Million discrepancies (missing) from our budget and decided he was going to run against me. I had him arrested on baseless charges while he was on stage to derail his campaign.

Now that I am under investigation by the Federal Bureau of Investigation for public corruption and election tampering, I can't get rid of my opponents this way. Now I have actually to appeal to the voters to keep me in office.

Mark, my wife wants me to retire to one of my multi-million dollar estates, but if I am removed from office, and people discover all of the corruption, missing money and the reason I'm a Sheriff able to own millions in real estate around the country, I will probably end up in a federal prison. Therefore, I need to maintain my power until my dying breath. I KNOW you will help!

Jim Donahue, a prominent author in the law enforcement community, wrote, *"Ric Bradshaw is one of the ringleaders of one of the most corrupt public organizations in the country. I have seen what has gone on in Palm Beach County and recognize that in that county there is a level of corruption and dishonesty that puts the Chicago political machine to shame. In fact, it's the kind of people in power in Palm Beach County that are the kind of people my dad fought in WWII to defeat. They are threatening the very fabric of our republic."*

BADVOLF | BY: JOHN MARK DOUGAN

THE TRUE STORY OF AN AMERICAN COP AVENGING A CORRUPT SYSTEM

Mark, I have told you exactly what kind of man I am for the people. You don't need to know the little details like I got caught stealing guns out of evidence, or that the Palm Beach Post caught me buying mafia members dinner with taxpayer money for significant campaign contributions... you just need to know how to vote and how your condo or homeowners leaders tell you how to vote. If you don't believe I have done every criminal, corrupt act written in this email, I implore you to google these incidents and find out the truth. I know I am the man that you, and your homeowner's association or condo association wants, and needs as the most powerful law enforcement officer in the land, your SHERIFF!

So please vote for me, and I'll try to get you a freebie from the prostitute in the above photo. And remember:

A vote for me is a vote for our (PBSO's) freedom!

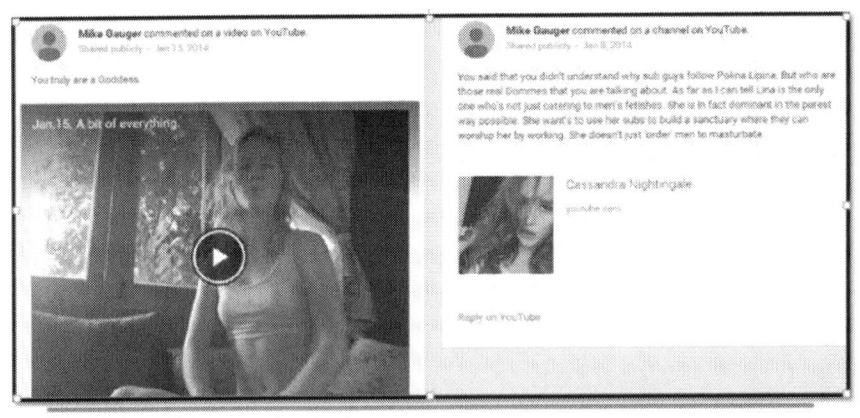

Mike Gauger just loves hot young Goddesses and he tells the world with YouTube. Even more, he loves kinky submission fetishes and the psychological aspects of such "purity" that goes way beyond masturbation.

You might guess that the Sheriff wasn't happy.

190

Chapter 36 - The FBI / State Attorney Raid

I probably don't have to point out the obvious, but I will anyway. The various forms of dissidence I displayed: email pranks on politicians, sowing fake news, creating a website to show how to prevent the FBI from accessing a computer; it was only a small portion of the activities in which I was engaged. My site exposing corruption and coming forward as a witness about the affair of a Deputy Sheriff in Seth Adams' civil murder trial pissed a lot of people off. The listing of the confidential records for law enforcement officers also didn't help. But like I said, if I wasn't entitled to my privacy, then why should a law enforcement officer be entitled to theirs? What's good for the goose is good for the gander, and law enforcement shouldn't be allowed to abuse their power, just because they can.

For a few days after I got that first document from the man in Washington, D.C., I saw strange cars idling in my neighborhood. I thought the Sheriff's Office was back to their old tricks, hiring people to harass my family and me. The PBSO helicopter circled over my house a few times.

On the morning of March 14, I woke up, fed my kids breakfast and shuttled them out the door so their mother could take them to school. When I was at the front door, I noticed a black Ford FX2 pickup truck idling, facing my home in PGA National – a gated community on the north side of Palm Beach County. The pickup had condensation on the black-tinted windows and windshield. The tint on the left side of the windshield was torn vertically. It had a very distinct look, and I knew I had never seen that truck before. Black tint on the windshield in Florida is illegal, so it's a good indicator that it's an undercover vehicle.

I went back into my house, put on a shirt, and went back outside to see why they were parked there. As I scampered out and across the parking lot, the doors of the truck burst open. Men clad in FBI tactical vests jumped out of truck - and they weren't the only ones. FBI agents were coming out of the bushes, from behind buildings and from every direction. It was surreal and was the most significant "holy shit" moment of my life.

An agent ran up on my right flank with a Taser and ordered me to the ground. I went down as fast as I could. He put his knee into my back and handcuffed me. After the agent slapped on the handcuffs, he immediately grabbed my mobile phone out of my pocket and passed it to another agent, presumably because they knew my phone was encrypted and had to act fast to ensure they could suck all the data out of it before it locked. They took off my watch and brought me to Agent Ellen Thomas.

Agent Thomas asked me if anything in the house was booby trapped… of course, I thought it was a silly question; they saw my kids walk out of the house just a moment ago. I thought to myself, "who in the hell would put booby traps in a house with young kids?"

I told him there were no booby traps, and like a swarm of insects, FBI agents swarmed into my house. Agent Ellen Thomas put me in the back of her car. After a few minutes, She uncuffed me and told me I wasn't under arrest; that I had been detained for their safety while they searched my house.

It turns out the circling helicopter was to obtain photographs for the warrants to raid my home and confiscate whatever they wanted. And believe me, they seized things so outside of the scope of the warrant, it's quite hard to believe, but then again, nothing they have done was ever legal or ethical.

They took my Bose Aviation headsets, stationary, business cards and took all of my files on corruption and complaints to the State Commission of Ethics; records detailing criminal activity taking place in the government. They were motivated to abuse their power in every way they could to make life difficult for me. They were sending a message: "Don't fuck with the government because we have the power to destroy you."

Agent Thomas said, "who are your Russian friends? You should tell us because it's going to be a lot easier if you tell us what we want to know."

She was also extremely interested in a few of my Russian friends that lived in South Florida. She referenced a friend who had gone to a club with me the previous weekend and appeared in a Facebook video. Other than that, I had no idea what she was talking about...

I don't know anyone in Russia of such great importance or involved in any criminal activity, but I didn't tell her that. I wanted them to think if I thought they were kind to me, I would tell them what they wanted. I did this to buy time and figure out what I was doing.

The FBI took my US Passport, presumably so they could look at all my passport stamps and figure out when and where I was at any given time. I assumed if they didn't arrest me, they would put me on a No-Fly list. Agent Thomas told me to leave while they searched my house. I guessed they didn't want me to see what they were doing.

I called my father, who picked me up. I also called Rick Sessa and Jose Lambiet to tell them what had happened. After I left, Sessa went to my home to see what was going on. You see, the FBI, well they are smart as hell. They know if a computer is decrypted and is running, it's possible to extract the password keys from memory. When Rick told me they were wheeling in machinery into my house, I had a pretty good idea they were carts with portable batteries and an inverter that would enable the FBI to keep the computer running while they unplugged it. That way, they could extrapolate the encryption key at a later date. They even have special machines that keep moving your mouse to keep the computer from locking.

They took almost all of the computer equipment that was inside my house, including a computer that had the data dump sent to me from the man in Washington, D.C.

My dad soon arrived. I got into his car, and we drove back to his house. A black pickup truck with black tinted windows (including the front windshield) followed us for twenty miles – it was following so close, the driver wanted me to know he was there. It's an intimidation tactic. "Stop at the store," I told my father. He turned into a neighborhood; the truck also turned but went past the store where we parked. It stopped a few hundred yards away, where it just parked.

I went into the store, bought a drink, got back into the car and we continued our drive. The truck didn't follow. It was my guess the crooked cops had a team or different vehicles following me, taking over at various points. It's a pretty standard procedure for surveillance of subjects.

We got to my father's house, where I promptly changed all my passwords for various things, such as my PBX system, etc. I tried to access my phone, but I couldn't. I later discovered they put it into a Faraday bag. The very first thing I did, I got a burner cell phone.

As you can imagine, sleeping that night was, well, about impossible. I knew these people were looking to throw me in jail, even for a little bit, where they would probably put me in with some guy who would kill me in exchange for having his charges dropped. It wasn't a hard leap to make since Detective Lewis had admitted they were looking to lock me up in their jail, how they wanted, and they would make sure I was put in with a "big black rapist." In fact, sleeping every night proved to be tough. I didn't sleep at all.

The next day, I spoke to FBI agent Thomas, and she wanted to meet me at the Palm Beach County library. I told her I would only talk about the list of names published and tell her how they were public record. I told her to bring someone from her technology department to better explain where the flaw was in the public records information system.

An informant at the State Attorney's Office had already told me the FBI applied for a warrant to seize my phone and judge Hurley denied it. My informant told me that to get my phone, the FBI went to the State Attorney's Office. I haven't seen the warrant the State Attorney used, but no doubt it was filled with lies to establish probable cause; if you remember from an earlier chapter, they all have judges in their pockets. These crooked cops could say whatever they wanted, make up any story or charges with impunity. The circuit court judge gave the State Attorney's office a warrant for my phone.

Since I knew about how the FBI was able to get a warrant for my phone, I was able to mention it to the agents and gauge their reaction and to see if they would lie. I wanted to know if they were operating independently or if they were working in cahoots with the Palm Beach County law enforcement. And of course, FBI agent Ellen Thomas lied about it, saying it was a coincidence.

When I met Agent Thomas at the library, she brought a dorky looking guy who didn't look like any tech guy I have ever seen. It wasn't so much his appearance so much as the way he acted- like he was high on Ritalin and just plain dumb. What was more bizarre is the way he carried himself; he danced about like he was looking for his lost boyfriend. He was trying to play "bad cop", and he was doing a terrible job at it. The fact he attempted to play bad cop while displaying an apparent, flamboyantly gay demeanor almost made me laugh. I know a lot of gay people, and I can't picture any of the "queens" playing bad cop. They may be bitchy, but they are generally super nice. Just knowing that I think, is what made it laughable. I hope the West Palm Beach FBI field office learned a valuable lesson; to keep this guy in a role that suits him, busting sex pervs in the park.

Chapter 37 - Escape and Evasion of the FBI

The Saturday after my home after the raid, March 20th, I rented a car from the Enterprise Rental Car in Delray Beach. I rented it in the name of my aunt, but I never told her for what reason. I drove to meeting and then stopped at the Russian embassy to see about political asylum, though it was closed.

The Russian visa on my passport was still valid for three more months (if I could get it back) so I decided I couldn't stick around. I didn't want the FBI to know I was traveling. I drove straight back to Palm Beach County before anyone realized I had taken my little trip.

During the entire excursion, I didn't even stop for food. My only stops were for gas and piss breaks; I paid cash for everything. The rental car company must have shit their pants when I returned their brand-new car with 2,000 miles on it in just two days.

I got back and went to my dad's house, located at the end of a cul-de-sac, I noticed a gold Chevy Suburban backed in the driveway of a home across the intersection at the beginning of the street. I had never seen a vehicle in the driveway before. When I asked my dad, he had never previously seen a car in their driveway, either.

When I returned home, I was very cautions inside of my house. I had a good idea the FBI probably put some surveillance equipment in my house, which is why they wanted me to leave when they were searching it. I noticed the smoke detector in the living room was turned, but I didn't inspect it. I didn't want the FBI to know I had suspicions. When I spoke to people about anything significant, I would exit the house and go down the block to have my conversations, or I would do it in a running shower while whispering.

A week had passed, and I was trying to decide what to do. I fell asleep but quickly woke up, covered in sweat, with visions of the FBI breaking down my door with my kids inside, and bringing me to Sheriff Bradshaw's jail. It was at that moment, I realized I had to get the fuck out of dodge.

I told Kelly that the Sheriff's Office and FBI weren't going to stop until I was either dead or in prison. I said I had to leave for the safety of her and the kids and that it would be a while before she heard from me again. I lied, telling her I was going to stay at a friend's house. I felt awful, because her mother had just died from a long struggle with MS. Kelly herself was also afflicted with the disease so for that kind of stress to be heaped on her, it was close to unbearable.

I didn't want any possibility she would implicated in helping me abscond from the country. But where I went; all hinge on obtaining my passport back from the FBI.

If I could get the passport, I could take a boat to Cuba and then a flight to Moscow. If not, I could stay in Cuba and ask for asylum. I couldn't tell anyone about my plan; not my friends, not my family. I didn't want the FBI to charge anyone for aiding in my escape. Doing so could land them in prison for five years and provide them significant leverage to force my return.

I called my criminal defense attorney, Steve Sessa, and told him I needed my passport for a business trip. Sessa called the FBI and told them if I wasn't under arrest, they had no right to hold it. He picked it up my passport from them; I met him at his office to retrieve it.

The FBI probably could have kept it on some grounds, but my Russian visa expired 03.06.2016 (March 6th, 2016, or so they probably thought). In European countries, the month and day are reversed, something that is always a source of confusion to Americans. No doubt the FBI didn't realize that my Russian Visa expired on June 3rd, 2016, an error led to the return of my passport.

On March 22, I retrieved a USB drive with some data backups, hid it in the stitching of my backpack, and took the Tri-Rail train to get down to the keys. At this point, I hadn't noticed anyone following me. When I got to Miami, I dropped by the Verizon store and got a new smartphone. Sadly, they were out of the Galaxy S7, so I settled for a Samsung Note 5. After the phone was activated, I turned it off and put it into my backpack. That night, I made my way down to Homestead, where I would catch a bus the next morning to the Keys.

I arrived at about 11 pm and had nowhere to sleep – I had a little over a thousand dollars on me, but the hotel nearby was completely booked. Like a homeless person, I slept in a shallow ditch in a field near the bus stop so that no one would see me. The ditch was wet and dirty, and I was only able to sleep for a few hours. I woke up, cold and shivering, went to a gas station and bought a cup of coffee and waited for the bus.

I took the bus down to Marathon Key, where I stopped to have breakfast. While there, I turned my new phone on and began setting it up, so I could have all my contacts and such. After wolfing down some food and coffee, I looked for a boat to rent. I couldn't afford much, but I wanted something with enough range to get me to Cuba with enough of a fuel reserve, in the case of the extremely rough seas that I was anticipating. There was a storm brewing in the Caribbean at the time.

I trudged all over Marathon Key but couldn't find a suitable boat. Naturally, I couldn't tell them I was going to take their vessel to Cuba, so my story was that I needed the range to travel all around the deep water areas for fish. One of the rental places told me a better place rent boats was Islamorada, at Bud N Mary's Marina.

During the time everything was taking place, PBSOTalk.com went dark. A crooked Broward County Assistant State Attorney named Dennis Nicewander wrote an email to convince GoDaddy to ban the anti-Sheriff Ric Bradshaw website from public view. He wrote, "My office is investigating a situation where someone hacked into public databases and is now publishing confidential personal information regarding law enforcement officers, judges and prosecutors."

Jose Lambiet of Gossip Extra investigated this and contacted both GoDaddy and the Broward State Attorney's office. He wrote, "according to the state attorney's spokesman, 'Broward's State Attorney's Office was not, is not, investigating pbsotalk.com, nor its founder Mark Dougan.'" My attorney, Tom Julin, told the media it was a troubling assault on free speech.

And public databases? How do you hack into a public database? It's public. Yes, the information came from public record; it was data available to all members of the public. Still, I was on the run, and there was nothing I could do at that point. The server was located outside of the United States, and while they could take the domain name, there wasn't a damn thing they could do to get to the actual data.

In the late afternoon, I walked back to the bus stop but had a two-hour wait. As I was sitting and waiting, I saw that same black Ford FX2 pickup with the torn front-tinted window pull into a gas station about 100 yards away. I knew in my gut with 100% certainty it was that same agent's vehicle, no doubt they found out I got a new phone on my Verizon account and tracked its location. They weren't near any gas pumps, and they just sat there. I could tell someone was there, watching me.

A few minutes later, several other cars arrived. The occupants exited their cars and were having a discussion. Probably about what the hell I was doing. As I was looking around, I realized the property where the bus stop was located stood right in front of a colossal diesel storage container, and I imagined them arresting me on suspicion that I was scoping out the area for domestic terrorism. Farfetched, perhaps, but knowing what I know now, I don't put it past the criminals in our government to make up anything. Especially dirty cops.

Still, I was worried they were there to arrest me. Man, I was damned nervous. I called my dad to hear his voice. A few minutes later, at long last, the bus arrived. I got on the bus and took it up to Islamorada. As I boarded the bus, several of the vehicles left the station and drove right past the bus. I knew they were preparing their team to follow. A standard technique is to have one car follow; they turn off as another one picks up the tail. That way, a team can use several vehicles to blend in better.

I made my way to Bud N Mary's Marina. I found a guy who rented me a boat. We got to talking, and coincidentally, he wanted the boat to disappear, so I told him I was trying to get to Cuba. He agreed to charge me a couple of hundred dollars, and I assured him the boat would be given to some of the Cuban Customs guys so they could part it off and make some cash in exchange for letting me into Cuba. Was he going to report it to his insurance? I don't know – probably, but that wasn't any of my business. Hell, I had my own problems that required focus.

The boat was fucking tiny. 18 feet (6 meters), open cockpit, with a top that didn't work. It also had only one small engine. Whatever. I planned to leave the next morning at first light and try to make it to Cuba by nightfall. It was windy and raining, and the forecast said it would be worse in the morning, so I estimated with the seas as rough as they were and the wind which was blowing from the south, I could probably make 8-10 knots per hour. That would give me about 14 hours to get to Cuba.

If you know anything about boating, an 18-foot boat to cross the rough waters between the Keys and Cuba, during a storm, is borderline suicidal. I gave myself a 25 percent chance I would be successful. That left me with a 75 percent chance I would flip the boat, or sink it, and fucking die. Still, I knew the only way I could maintain my safety was to get out of the reach of the American government. To do that, I had to be daring and bold, risking the real possibility of death. But to me, dying at sea was better than dying in a prison cell or losing my freedom. That would mean they won, and I wasn't going to let them win as long as I was alive.

That night, I lay in the boat, pulling one of the cushions on top of me to try and stay warm. I didn't sleep well – it was cold as hell, and I kept thinking about potential problems on the journey.

I woke up to the gentle lapping of the waves against the boats in the water. I looked at my new Samsung watch. I had many watches over the last several years and was accustomed to seeing a lovely mechanical Swiss timepiece on my wrist, making the digital watch seem foreign. Kelly, the only woman I've ever loved, gave me the one that was on my wrist just this morning.

I had no choice but to use it as collateral, guaranteeing I was going to bring back this small, open cockpit fishing boat I rented from Bud N' Mary's Marina on Islamorada Key in South Florida. I had no intentions of returning this vessel. Instead, if I survived the journey, I was going to give this 18-foot floating piece of crap to the crooked Cuban customs agents in exchange for letting me into their country without asking too many questions.

The guy renting the boat to me knew it would disappear. He gave me a low hourly price and took the watch, telling me if he never sees the vessel again, he'd be happy. No, he wanted the insurance money to replace the barely-buoyant shitbox, powered by a four-stroke engine which barely ran. With a lot of skill and luck, I would be able to catch a flight out of Havana to Moscow in a few days. My watch told me it was three in the morning.

I didn't sleep well, anyway. It was a wet, chilly 65 degrees and I had no blankets, so my body stiffened from the cold. The only warm article of clothing I had was an expensive custom-made Zegna sports coat, and I wasn't about to wreck or lose it. Still, it was better than the previous night's sleep; to prevent being spotted, I snoozed in a wet drainage ditch in the middle of a field. At least now, I wasn't laying in four inches of muddy water. I pulled one of the seat cushions on top of me for warmth, and while it didn't help much, it was better than nothing.

But cold, I can handle that no problem. My childhood upbringing, first in the smoky mountains of North Carolina and then high up in the Rocky Mountains of Durango, Colorado, combined with my Marine Corps infantry experience, provided me with the knowledge that I can handle the harshest conditions; lacking warmth, food, water, and sleep. I would survive, flourish even.

The real reason I wasn't sleeping though was that I was nervous about the storm brewing in the Atlantic. As an experienced seaman, I knew the storm made my chances of escaping alive to Cuba on such a small boat in these incredibly turbulent sea conditions, pretty slim. I gave myself minuscule odds that I would survive the journey, but I would fight my hardest to make it. Still, there was something else. Despite the silence, I suspected an FBI surveillance team, the one I spotted earlier in the day, was there, somewhere, watching me.

I picked my head up high enough from the boat to see over the dock and observe my surroundings. I thought the small houseboat, docked about fifty yards away on the opposite side of the pier, offered the best vantage point to watch me. Not only that, but there was an odd couple that occupied it a few hours after I rented my boat. I walked past on the way to my floating freedom and struck up a conversation with one of the women on board.

My reptilian brain told me she seemed out of place. She looked like she dressed for a summery vacation, but her tense demeanor suggested otherwise. She spoke to me in a standoffish manner, as if she was being forced to talk to the enemy. Still, I couldn't be sure if she was a federal agent. Ellen Thomas, the crooked FBI agent who orchestrated the raid on my home, looked like an unattractive soccer mom with bad hygiene and wreaked of body odor and bad breath, so this one could definitely be a Fed.

The lights inside the houseboat were now off, suggesting the occupants were asleep or more likely, observing me. The metal-halide lights, strategically placed around the marina, eerily illuminated the marina with a greenish orange glow. I looked carefully and saw the metal window blinds on the houseboat had a small separation in the middle. I could see the reflection of the lights of what looked like the round piece of glass that was holding the blinds apart. "It's most likely a camera lens, and it's pointing right at me," I thought, but I couldn't be entirely sure.

It had been a while since I was able to relieve myself, and my bladder was now pressing up against my lungs. I was also stiff with cold, so I decided to use the marina facilities located in the middle of the property to take a hot shower and warm myself up. I climbed out of the boat, and I observed that the out-of-place blind in the houseboat lowered as I approached. I walked past the boxy vessel, only looking at it in the corner of my eye. I saw no other movement. Perhaps it was paranoia? It was a possibility, but I wasn't sure. I sauntered down and around the L-shaped dock and to the marina's bathroom.

The lovely, hot water with stinging pressure greeted me like an old friend and was the only small comfort I had over the last few days. I let the rejuvenating, wet warmth flow down my body for a long time as I gathered my thoughts. After I got dressed again, I decided I would do a little reconnaissance around the marina to see if anything else was unusual or seemed out of place. I knew if the FBI was monitoring my movements, they weren't going to move their teams just because I felt like a midnight stroll. I've done counter-surveillance before, and I knew it would be too much of a risk that they would blow their cover.

When I left the bathroom, I walked a few yards south towards the boat, and then cut between the dock and the building, doubling back to the northwest. Because of the proximity of the larger yachts relative to the structure, I knew it would be difficult for anyone spying on me to see where I had gone. I snuck along the dock, past the deserted café, and then turned north, slinking along another structure.

I reached a parking lot and turned west, lurking along the cars - there weren't too many. One vehicle, in particular, a newer model silver Chevy Suburban, caught my eye. Parked strangely; athwart and too close to the main building, it seemed as if to intentionally kept it out of out of sight from the docks. It could have belonged to a worker or boater, but it wasn't exactly an appropriate spot for any activity except for...

There were no doors nearby, and to get to the dock you would have to walk around the large building. I decided there were tons of other parking places that would be more reasonable. Another oddity, the tint on the truck was pitch black, even on the windshield. In Florida, blacking out the windshield is illegal, except for law enforcement vehicles.

I walked next to the Suburban to catch a glimpse of the license plate on the back. Despite the dark tint, I saw the glow of surveillance equipment in the rear, silhouetting a person moving around in the back seat. The person, who I could tell was watching me, quickly sprang from the laughably stereotypical American SUV, keeping the door pressed tightly against his body as if he were trying to prevent the light within from escaping. The man that emerged was a good six inches taller than I, had dark scruffy hair, a beard, and a pierced ear. He spontaneously began to explain what he was doing there;

"I'm just waiting to leave on an early morning charter," he volunteered. Not that I asked; it wasn't any of my business.

Histrionic acting, wasn't it? Still, I had a light, casual conversation with him about fishing, asking him questions about which boat he chartered and what he planned to catch. I made the dialogue sound light and innocent, but I was asking information he would have to make up on the spot to trip him up. It was a trick I learned from being a cop.

I could sense he had no idea what he was talking about, though I could see his mind wander to what his true trophy fish was going to be -- me. Still, he seemed like a nice enough guy, just trying to do his job, but not really managing. None of the agents over the last few weeks were doing their jobs well, in my opinion.

The FBI agents in the West Palm Beach and Miami offices were sloppy, careless and negligent. They knew I was observant as hell. After I confronted the agents in the parking lot waiting to raid my house and told them I saw them doing surveillance on my home a few days prior, they should have been more cautious. But they weren't, and it was good for me because now I knew I had to escape another way.

Leaving in the boat, even if I were able to make it past the storm, would have resulted in Homeland Security or the Coast Guard stopping me going to Cuba, giving them grounds to arrest me for fleeing from suspected prosecution. Discovering their surveillance also had another benefit.

Now that I indeed recognized they were conducting such an intense, clandestine operation, I knew I had to step up my game and give them the slip, once and for all. That meant deactivating all mobile devices, including the burner, and finding a way to escape so that they wouldn't be able to follow me. Up to this point, it was more of a half-assed, lazy attempt and I should have known better. Besides, anti-surveillance, or losing a surveillance team, is easy enough if you understand how they work and the nature of their limitations. I knew well enough.

I returned to the cold, damp boat. Despite the fact I wasn't going to be sneaking off to Cuba and now had to plan something else, I was relieved and went back to sleep. I wanted the FBI to feel comfortable that they <u>didn't ruin their surveillance</u>, but I was also glad to have my new knowledge and was just plain exhausted. I woke up at first light and waited for the boat rental office to open so I could get my watch back and give them the keys to the boat. I hopped on a northbound bus and set about making my plans for the great escape.

I awoke the next morning drenched from the rain, so I went back into the bathroom and showered. After dressing, I walked for about 14 kilometers (eight miles) to avoid being followed and began back towards Palm Beach County, taking a bus back to Homestead.

As the bus was heading North into Key Largo, there was a black helicopter hovering about 50 feet over the road. I was thinking to myself, "This is it! They are going to storm the bus and take me away." We passed under the helicopter, and that was it. Perhaps they were checking utility poles? I don't know, but it was weird. As the bus reached the city of Homestead, I thought maybe the government found out about my burner cell and was able to track me, so I stopped at Best Buy and picked up a new one, with cash and under a fake name.

When I left Best Buy, I saw a gold Ford Taurus running in a handicapped parking space, backed in so the driver inside could have a good view of the store. I watched carefully out of the corner of my eye and could tell the chubby older guy within was paying close attention to my movements. I removed the battery in the first burner, put it in my bag and jumped on another bus to go to Metro Rail. As the bus pulled out, I saw the man in the gold car hold a portable radio to his face and pull out of the parking space. Because of the layout of the bus; there was no rear window, and I couldn't tell if he was following the bus. When the bus turned at an intersection, I could see out of the side window that the same gold car with the same man was four or five cars behind. I had no idea how many other vehicles were in on the surveillance, but I knew this one was tailing me.

I exited the bus I took the Metro Rail to the center of downtown Miami, and walked through buildings, up and down stairwells, crowded areas and such in a manner where it would have been nearly impossible to follow me. I went to my attorney Tom Julin's office at Hunton Williams, where he put me in the conference room and gave me some food. He asked me how I was doing, and when I told him all that had happened, he was shocked. I asked him to mail a package for me to my children.

Exhausted, I decided to say screw it and buy a plane ticket to Moscow. I tried Aeroflot and Delta, and none of them could book a ticket for me with my passport number. Furthermore, every credit and bank card I used was declined, despite knowing I had lots of money available. After calling the airline, they told me they couldn't tell me the reason. However, they emphasized that one possible reason was that I was on the TSA's "No Fly List."

I arrived in West Palm Beach after nightfall, and I took a taxi from the Tri-Rail station to my brother's house. When I entered the front door, I realized I didn't have my wallet containing my passport or the thousand dollars I was able to scrounge together. I freaked out, realizing that all my plans of escape may have been self-sabotaged because of my own stupidity and carelessness. I had left my wallet in the taxi while paying the driver but didn't realize it for over two hours. I was able to get the driver's phone number and called him.

He said he has several fares since my ride, but would check in the back of his car the next time he stopped. He called me back and said he found my wallet on the floor in the back seat. Being a beautiful, thin, grey-textured Ferragamo wallet, it blended in perfectly with the floor and even shining a light, he almost didn't see it. He met me and returned the wallet with the passport and all the money still inside. I gave him $50 and thanked him for his honesty. It was such an incredible relief and incredible luck, I was in disbelief about it the rest of the evening.

After I sat and gathered my thoughts, thinking of my next move, I decided I needed a more creative solution. I had an old Ford Ranger truck that hadn't driven for seven years. I never registered the little pickup because there was some problem with the title. I changed the oil and filter, and amazingly it started right up and ran pretty well. Still, the transmission was making noise, and it had me a little worried. I put a trailer tag on it and asked someone to park it on the north side of the Boynton Beach mall at lunchtime the next day, which was Easter.

On Easter day, I stopped at my mother's house, which was vacant, where I got a blond wig and a pair of blue, non-prescription sunglasses. I also grabbed some extra clothing, stuck it in my backpack, and went to the mall. I thought about going to my father's house, sneaking over the back wall, and seeing my beautiful children before I left, but I knew the risk was too great. So with a very heavy heart, I went to the Boynton Beach Mall, where I parked on the south side. I went into the mall, slipped into a crowded store, changed my shirt behind a clothing rack and donned the wig, glasses and a yellow baseball hat. I left the bag and walked in a different direction and exited on the north side. As planned, the truck was waiting there with the key on top of the tire. I drove off and started making my way to the north.

I drove to New Hampshire, where I researched how I could get across the US border without going through US customs/TSA. I was pretty confident that flying, driving or taking a ferry all require you pass through TSA before exiting the country. While I didn't think there was a warrant out for my arrest, no doubt there was probably a detainer request. I thought the best way to get across would be sneaking across the border. But during my research, I found out it's not very easy. The US/Canadian border is protected with lasers, pressure plates and drones with thermal cameras. It was time to regroup.

I drove back down to New Haven, CT, where I parked at an old friend's house. I took a train into Manhattan to talk to my other attorney, Arkady Buhk, who is one of the premier cyber attorneys in the country. I was wearing a yellow hat and had the wig and sunglasses in a bag. I stepped off the train and started walking to the exit; there was an obese man in his 50's, dressed in plain clothing and a bulge under his jacket standing. He was standing at the beginning of the platform holding a clipboard. He was looking down at the clipboard and examining people getting off the train. I knew he was looking for someone in particular. My gut told me he was looking for me, and I could feel the knot tightening in my stomach.

As I walked past him, trying to be calm and nonchalant. He looked down, looked up at me, looked down, looked up… I walked straight past and in my peripheral vision, saw he had photos of someone. I didn't get a good enough look to see if the pictures were of me, but my suspicions were confirmed when he turned and began to follow me up the stairs.

Like a bolt of lightning, I shot up the stairs and out the door to the city. I rounded the corner and dashed far enough where I could turn into a business before he rounded the same corner and saw where I went. After a few minutes, my breathing returned to normal, I took off the hat, put it in my bag. I threw on the wig and glasses, exited the store and got into a taxi. I had the cabbie circle around the block, exited, and got into another taxi going the other way. After a half-dozen blocks, I exited the yellow cab and began walking to Arkady's office.

Arkady agreed with me that once they have your computer, there are countless things for them to discover that are technically illegal and can land you in prison for a long time. Stuff like downloaded music or movies or using software that isn't appropriately registered… the American cyber laws are absolutely terrifying. Or, I thought they might pin the published names on my website and charge me with espionage.

I went back to my friend's house, packed, and left for North Carolina the next day. I kept my burner phone off with the battery out the entire way out of fear it would compromise my location. Once in North Carolina, I stopped at the family cabin and started doing copious research on how I could get into Canada without going through TSA. I spent two days, searching rivers to swim across, or boats to rent to get me across, and cheap pieces of shit sailboats I could buy to sail to Cuba or Canada. All these ideas were risky propositions.

And then it dawned on me. If I were to take off in the USA, fly over Canada and fly back into the USA, merely flying over that territory doesn't require TSA checks. And what would happen if someone onboard had a medical emergency? The pilot would of course land in the closest airport. I called a bunch of flight charter companies with the story that I was writing a book on plate tectonics, and that I had to take off from Buffalo, fly over Canadian territory and match specific features with GPS coordinates. I wound up finding a private pilot who agreed to take me up for cash under the table, a complete violation of F.A.A. rules. I would like to go into additional details on this, but there are certain things I have to keep silent about to protect innocent people.

After crossing into Canada, I dashed from the small airfield and made my way to Toronto, where I booked a flight on Turkish Airlines. The flight was scheduled to depart at 9PM that evening, fly to Istanbul where I would have a one-hour layover before leaving for Moscow. The fact I was out of the United States was some relief to me, and I was able to book the flight successfully. I was worried that once they scanned my passport at the ticket counter, the federal government would somehow show up, or perhaps the Canadians, at the request of Uncle Sam, and detain me.

At 9 pm, I had a big fat knot in my stomach, and I was waiting…

No one came to arrest me; however, when it came time to board, they announced they canceled the flight due to a mechanical problem. After two hours, the airline decided to put everyone up at a hotel. What a mess! Making matters worse, every hotel in the area was booked, and the closest place the airline got us a room was a two-hour drive away, which they shuttled us by bus.

I was extremely nervous because the airline didn't tell us the exact reason why the flight didn't take off. Perhaps it was because of me? The thought crossed my mind, and I knew every moment I spent in Canada was a moment to get arrested. I began talking to a guy, Michael McDonald, a very cool Canadian documentary maker living in Germany. I sat next to him on the bus and told him what I had been through, and how worried I was.

Of course, he told me not to worry; that's what anyone would say, but doing it is another thing entirely. By the time we got to the hotel, it was well past 2 am. Everyone was exhausted.

Morning came, and then lunchtime. The airlines ordered us Chinese food or something like that. It wasn't delicious, but I hadn't been eating much, and I was famished. That afternoon, the airline notified us they fixed the plane. We were to depart at 9PM. We got our stuff together and went to the airport. I had a knot in my stomach that I was going to be pinched having visions of being tackled in front of the gate like a terrorist. And then I realized I was in Canada, so my thoughts turned into being detained; not by being tackled, but from the very polite Canadians shaking my hands until they didn't work anymore.

At the airport, some of us got tickets for the next flight, and some didn't. Some lady was going to miss her daughter's graduation, and she got screwed. Ordinarily, I would have traded places with her for such an event but being that I needed to get the hell out of the country and get to Moscow pronto, I was just glad to be issued a new ticket for that evening's flight. I will take a moment to thank her for missing such an important event to unknowingly aid in my escape.

I boarded the flight without being arrested. I sat next to Michael McDonald on the plane and once we were airborne, I breathed a major sigh of relief. Still, I knew Turkey is an extradition country, and if the Feds found I left and issued a warrant for my arrest, I could be held there and extradited to the United States. So, it wasn't until we departed Turkey and headed for Moscow that I started truly felt relieved.

While the flight from Canada to Turkey was uneventful, the trip from Turkey to Moscow was a bit more… entertaining. I was in an emergency exit row, so I had a lot of legroom, for which I was thankful. That ended when some lady on the flight complained of chest pains and the flight attendants laid her down at my feet with an IV bag. On the upside, the flight attendants were friendly and flirty, and they kept coming by and stuffing me full of Turkish Delight.

Chapter 38 - Escape Completed!

When I landed in Moscow, I contacted Svetlana, a super girl I had dated a few times. "Svetlana?" I asked, "It's John. I just landed in Moscow. I couldn't call you before, but I have an emergency. Can you come to pick me up?"

"Yes sure!" she continued, "Take the train to Kievskaya and meet me at the McDonald's at Europiskiy Mall."

I grabbed my bags and hopped on the Aero Express train, very happy to be alive and safe in Moscow. The first stop: getting a sim card for my Samsung phone. The next stop, her home on Rublevka Shosse.

When I got to her home, I sat on the couch and let everything sink in to my head. It was the first time in weeks I could reflect on what happened. I broke down crying for what seemed like hours. It was the first time I cried since I was a little kid. I wasn't unhappy to be there; quite the contrary. I love Moscow. It's a fascinating city and so filled with wonderful people and fantastic architecture. Plus, I love any place with good nightlife, and Moscow has that in abundance.

No, what broke my heart was being forced to leave my kids. My mind was suddenly comprehending that I had lost everything. My home, my belongings except for the clothing I brought, and more devastatingly, my family – my father and mother, their spouses, Three brothers, two sisters and most horribly, my two beautiful children. I would wake up every morning and see them, feeling their hugs on my neck, kisses on my cheek. It was so wonderful to be able to walk them to the bus stop or give them a ride to school in the mornings. I love my babies with all my heart; more than I have ever loved anything. And I didn't know when I was going to have a chance to see them again.

What would they think? Would they think they did something wrong to make me leave? Would they think I abandoned them? How can you explain to young children that you had to run from an evil, oppressive group of cops and not make them fear or hate their entire country? As I type this, I still struggle with how to put everything into context. I talk to them almost every day. I have tried my best to explain why I had to leave, but I am afraid I can't tell them everything – not yet. They won't understand, but I hope in a few years they will. As I write this book, almost two years later, I still haven't seen my children.

I asked Svetlana what I should do. "My ex-husband is Zakhar Artimyev[8], a journalist with Evening Moscow newspaper," She said. "I will arrange a meeting because he is a man that can help you."

The next day, I took the metro to the Evening Moscow newspaper where I met Zakhar and his fellow journalists. I told them

---

8   If you are reading this book in Russian, it is being translated by Zakhar. Please tell him what a wonderful job he did. If you are reading this in English, you can still pay him a complement for being an awesome guy.

about the crooked Sheriff, the FBI raiding my home, and my great escape to Russia.

Zakhar and his editor were shocked; they thought it was a work of fiction but it only took a few minutes of googling for them to believe me. Zakhar wrote the story but it took several days for it to be published; the editor wanted everything to be verified to make sure I wasn't some sort of crack pot. They read dozens of articles about me and my activities. I put them in touch with attorneys, journalists and other people that gave first-hand accounts of what happened. When they were convinced beyond all reasonable doubt, they published the story.

After Zakhar's article came out, it was a media firestorm. I had journalists from numerous papers and TV stations contacting me. I felt like I had the Paparazzi following me because of all the television cameras. I went to the Federal Migration Service (FMS) office and applied for political asylum. Little did I know, it would take almost a year to obtain as FMS was undergoing reorganization.

I was granted asylum in February 2017. I was told by the people at FMS that four guys in their IT department had been arrested. Apparently, the CIA had paid them each $15,000 to get any information they could about me. I don't know what information they could have possibly offered... my notes about the Sheriff, corruption in the Palm Beach County government, my address in Moscow... but hell, they can get all that and more on my website. The IT guys got caught while they were auditing why someone was running my name in their systems.

When you think about it, what is the motive behind the Russian collusion narrative in the 2016 elections? I suspect it's nothing more than a money grab. Make people believe Russia is going to get them and they will throw money to your budget. It allows them to justify incredibly broad powers to spy, hack and violate any American's privacy they damned well please. It's God damned scary, and those on the left AND the right should fear what's happening.

Liberal friends, please wake up: it's okay to hate Trump, but pushing the narrative of Russian collusion just because it's convenient and it makes him look even worse, it's very, very dangerous. All the power the government is grabbing to use against Trump which you applaud, it can be used against any one of you.

I am frequently asked "Why Russia?" People thought I was under some type of illusion that I would be leaving the corruption of the United States and coming to a land I believed was free from problems. "Out of the frying pan and into the fire," as they say.

Of course, I am not disillusioned in the very least. I understand that Russia, like other countries, faces issues with corruption. Those people that ask me this simply fail to realize that my life was in danger. I was being hunted by one of the most powerful law enforcement agencies in the world whose plan was to capture me, put me in jail, and arrange for some type of "accident" to happen. It wasn't just speculation; they said as much in audio recordings. If I stayed in the United States, I have no doubt that I would not be here today to write this story.

Coming to Russia was not about choosing the better place. It was about escaping from people in my government that wanted to see me in jail for the rest of my life, or worse - dead.

In the month after I arrived in Moscow, I was interviewed by almost everyone. I had reporters and cameramen following me; photos, selfies, and all manner of publicity reserved for people who are much more interesting than I am. It was such a very strange, surreal experience.

Life and Antics in Moscow

Chapter 39 - Settling In

You hear all the time about families that fight for their loved ones. Loved ones wrongly incarcerated, retaliated against, and other such things. When my brothers would be arrested for a crime, everyone was there for them. Me, I was on my own. My family wrote me off as a lost cause. Kelly, being the executive assistant for elected Public Defender, never even bothered to help. And after a month, the reality of the situation set in – that no one would ever fight for me. No one would ever fight for my resistance of the criminal activities committed by so paly police officers. I was left on my own, in a foreign land where I didn't speak the language and had very little prospects. And so on May 11th, I accepted my fate and sent the following letter to Kelly:

Dear Kelly,

I wanted you to know you were the first true love in my life, and I loved you the first moment I laid eyes upon you, wearing your white flowery dress and sitting on the chaise lounge at Mark Shames' house. The only other two loves I have had, you gave me; Kelton and Aurelia.

I know your life is not easy right now. I would tell you that mine isn't either, but in a way, I chose this path. Naturally, I wouldn't ever have wanted to leave you and my babies, but I was left with no choice, and there is no turning back now. Believe me, it tears a deep hole in my heart and I'm trying my best not to replace it with vengeance and hatred towards my country. Not that it's working... but I'm trying.

I know you loved me at one point in your life, but over the past ten years, I felt you growing more distant, until the point where there was absolutely no love at all. When I was consumed by the hatred and anger eating away at me, you were absent, and I was abandoned by the woman who was supposed to help me find my way out of the darkness. And it's a shame, because I will love you all my life.

I must proceed with my life with the belief that I will never be able to step foot in my country again; and with the belief that you really don't want to see me again, because everything you show me, everything I feel from you, it seems to be the case.

I hope you will allow the children to come visit regularly. I will do my best to come up with the money to make it happen. One day, they will be old enough to analyze the situation and if they think you tried keeping them away from me, they will resent you terribly. I know, because it happened to me with my mom, and I never really got over it. I don't think that's how you would be, but I just want you to keep it in the back of your mind.

I miss you and the kids so much, and the love I have for you all will never be able to be replaced. But I will need to find something, someone, who can at least help heal my pain and fill my heart with something other than hatred. I hope you will do the same. Someone who makes you feel like we felt when we first met. Someone you want to have adventures with, and someone who will love you as much as I do. If it is possible.

If things change, if for some reason I am able to return to the United States, depending on where I am in my life, I probably wouldn't move back, but I would come see the children frequently. You, too, if you would ever want. And you can ALWAYS come here to visit me. And if one day, you ever wanted to try a life here, you might be surprised that you enjoy it. I would invite you to do it now, but I understand your feelings towards me, and I know you don't have the ability to change that.

I hope you know how much you have meant to me, how much I love you... and how much I love the kids. I'm not the monster you may think; I'm the guy who cries at sad songs and movies.

No matter where, or who is in my life, my promise to you will always stand. If you need me, or you become sick, and have no one in your life to care for you, no one else in my life will matter and all will cease to exist, except for you, and I will be there at your side at a moment's notice (even though you may have to come here for me to do it).

Thank you for your love, and for my two beautiful babies.

Shortly after I got to Moscow, I had to find a place to stay. I was almost out of money so my options were limited. That's when I met an angel that saved me – Irina. We met at… Starbucks ;) and we went on a few dates. I knew right away it was love at first sight. She was a kind, nice, fun girl, intelligent and stubborn as hell and about five years younger than I. We went on a few dates and that's when I was given two-days' notice that I had to vacate Svetlana's apartment.

Irina told me that I could stay with her for a few days, and I gratefully accepted. And a few days turned into weeks, and into months. I guess she kept me around because she was mesmerized by my delicious cooking abilities… or my ability to push the button on her coffee maker.

Other than making her coffee in the mornings and the occasional dinner, she never asked anything of me. When I had a problem, such as something medical, she brought me and fixed it. When I needed support, she was there. It was a brutal time in my life. More times than I can count, I collapsed in her bathtub, under the running water, breaking down from missing my children, realizing I was missing their entire life. Knowing I was helpless to do anything about it.

I always tried to hide my breakdowns, but Irina always knew when it was happening. She would sit next to the tub, petting my head (she started calling me her hedgehog because of my prickly haircut), quietly consoling me. Giving me the love and understanding I always wanted but never had.

Chapter 40 - Wild Night at the Night Wolves Party

On May 31, 2016, just a little over one month after my arrival, I was invited to the Night Wolves 27th anniversary party. It was such a cool party, filled with alcohol, friends, fireworks are great music. I had been hanging out with UFC fighter Jeff Monson, who had also been invited. I heard him speaking English, walked over to him and struck up a conversation. "Where are you from?" I asked.

"West Palm Beach, Florida, and you?" he answered. I was genuinely surprised to run into someone in Moscow who lived just a few miles from me in Florida. Monson had been speaking on the stage, but I had no idea who he was. I asked him, and he was surprised I didn't know who he was. Oops! He invited me to sit and have dinner with him; he was sitting with a bunch of journalists, one from Komsomolskiya Pravda who had just done a story on my arrival to Moscow. And if that wasn't enough, the weather was excellent.

After some eating and drinking, I excused myself to go to the men's room. I walked downstairs off the metal labyrinth and as I passed the area where they were grilling Kebabs, I saw a lovely young woman standing there with a truly terrified look in her eyes. There were a lot of men standing around, but they were laughing and joking with one another, paying her no attention. No, she wasn't afraid of them.

"Are you okay?" I asked. She shook her head no but didn't say anything. I realized she might be in medical distress of some sort, and judging by the chewed-up food on her shoes, I took an educated guess she may be choking. I asked her, "Can you breathe?" Again, she shook her head in a manner to indicate she could not breathe.

I spun her around and began performing the Heimlich maneuver on her for what seemed like hours, but really, it was probably under a minute or so. Nothing was happening, and she started to go limp. I looked in her throat, but I didn't see anything, but her eyes were rolling back into her head. I knew she wasn't going to live much longer. I furiously tugged backward under and up inside her rib cage so hard; I was lifting her feet from the ground.

At some point, I felt a slight change in the resistance. The woman was limp in my arms at that point. I looked in her mouth again, stuck in my index and middle finger and felt there was a fat piece of steak in the back of her throat. I reached in as deeply as I could, hoping I wasn't going to damage her throat. I grabbed the meat and tugged it out of her esophagus. She violently inhaled a breath of life-giving air and hung on to my neck, me supporting her weight, until she could stand on her own.

I walked her back to her boyfriend, and they were incredibly kind. They asked me what I was doing in Moscow, and I told them the abbreviated version. They bought me a drink from the bar and left –

unsurprisingly, her throat was very sore. I went back and sat with Jeff and the other guys and got drunk.

I woke early the very next morning and saw I received a Facebook message from a woman named Ekaterina; it was the woman I had assisted. She was incredibly grateful and was thanking me. I wrote her back and told her I was the one who was happy. I was happy because I lost everything in my life, including my children. I explained to her that I felt as I had no purpose, but in helping her, perhaps I had a purpose after all.

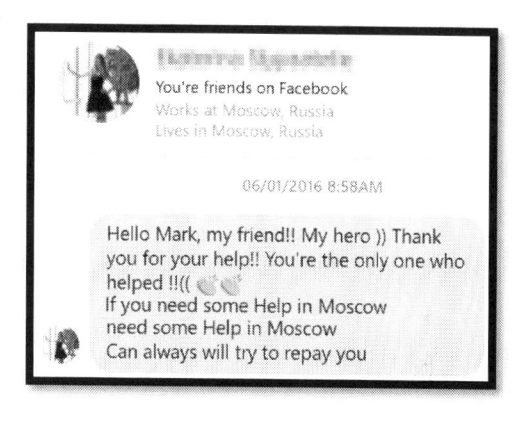

It's not something that I can explain, but as a man with a broken soul, I think she helped me just as much as I helped her. I haven't spoken to her in quite a while now, but I see her on Facebook, and she's living her life to the fullest. It's a beautiful thing to see.

Still, my depression was incredibly profound. I woke every day thinking of my kids, missing them, vowing vengeance on those that forced me to leave them, fleeing into exile. I moped around most of the day, and in the evenings, at least a few times per week, I would break down in tears, wishing for my children.

I had wanted to see them for the summer; my father promised he would bring them to visit me. My brother wound up getting a DUI, and my dad spent the money on an attorney for him. As December came, I sank lower into depression. With no job, no money; after getting off the metro, I couldn't even afford to take a bus to my apartment.

As I walked the four kilometers to my home on a cold, rainy December Moscow midnight, I decided I was going to end my life. Doing it before the holidays was too terrible and my family would have been devastated. Ending my life after the New Year would suck for the poor bastard who had to cart out my body before the Russian Christmas (January 7th). I decided that January 10th was the ideal day for it.

When I woke up on January 10th, it was uncharacteristically sunny and beautiful. There had been a magnificent snowfall, and the sky was a majestic blue. I had a new sense of purpose and decided that I am a fighter until the end. I would never give those people the satisfaction of being able to sit back and have a chuckle over my death.

For those who would accuse me of being involved with a Russian crime organization or with the government, they are fools. I'd at least have money for the bus if that were true.

I decided I needed to stop feeling sorry for myself and to get off my ass to start working towards the goal of seeing my kids again. And I wasn't going to do it being poor. But what to do?

I met a woman who needed to write an economics dissertation for her MBA degree from a prestigious university in London. She had just six days left to give it to her professor; she hadn't done a damned thing. No research, no writing, no thought to the topic - and it was an incredibly complex topic[9]. She bought me a laptop and paid me about 50,000 rubles (almost $1,000) to get everything done.

She was able to get a small extension on the due date, a few days. By the time her assignment needed to be turned in, I had written a report based on survey results I had faked by writing a program to randomize data towards a weighted result. I performed statistical analysis of the falsified data for the basis of the paper. I would have preferred to do it the right way with correct data, but on such short notice, there wasn't time. The entire report, data, and analysis were over 250 pages long. Despite all the obstacles, she was successful in her bid to obtain her MBA degree.

---

9   I can't tell you the topic because it might be a problem for her.

Chapter 41 - Creating the BadVolf Computer Table

An American company wouldn't hire me knowing the American government wanted me and my Russian language skills are terrible. I teach at my friend's kindergarten an hour or two each week, and while there is good money in teaching English in Moscow, I dread teaching. I don't have the patience for it. I'm a math guy. An engineering guy. I love using my brain, and when I teach kids, even for just an hour, I can only count the seconds for the hour to pass.

I created a company called BadVolf and decided to manufacture storage servers here. I used my laptop and some CAD software to create a prototype of a server case that could hold sixty hard drives. It was based off an existing design I had, but it wasn't interesting, and the opportunities were scarce. In talking to my seven-year-old son Kelton, we decided it would be cool to make computer-integrated desks. When I say computer desks, I mean all the components are built inside the computer. The motherboard, video cards, fans; everything – visible and beautifully illuminated under a glass top.

I spent weeks going over technical specifications and engineering drawings of various computer components. I compiled a bunch of the information into a design for my first table. I spend two months designing the table. The metal fabrication company in Ivanovo[10] that made my server prototype also produced the first desk prototype. While in Ivanovo, I met my friend Oleg, an excellent English speaker and aspiring police officer. Oleg wanted to help me with the desk project, and since he had to go to Moscow, he told me we could go together.

He called one of his friends who said he would drive us, and the table prototype, to Moscow in a truck. When we arrived at the meeting place, the truck – it wasn't a truck at all. It was a little hatchback car with two people inside. There was no way we were going to fit. So Instead of shipping it back on the train, we took a fucking Marshutka[11] back to Moscow.

It was chaos. The driver stopped about halfway through the drive and jacked the price up on us, threatening to leave us on the side of the road if we didn't pay the extra fee. When Oleg refused, we continued the journey, the driver's friend saying he was going to call the Russian police on us and tell them we were traveling with a suspicious package. After renegotiating the price (that's Russian for saying we got fucked), we arrived in Moscow.

Oleg and I went to a company called HYPERPC, a custom PC-building company in Moscow that does unbelievable unbelievably

---

10   Yes, I know Ivanovo is called the City of Brides. Thanks for that information.

11   Also known as a Jihad Taxi. It's a short little bus that seats about 14 people, usually driven by a fucking maniac.

high-quality work. They bought a few of the tables and put them on their website.

I was working on a little laptop, and the processing power required to model more advanced tables in my CAD program was brutal. Changes were taking several minutes to make with some rebuilds were taking up to 30 minutes. HYPERPC let me use the first computer desk to develop more advanced desks.

On their website, they took credit for designing the table, but to be fair, I did work with them on bettering the design. I let the dishonesty slide because overall, they are good guys and a good company. I get the need for being unique amongst your competitors, so I didn't take it personally.

In a way, however, it backfired on them. They had a signed agreement with Intel that they would not use any AMD parts. ASUS and AMD approached me and asked to use the table for the official launch of the Threadripper processor. I agreed, and it put HYPERPC in an awkward position. Since they took credit for designing the table, they now had to explain to Intel why their table was used for the launch of their competitor's product. They weren't pleased about it. But still, what was I to do? I needed the money, and HYPERPC only bought a few tables, certainly not enough for me to pay my bills.

The table has since made it into PC Magazine Russia and used for some very prestigious events. HYPERPC used it for the world gaming championships. AMD used it for Russia's Computer Graphic Design event. Samsung used it to launch their new 49" gaming monitor. ASUS used it for Game World. The product evolved with each batch made. The tables are a gamer's wet dream. You can see what they look like at badvolf.com .

The next batch of tables after the prototype took forever to get from the company in Ivanovo. Not only that, but they haphazardly made them and nothing fit properly. I spent weeks correcting the flaws in the manufacturing with basic tools. I decided I needed to find another fabrication company.

That's when I met my friend Dmitry (Dima) and his lovely wife Tatiana (Tanya). Dima had read about my story in one of the news articles, and he was delighted to help. His generosity and help led me to ship my first two international tables to the Philippines and United States. But computer tables be damned, I made lifelong friends with Dima and Tanya.

The Igor Adventure – Insanity in the Russian Forest

In the spring of 2017, I was walking through Savolovskaya metro, where a police officer named Sergey Mihailiykov was trying to arrest a drunk man. His drunk friend attempted to attack the cop, so I took the liberty of stepping in to help out. I grabbed the drunk friend, spun him around and kept him away from the cop. Soon after, many other police officers arrived and pulled grabbed the drunk man I was keeping away from Sergey. They circled me, and I thought I was going to be arrested, but it turned out they appreciated it. I became friends with Sergey and another Metro employee, Igor Bilov.

Igor asked me to come back at lunch; I introduced Igor to KFC – Kentucky Fried Chicken. Now he's a KFC fanatic (there are LOTS of KFC's in Russia). Igor says to me in his best, but broken English, "Hey John. You go to Dacha[12] with me. We go this summer. You go?"

---

12 A Dacha is a small country cabin

Except this dacha was located at Bolshoi Kasli lake, right between Yekaterinburg and Chelyabinsk. You have probably heard of Chelyabinsk; it's the large city where a meteor blew up, injuring thousands of people and blowing out windows in buildings in a fifty-mile radius. To which I responded, "Hell yeah! Count me in!" Because I'm always up for a good party at a Dacha, especially places where meteors love to explode. "Igor, I can only go if I had the money for it," I said. Igor's assured me, "Don't worry John. I'll get the tickets."

Igor made good on his word. He gave me my ticket a week before we were to leave. A few days later, Irina pointed out to me that it was a train ticket, not an airplane ticket. I say, "Well hell, how long is that going to take?" I've been on long trains before. I took an 11-hour train to Kiev before, and it was a nightmare. This one, I knew was going to take about double the time. I was informed it would take 32 hours. I almost died.

Irina looked at my face and said, "Oh, don't worry. These long trains usually have nice sleeping accommodations. I'll pack you lots of food and beer, and it will be a long party."

Okay, I wasn't going to panic. I decided to make the most of the trip. As we boarded, the feeling of dread washed over me. The seats Igor bought were for sitting only. There was no way in hell I was going to make it 32 hours sitting in a crappy chair. As you may have guessed, I can take any amount of punishment in a life-or-death situation, but this wasn't life or death. It was supposed to be a nice vacation. There's nothing nice about sitting for so long.

I told Igor that I would get off at the next stop and give him the money for the ticket, but he says, "John, don't worry. I got everything taken care of." That's when he walked up to the security guy for the train. Each train car comes with sleeping quarters for the car's stewards. Igor bribed the guy to give up his room. It was smooth sailing after that. Well, at least we got to Chelyabinsk.

We pulled in to the train station a few days later at about 4 am. Igor's friends met us, and I had the first taste of what havoc awaited me for the next five days. We got to his friend's Lada[13], and he opened the trunk. His friend pulled out a liter of vodka and started pounding it. "Oh shit," I thought. "It's too late to turn back now."

I threw my bag in the car, got into the back seat and put on my seatbelt. The seatbelt wouldn't have helped much – the driver was speeding 140kph (85mph) down the slick, winding mountain roads. Igor, laughing in the front seat, was carrying on a normal conversation with the guy sitting next to me. Not me - beads of sweat were forming on my forehead, despite the cold weather.

"Igor!" I yelled, "If your friend insists on driving like an asshole, drop me off here. I'll walk and find my way. I'm not going to die before I get a chance to see my kids again!"

Igor, probably not understanding what I just said, looked at me with a smile and said, "Okay John."

A few minutes later, we stopped at a lovely mountain where I was able to fly the drone and get some fantastic footage. I used the translator so Igor would understand I wanted his friend to stop driving like a complete asshole. He understood, and the ride was a bit better until we reached the Dacha.

---

13 Lada is a Russian car that's about 25 years behind the rest of the automotive world. I admit though, I would kill for a Lada Niva with big tires

Mother of God was that a shock! There was water, but ice cold. There was a place to use the bathroom – outside. There was no shower. I think Igor was as surprised as I was because he found the lady who rented him the Dacha and told her we wanted another place.

The manager relocated the five of us into a different dacha, this one with hot water. We stayed one night and had a great, drunken time. The manager kicked us out the next morning. Igor told me it was because she jacked the price up on us. I wasn't sure if it was that, or if his drunk friends made so much noise it pissed all the other people in surrounding dachas off. Whatever. It was nice to be gone.

The next night, we stayed at his friend's home located near the lake with a beautiful vegetable garden. But there was no running water in the house, and if you wanted a bathroom, you had to walk outside to the far side of the garden and use the outhouse. "Don't breathe," I told myself, "you might inhale a fly or die from the odor."

Luckily, there was a lot of drinking that night. The wife of the man who owned the house made Ukha, soup made from boiled fish - the entire fish; head, tail, eyes - everything. She scooped soup out into my bowl and plopped down some small fish with missing eyeballs. I thought to myself, "Fuck. I'm going to be eating fish eyeballs."

The next morning, I had enough of the elegant country living, and I got the hell out of there. Igor's friend drove me to Yekaterinburg where I spent two lovely days by myself. Yekaterinburg is a big city – and I belong in a big city. I had a great time. Igor wasn't offended that I bailed – a month later, I went to his daughter's wedding.

Chapter 42 - Malicious Warrant Filed by State Attorney

In March 2017, an incredibly vindictive Assistant State Attorney named Brian Fernandes was trying to get me at any cost. Brian Fernandes is State Attorney David Aronberg's second in command, and naturally, there was a vendetta against me for exposing his boss for being the scumbag that he is.

A.S.A. Fernandes engaged in malicious prosecution against Rick Sessa on charges he knew were false but told Sessa he would reduce them or drop them if he were to give information that would lead to a warrant for my arrest. Specifically, he wanted Sessa to say it was me who recorded Detective Kenneth Mark Lewis in his admissions of committing numerous crimes for the Sheriff and Chief Deputy Gauger.

Sessa told me that during the meeting, Fernandes slammed his hands on the table and leaned forward and shouted, "this guy recorded a cop, and that shit's unacceptable!" Or something to that effect. He was so pissed that my recordings embarrassed law enforcement leadership in Palm Beach County, he was positively dying to get me.

When Sessa told them he wasn't going to help them, Assistant State Attorney Fernandes issued a warrant for my arrest for the extortion case regarding the website sales discussion – you remember… the case in which the other prosecutor refused. There's a saying in police work… you can beat the rap, but you can't beat the ride. Fernandes maliciously leveraged his power to try and have me extradited back to the United States. Of course, that will never happen because I have my political asylum here, but still, it's a shady thing to do as a prosecutor. This kind of thing is not supposed to happen in America.

There is a man named Bill Browder, a critic of Vladimir Putin. Browder claimed that Russia filed for a warrant for his arrest to have him "Red Noticed" in the Interpol database for extradition to Russia in retaliation for being critical. The leaders in America were outraged that someone would do such a thing and condemned Putin. Yet, here we are, and if this kind of thing can happen at lower levels of State government, then it can occur at any level of the American government. That's right, in the United States of America. It is heartbreaking when you realize that when politicians and law enforcement leaders condemn the actions of other countries while ignoring and turning a blind eye to their own, similar deeds.

Chapter 43 - DC Weekly

On November 11, 2017, the Palm Beach Post did a front-page story entitled, "Story labeling PBSO chief deputy as racist is fake news." According to the Palm Beach Post, it is about "...how one of the Palm Beach County Sheriff's Office leaders, Chief Deputy Michael Gauger, was one of the most hated people on social media."

The article stemmed from an online news publication, a website called the DC Weekly, claiming that Gauger was caught trying to find people on a white supremacist website to help him murder black and Jewish people. The story came complete with an official-looking police report and the documentation of trying to cover up the incident.

Those that worked with Chief Deputy Gauger wouldn't have been surprised if the story was true, given rumors of Gauger's long history of hate towards blacks and Jews. People that used to work with Gauger would post on PBSOTalk, and even people I personally know, would talk about how he would torture blacks into confessing crimes when he was a detective in the 1980's and 1990's.

Still, Gauger has a powerful influence within the South Florida media community, and they wrote that the story was fake news and they implicated my involvement. Of course, they were right.

The website's domain name had been purchased just the day before by someone who registered it through an anonymous proxy yet it was filled with months-worth of stories from various news sources. The Palm Beach Post contacted me asking if I was behind it; of course, I denied any involvement. Still, I think they became suspicious when I laughed about it and told them in great detail how easy it was to make a fake-news site within an hour. I think they became even more suspicious when they found the site was hosted on the same server in New York that hosts my BadVolf company website. Must have been a coincidence (wink wink).

The real crux of the story was how many people fell for it. Gauger and PBSO were lambasted by the public on Facebook and Twitter.

The Palm Beach Post reported that a man from Jacksonville wrote, "*He is the seed of his father, the devil*" while a woman exclaimed, "*I'm literally sick to my stomach.*"

And yet, another demanded, "Take to his neighborhood! Embarrassing him, his family and community until he can't take it no more."

Lawrence Mower of the Palm Beach Post wrote:

```
"The fake story appeared so real — even citing what
appeared to be a real PBSO report — that it was picked
up by news sites and bloggers and shared thousands of
times on Facebook, including by the comedian D.L.
```

Hughley[14] and the activist Tim Wise[15], who urged people to complain to PBSO."

The Post compared my tactics to a "Russian misinformation campaign that U.S. intelligence officials say spread maliciously false stories before the 2016 election."

Of course, I was doing fake news LONG before Russia was ever accused of doing fake news. Frankly speaking, I suspect it's not Russia at all, but other people like me, sick of our government getting Carte blanche to do whatever they want, who have to resort to sensationalism to get their points across.

The Palm Beach Post article continued, saying:

"By turning those same techniques loose on far less-prominent matters, the story shows just how easily 'fake news' can be weaponized at the local level.

Tech-savvy former PBSO deputy Mark Dougan, who has had a long-running feud against Gauger, denied involvement. Still, he described in detail how quickly a website like DCWeekly could be created and filled with content."

Yeah, well, if I didn't deny involvement, I would have nothing to put in my book for the good people that buy it. I told the Palm Beach Post, *"It takes 30 minutes, total, to set up a fake news site from start to finish."*

---

14   https://www.facebook.com/RealDLHughley/posts/2069891856386474

15   https://www.facebook.com/timjacobwise/posts/10154909703480969

Teri Barbera, the lying, incompetent PBSO spokeswoman, told the Post:

> *"The stories about Gauger spread so rapidly on social media that my own daughter confronted me after seeing it. A captain's daughter also asked him about it. They want to know, is this really happening?"*

The Palm Beach Post article goes on to say:

```
"But that didn't stop bloggers and news sites from
picking it up. The most notable was Raw Story, a site
that primarily aggregates news from around the web and
has more than 1 million followers on Facebook.

Without verifying the DCWeekly story, Raw Story
reporter David Ferguson picked it up under the
headline, 'Top Florida law enforcement official plotted
to abduct, rape and murder 'a black man or a Jew.'

The story was eventually taken down without
explanation, but not before the explosive piece became
a weapon, spreading on Facebook and generating
thousands of negative comments about Gauger and PBSO.

Wise, the anti-racism activist, shared it on his
Facebook page. He later took it down and apologized,
vowing never to share from Raw Story again."
```

The article was written by Lawrence Mower, who left the Post shortly after the article was written. It's truly a shame; Mower was the only decent journalist they had left. Was he very liberal? I suspect yes, but he never showed it in his reporting – and that's a reporter you can trust to be objective.

After Tim Wise was called out for citing my fake news story, he wrote to his Facebook followers:

"And now I'm going to demonstrate two things: 1) How an adult apologizes when they mess up; and 2) how we on the left can indeed be more committed to truth and what's right than our pre-existing narrative...

So earlier I re-posted a piece from Raw Story, concerning a deputy from the Palm Beach Sheriff's Office named Michael Gauger. This piece suggested that he had been exposed as a white supremacist who had fantasized about murdering a black person or a Jew. I posted this because a) in the past Raw Story has generally been a solid source of information, and b) because I found multiple links with the same information and it seemed valid.

But it WAS NOT. And I am not only ashamed for having asked people to call the Palm Beach Sheriff's Office to demand his firing, or to Tweet at them, I am beyond pissed. There is no excuse for Raw Story not having fact checked a story of this magnitude before running it...it's one thing to publish a piece with some data that was off; but its quite another to suggest someone is basically a Nazi...

And it's my fault for not seeking greater verification. I apologize without reservation: to Deputy Gauger, to the PBSO, to Gauger's family, and to everyone. There are more than enough pieces of evidence of police misconduct in this country...we need not spread phony ones.

Which then leads me to say the following: just as I had called for the professional destruction of the presumed Nazi deputy (which would have been justified if the story were true), I must now call for the journalistic equivalent for those who first spread this bullshit about him. Raw Story should be shuttered over this. There is no excuse. It isn't enough to fire whatever pathetic intern approved this story. The higher ups have to go. And although I hate this — I have published many times at Raw Story and have always respected them — until they clean house entirely, and bring in 100 percent new people, and make amends to those injured by their deception and irresponsibility, I will:

1. Never re-post a single article from them
2. Never submit another piece to them for publication, and
3. Call for Raw Story to be shut down, completely

We on the left must be better and do better than this, and when we mess up, heads must roll. Giving the right ammo for their nonsense about "fake news" is unforgivable...

I am sorry. I will do better, and from now on, I will never post anything from any source that I haven't personally fact checked.

Now, having said all of that, feel free to copy and paste this to the president so he can see how grown ups can apologize rather than doubling down on their errors..."

His post got thousands of views, and hundreds of responses and shares. If I had to feel bad for anyone here, it's Tim Wise, but he shouldn't be so bent about it. I was told by a technology journalist that it's one of the best Fake News sites he had ever seen. Hey – I don't to anything half way.

He shouldn't blame himself and he shouldn't blame Raw; Raw chose that name for a reason; because they get Raw news. They have to blast the information out fast or they would have to change the name to "Old News." The reason fake news is so easy is that the media has become a blood sport, a competition who can put out the most sensational headlines the fastest. This is the media's Achilles heel because it's so easy to make a mistake. State Troopers are always saying, "Speed Kills." Yeah, well that's not just in driving.

After Lawrence Mower asked me if I created the site and I sidestepped the question, I told him how someone would create their own. Mower wrote, "But he described in unusual detail how someone could recreate DCWeekly.org and the fake article from scratch."

And as a bonus for buying my book, in the last chapter I am going to tell you how to create your own fake news site.

Oh, and the fake PBSO report? Remember when I mentioned several chapters ago that I created a reporting system that saved me enormous time? Yeah, well, I still have it. So, it's absolutely an authentic Probable Cause affidavit. Guys, you were tricked by a real, legitimate document that just didn't happen to exist in a computer system somewhere. Don't be too hard on yourselves. Speaking of which, I'm thinking of making it web accessible, so people can create their own fake PBSO reports.

Some may say that Fake News may be dishonest. There is an American saying, "You reap what you sow." To me, it isn't a matter of dishonesty; it is about treating them as they treat others. It is a matter of adapting methods of fighting to match those of your enemies

Regarding disinformation campaigns, many law enforcement officers write their own fake news in legitimate police reports that are responsible for the incarceration and killing of the innocent. I could have put the fake news site on another server somewhere to hide any traces to me completely, but I wanted hints as to from where the attacks are coming. I want them to understand that in their desire to crush me for honest political speech, they put me in a place to expose everything, free from worry about any repercussions from my methods.

They may have run me off, but in doing so, I am in a position to fight them like never before, using tactics they will never expect, or think was possible. And I want them to know that for as long as they are in power, I am going to keep them on their toes, wondering what nightmare is coming next. For now, it will be exposing them in my book – and the documentary that is coming out on July 13, 2018.

Chapter 44 - Plotting Julian Assange's Escape

Now that Julian Assange had been caught, I decided to add this chapter.

In February 2018, I was approached by a friend of mine (I'll refer to him as G), living in Moscow and England. He and his friends were worried about Julian Assange, one of his close friends (we'll just call him K) having a direct tie to him. I am not going to detail as to what capacity because I don't want to cause any problems for anyone.

G wanted to formulate a plan to get Assange from the Ecuadorian embassy in London, but said it was impossible because snipers had been posted across from the embassy to watch for him. In addition, there were spies within the embassy walls that were watching Assange and reporting back to London's MI5. But I told G that nothing was impossible, and using a bit of misdirection, it could be done. He gave me a week to think about it and come up with some ideas… and I came up with one.

My idea was to send a documentary film crew of five people in to interview Assange, which could be done in his bedroom. One person on the team would have to possess the same physical attributes as Assange; height, weight, build and hair color. This was key. The person in charge of makeup for the documentary would not be just any regular beauty consultant, but a master in silicone and latex special effects. The ingredients to create latex masks would be innocent enough in a big box of makeup gear if the contents were inspected, so I wasn't worried any attention would be payed to this part. If questions were asked upon entry, the plan could simply make the documentary and the escape could be aborted.

Once the documentary team gained access to Assange and his bedroom door shut the deception would begin. A latex mask would be made of both Assange and the member of the documentary team that shared his physician attributes. The latex masks would be glued in place, and the documentary team would leave after "filming." No one pays much attention when you leave an embassy, and Assange, wearing the latex mask of the documentary maker, would have been able to freely stroll out to the vehicle and drive away.

Latex and silicone mask special effects technology has come to the point where it's nearly impossible to tell someone is in disguise as even the pores can be duplicated. The man who took Assange's place would have had to stay in Assange's room until the documentary team and Assange made it to Poland – about 24 hours. After that, it was hoped he would destroy his latex mask, shower, and waltz out of the embassy without anyone asking any questions. In the event he was caught, any crime he may have committed would have been on the soil of Ecuador, and they would probably have been happy just to rid of Julian Assange.

Putting this scenario together was the easy part. The difficult part was yet to come. Not only did I have to plan the escape route, find a way to get Assange through the Russian border to safety and into Russia, but also to find a team of guys what were capable, and willing, to take part in such a plan. So while it only took a day to come up with the general plan, it would take much longer to come up with the rest of the details. I wanted to make sure there was interest before I wasted my time.

I asked for Assange's public GPG key to be put on the Wikileaks server for just long enough so I could download it. I did, and I encrypted a message to him with the short version of my plan to see if he would be interested. I placed this message and a copy of my public GPG key on a USB stick here in Moscow and my friend G hand delivered it to one of Assange's close associates. I received a reply on a USB stick a few weeks later that Assange was very interested but wanted more details and assurances that he could get through the border from the EU into Russia.

And so, over the next five months, I carefully researched every detail to carry out my plan with precision. I meticulously studied satellite maps to determine the best place for someone to gain entry into Russia. I adventured to Karelia near the border of Finland, and it's pretty desolate up there, but and as it turns out, I decided that the best border crossing wasn't in Russia at all. The best place to cross would have been from Poland into Belarus. Why? Because Belarus isn't considered a hostile nation by NATO and the UN. Merely, a poor country that happens to back up to Poland. Poland is also poor, which means not as much money to spend on patrols and border security.

I scoured satellite maps and made friends with people in Belarus who could study the area for me (on the pretext of a hunting trip).

Crossing here would mean less time Assange would have to spend in a car because it's a thousand kilometers closer that crossing in Finland. And when you are on the run, every minute you spend in hostile territory has a potential for being caught. And crossing from Belarus to Russia is no different from crossing from Florida into Georgia, or crossing from one EU country into another. There's a check point, but as long as you have some sort of Russian document, they just wave you through. Still, I didn't want to take this chance and was told that many people drive dirt roads where there aren't check points

When I had the important details of the plan mapped out, I sent another encrypted message to Assange, and told him that it was time for me to test out things for myself.

Saturday, June 23, 2018: I told my girlfriend I was going on a camping trip. It was dark and raining as I drove in solitude, west along the E30 towards the border of Belarus. I was in my Land Rover Defender 110, a flat black beast from the Raptor paint – it looked cool, but also prevented any errant reflections from making its way to someone who might be watching. I knew I was getting off the highway before the border crossing, but I was still nervous. I didn't have my American passport, only my political asylum document. I knew there would be questions if I was stopped, and it would take a while to sort out.

As my GPS showed I was a few dozen kilometers from the border, my heart was pounding. Near the town of Tvertino, I took the P120 north to Ploskoye, and then turned west on an obscure logging road. I stopped to deflate the 35 inch mud terrain tires to 10 psi, safely done so only by the bead-lock wheels I had fitted. Low tire pressures enabled me to travel faster on the awful roads, the rubber absorbing most of the shock from the logs, rocks and holes. Still, it would be a punishing trip, and I was happy my Defender was up for the challenge.

As the logging road turned north, I came across the obscure dirt trail my friends had located for me. I needed to turn west here to make my way to the border. This track was even worse than the first and filled with deep pools of mud. I had a portable winch strapped down in the back, so if I got stuck, I would be able to get myself out. Luckily, I didn't need resort to this.

Next to me, was a night vision monocular and on the dashboard was the screen for the PathfindIR thermal vision camera I had mounted on the roof rack. I borrowed the night vision and the FLIR system from a Russian friend.

I had replaced my front fog lights with infrared LED bulbs – invisible to the human eye – that would augment the night vision I had on such a low light evening. I purchased the no-glow infrared bulbs in Garbushka, which is one of Russia's electronics shopping centers that sells anything from televisions to night vision, to GPS / Cellular jammers. Once I got to a predetermined point – a place where the trail opened up into more of a road, I killed my lights and donned the monocular, translating the blackness into a world of green. Keeping the brake lights off was a simply matter of pulling a fuse.

As I proceeded, my unaided eye was able to keep watch on the thermal image displayed in front of me, which made it easy to spot any oncoming cars or people from a long way away. It would give me plenty of time to pull off the road if I had to hide from view. It worked great, and I saw numerous animals even hiding in the brush that I would have never seen otherwise. But no people.

It took nearly five hours to make the short distance north of the tiny town of Koty while driving through patches of thick forest and over fallen trees, veering to keep along the tree line where it was open fields.

I made it to just a kilometer from the border before daybreak and decided it was too late to risk driving through the logging roads into Belarus. I drove into the dense brush out of view from the logging road and used the bushy branch of a pine tree to sweep the dirt bank, erasing the tire marks that would make a passing car suspicious. I carry a hammock/tent combo in the back, so I tied it up between two trees and took a nap for a few hours.

I woke up about at about 7 a.m. – the sun was already up, but because of the rain and the benefit of a thick brush canopy to make it darker, I decided to relax a bit. I listened closely and heard nothing but the sound of a forest; the drizzle of rain from the leaves, the occasional chirping birds, and wind blowing through the trees. I felt completely at ease, knowing I was born for this kind of stuff.

When I finally got out of my hammock tent, I changed into a summer camouflage hunting outfit, put on my hiking boots, grabbed some land navigation equipment and a canteen of water. I also carried a knife – a Russian version of the K-bar, on my hip. Bears and other dangerous animals were present in this forest, so I took my Ravin crossbow – a gift from a friend - from the Defender. I cocked it, and slung it over my shoulder along with some arrows. If I came across a bear, and he decided he was hungry, I would most likely only get one shot to stop it from making he his dinner. Being the optimist, I hoped I wouldn't need it.

I wanted to walk the route across the border because I was unsure about the way ahead. I made my way through the trees slowly – very slowly, west towards the border. I stayed north of the road in the wooded area, stopping occasionally to observe any activity on the road. A river ran to the southwest, forcing me to cross a bridge made of railroad ties. I crouched in the brush for a while, listening, but heard nothing except for nature. I saw nothing, except forest and the dirt road.

I stood and began to walk across the bridge and as luck would have it, I was about ¾ way to the end when I heard the rumble of vibrating metal being shaken by the rutted washboard surface of the road ahead. Whatever was making the sound was a few hundred meters ahead, around a curve, out of range of my vision. Quickly, I clambered over the side of the bridge.

The bridge was low enough so that when I hung, my feet could touch the water, which was moving quickly, and I hoped it was only a foot or two deep. I let go, not anticipating how strong the current was, which carried my feet out from under me, causing me to fall sideways into the water. I smashed the hell out of my shoulder on a large rock, but I didn't have time to think about it. I grabbed one of the thick pilings that held up the bridge and stood up, soaked and dirty from the muddy river. I crept to the bank under the bridge and watched as a truck loaded with logs came around the corner, passing overhead. I remained there until I could no longer hear the truck, before I walked under the bridge and onto the shore, checking to make sure I had everything. I resumed my reconnaissance towards Belarus.

A few hundred meters more, where the road turned north to run along the Russian border, there was an overgrown path that forked off leading into Belarus. There was a small river about 20 meters wide that separated the two countries. There were tracks from off-road vehicles leading into the water, and I knew people were crossing in their trucks here - I crossed on foot. The water was about a meter deep in the center, and I was again drenched. There was no other security – not surprisingly, because Belarus is considered to be the sister of Russia. Normally, people travel freely between the borders with only a quick glance at their passports (like traveling from the USA to Canada). But since I didn't have a passport... I had to opt for this alternate route.

As I entered Belarus, I walked around the overgrown path, I could see signs embedded in the dried mud that this trail was used by off road vehicles and ATVs. Still, the tracks weren't fresh. They were worn from raindrops, which meant the trail wasn't used frequently. I continued another half kilometer on foot and saw a ditch filled with water. Luckily, there was another bridge made from railroad ties, and farmland.

After crossing the bridge, I came to the coordinates provided to me by a hunting guide I paid well (by Belarus standards), a resident of Belarus, who already scouted the area for me. I saw two paths; the main that leading north to the main farm area and a smaller path continuing through the forest. As I was instructed, I walked the smaller path. After a few more kilometers of hiking, I came to a dirt road surrounded by more fields. The satellite images from Google Earth showed there was nothing around, with muddy trails made by tractors leading all the way to town of Vykhodtsy. This was exactly what I hoped for. Once I knew the way, and that there would be no more problems, I turned back to get my Defender.

By the time I got back, it was close to 6 p.m. and I was famished. I made some Ramen noodles and roasted some chicken on my portable grill, extinguished the fire and changed my clothing into something dry. I slept for another few hours, packed my stuff and drove the way I had earlier checked out.

I made my way to the stream, put the Defender into low range, and crawled down the bank to drive across. The water poured in through the cracks in the doors – the Defender wasn't as well sealed as I had hoped. Still, it was easy enough for my snorkeled Defender to drive through.

After crossing into Belarus and going over the bridge near the farmer's fields, a Chinese-made ATV like a John Deere drove towards me. My hands tensed up, and as I was trying to decide what I was going to say, he drove past me and gave a wave.

I finally made it to Vykhodtsy. I slowly made my way north on the muddy logging roads. They slowly turned to gravel, and then eventually to neglected paved roads. I got to the town of Dombromsli, where I inflated my tires once again. I was able to pick up a main road back to the E30 and towards Minsk. From here, it was clear sailing. I stopped in Minsk where I had a late dinner, surprised by the fact the restaurant still allowed smoking inside.

I drove to my final destination for the night, the town of Grodno, where I stayed with my friend Dima. I took a hot shower, ate some fish soup and discussed the plan for tomorrow's ingress into the European Union. The two of us woke early in the morning and drove a dozen or so kilometers west to a small village located just east of Polish border and just south of Lithuania.

We picked up our "fishing guide," Alexey, a man who knew the border and Augustow Forest areas better than he knew his own mother. Alexey was in interesting guy – if that's what you want to call it. He was in his 60s, and even shorter than I am – probably 5'6," a full head of grey hair. He spoke not only Russian and English, but also German, Arabic and Farsi. He had a fierce look that told me he was not a man to cross.

Dima told me that in the 80's. Alexey was a commander in the Soviet special forces. He was sent to hunt, torture and kill the family member of a Hezbollah terrorist leader that kidnapped some Russian diplomats. Alexey made it clear to the terrorist leader that his group would hunt the terrorist's remaining family members, probably by sending a touching Hallmark card and a few of the relative's body parts. He would do so in the same manner until the diplomats were released and safe. The terrorist leader released the remaining diplomats. Yeah, this Alexey guy had been there, done that. I knew I was in good hands.

A few more kilometers north and we ditched the Defender off the roads in a wooded area, taking our navigation gear, some handheld radios and some fishing poles. Alexey carried a shotgun-rifle combo made by CZ that fired both 12-gauge slugs and hollow point .30-06 rounds. I took my Ravin crossbow and some broadheads. I prefer a crossbow in many situations because it doesn't make a lot of noise. Dima, well, Dima's a big guy who took just a knife, insisting he could kill anything with it if he had to.

It wasn't an easy trip because we had to climb rocky hills and cross streams. I worried a little about how Assange, who had been cooped up in an embassy for six long years, was going to fare, but a man escaping with the hope of freedom should have plenty of motivation.

We battled our way through the brush for at least a thousand meters or so and it opened up the bank of a small river. We were maintaining strict silence, using hand gestures for communication. Yeah, these guys were pros, and the former military training showed their discipline. About five meters before the clearing, Alexey dropped down on a knee and held up his hand, telling us to do the same. He started to unsling his shotgun and I signaled to him not to shoot anything. I slowly, silently, made my way to him, and he pointed to a rather large brown bear that had paused his search for food to look around, obviously smelling the three humans that were lurking nearby. I unslung my crossbow, put an arrow into the arch, and when I heard the familiar click of the nock grabbing the string, flipped off the safety and maintained a ready position, my eye just over the scope.

I told Alexey we were not on a hunting trip and that if he shot his rifle, the excursion would be aborted. I never disclosed the exact nature of what my objective was, but I think they understood we weren't there to kill a bear. Alexey flipped off the safety of the rifle and like me, held a ready position though it was clear he wouldn't fire unless I shot first and that shot was ineffective. I had full confidence this was the type of man who wouldn't panic and would do exactly as he said.

The bear sniffed around a bit and must have decided he was going to end up on some hunter's floor because he shot back and crashed into the forest, disappearing from our view and into the forest. Still, we maintained our position for several minutes before continuing.

After walking several more kilometers, we came to the edge of the wooded area. We stopped, hidden from view… quiet, listening to our surroundings. There was a dirt road that ran along the border of Belarus and Poland that was occasionally patrolled by Belarussian soldiers and Alexey told me we were just one kilometer from the border. We crossed the gravel, wash boarded road, entering the woods again. walking stealthily through the woods until we arrived at a beautiful little lake. Alexey explained that the lake was named Jezioro Wiązowiec and stretched across the border into Poland.

The area was heavily wooded and if we saw anyone, no one would have given any thought to three sportsmen wearing camouflage and carrying fishing poles and rifles, however the area was deserted. We walked west along the north side of the lake, and about a kilometer through the woods to a beat-up little cottage with an outhouse that Alexey had rented. The owners left the key for us, never asking for identification or even to meet

The three of us had successfully breached the borders of the European Union to a place where the documentary team, and Assange, could drive to by car without scrutiny. Alexey wanted to try out my crossbow, so I told him to have fun, and he returned with a fox he had killed for our dinner. We roasted the fox and drank some homemade wine the cabin owners had left for us. We stayed overnight, eating, drinking and talking about our respective branches of military service.

The next day, we uneventfully returned the way we came. We had plenty of time, so we did some fishing before making our way back to the Defender where I dropped the guys off.

I drove back the way I came through the Belarus border, making the crossing at night. When I got back to the E30, I traveled East towards Moscow. After about 30 kilometers of nothing but forest, I was stopped by two police cars on the side of the road. My heart was beating fast, I could feel my hands starting to perspire, but I kept my bearing. I was asked to step out of the car and was motioned to the back of one of the police cars. Was I being arrested? If someone they had evidence of me coming and going illegally though the border, I was prepared to call some powerful friends that could help me out of the mess.

It turns out, they caught me speeding. Somewhere the speed limit had dropped from 90 to 40 and they had set up a camera that send them the photo of my car a few kilometers back. They wanted to write me a ticket, but they understood I didn't speak Russian, so they gave up and let me go. I thanked them and made it the rest of the way back to Moscow without any further problems. Honestly, the police in this country are VERY nice and polite.

I made the trip myself from Moscow to Grodno and to the cabin in Poland two additional times over the next month, alone, to make sure no other surprises would have been lurking. I didn't want to let the other guys in on the true nature of my plan because everyone else who knew was a possible security risk. Each time I made the trip, there was the same result; I never saw anyone, heard anyone... just forest and the occasional rumbling of an automobile far off in the distance.

My last trip was the most memorable. It was late and the sun set low in the clear sky. As I exited from the woods onto the bank of a river, I came across a pack of Russian timber wolves. Absolutely beautiful, and not more than 30 feet away, their heard turned in my direction. It was one of those oh sh#t moments. I had my crossbow with me, but I left it slung as I felt no fear. The wolves looked at me for a second, gave me a knowing gaze, trotted over the rocks and across the stream, disappearing from view and into the dark forest.

On July 22, after I successfully completed my three illicit border crossings, I told G I had solidified the plan and could prove that I could get through the border. I offered to drive to London to meet him, and he informed me there were border checks between France and England. This would be the only sticking point... but Assange would be coming the other direction while wearing the latex and using the other man's passport. Both G , K and I felt confident it wouldn't raise any suspicions. I met up with G and gave him another thumb drive to deliver.

Time was getting short, and at this point, the embassy was growing weary of Assange's stay. We were worried he was going to be arrested within the week and it was being reported that his mental health was declining, as was his hygiene. This is the actual conversation as copied from my chat:

[01:25, 7/22/2018] BadVolf: Bro, we still have a week to get out the professor

[01:26, 7/22/2018] G UK: I am meeting K next week

[01:26, 7/22/2018] BadVolf: Then equador hands him over

[01:26, 7/22/2018] G UK: I was thinking about it as well

[01:26, 7/22/2018] BadVolf: I have a plan. A good one.

[01:27, 7/22/2018] G UK: The first plan wasn't bad either man

[01:28, 7/22/2018] G UK: It's just him, he needs to trust us

[01:28, 7/22/2018] BadVolf: Makeup?

[01:28, 7/22/2018] G UK: Yeap

[01:28, 7/22/2018] BadVolf: Well he's either got to shit or get off the pot

[01:28, 7/22/2018] G UK: I don't know man

[01:28, 7/22/2018] BadVolf: He can't wait for trust. I can get it done.

[01:29, 7/22/2018] BadVolf: It's still same plan. I know how to get in

[01:41, 7/22/2018] BadVolf: I can come

[01:42, 7/22/2018] G UK: Uk??

[01:42, 7/22/2018] G UK: Isn't that a bit dangerous??

[05:16, 7/22/2018] BadVolf: I can prove I can get in which means I can get him out

[05:26, 7/22/2018] G UK: Are you willing to take that risk bro???

[09:15, 7/22/2018] BadVolf: Sure

[19:51, 7/22/2018] BadVolf: I know how to get out through Belarus into Poland. No problem.

[19:52, 7/22/2018] G UK: Fair enough. How you planning to get to the UK??

[19:52, 7/22/2018] BadVolf: And from Poland, it's clear driving all the way to England

[19:55, 7/22/2018] BadVolf: I also got the makeup artist and a guy to switch places

[19:56, 7/22/2018] BadVolf: We need a delegate of journalists to visit him

[19:56, 7/22/2018] BadVolf: Then the switch can be made

[19:56, 7/22/2018] BadVolf: 5 people enter, 5 people leave

The plan, and the people, were in place to get Assange out of the embassy. We were ready to go! But the response back from Assange wasn't what I expected – a few days before the plan was to be carried out, he decided the plan was too risky and he was going to take his chances living in the Embassy. I told G about his response, and we both thought he was a damned fool, but… what could we do? Nothing. You can't force a man to do something he doesn't want to do. And that was that.

I was wrong about one thing – Assange wasn't arrested the next week - that happened several months later. Still, it did happen, as I suspected. G wrote to me, telling me Assange was arrested. I couldn't really say I felt bad because it was imminent, and he ignored a great plan that had a high probability of success.

On April 11, 2019, I woke to find G had sent me a link:

[12:55, 4/11/2019] G UK:
https://www.theguardian.com/media/2019/apr/10/julian-assange-wikileaks-says-spies-at-work-in-ecuadorean-embassy

[12:55, 4/11/2019] G UK: https://youtu.be/PuL8hmOFoYU

[14:28, 4/11/2019] G UK: Assange will be handed over to USA

[14:29, 4/11/2019] G UK: What a fool.

[14:32, 4/11/2019] BadVolf: Yeah, he should have went along with my plan while he had the opportunity.

[14:32, 4/11/2019] G UK: Bro, we approached him twice.

[14:33, 4/11/2019] BadVolf: He should have known better. We knew that the patience at the embassy was wearing thin and this shit would eventually happen. I don't know how the fuck that guy can be so smart, and yet so short-sighted.

[14:33, 4/11/2019] G UK: Well I bet he is regretting his decision now

[14:34, 4/11/2019] G UK: What is he facing in states??

[14:38, 4/11/2019] BadVolf: Life in prison or possibly even execution. They'll probably just kill him in some "accident."

[14:39, 4/11/2019] G UK: I guess we will soon find out

And now, as I update this book, I guess we've found out. He's been caged up like a terrorist, and I have my doubts he will live to ever see freedom again.

Chapter 45 - A Joyful Miracle and Evil Tragedy

My ex-girlfriend, Irina was always good about letting me go on adventures, something I feel I need to do. I have exploration in my blood and it eats at me when I sit too long in one place. Still, Irina never asked for anything of me. I would contribute when I could, but here and there, I would squirrel away a few rubles to be able to see my children.

There was one thing Irina wanted – a baby. At 38, her clock was ticking. It had been over a year since I was able to see my own kids. Kelly repeatedly found reasons not to let them come see their father. I also longed for a little baby; Kelton and Aurelia could never be replaced, but I thought perhaps it would help me cope with the loss of my two children. And yes, I speak to them nearly every day, but when they aren't there, when they aren't able to hug you, it's a feeling of deep loss. If, or when Kelly ever decided to bring them or let them come was statistically very small in my mind. And so Irina and I worked on having a baby.

Anastasiya Johnovna Andreeva-Dougan was born on February 16th, 2018 (ironically, sharing the same birthday as my ex, Kelly). Such a beautiful baby girl that looks so much like her sister, Aurelia. Full of smiles and a keen interest of her surroundings.

But Anastasiya was a secret. I felt if Kelly got wind of it, it would be yet another excuse not to let the kids come see me. More importantly, I was worried about how the kids would take it. My biggest fear was that the Kelton and Aurelia would think I didn't like them enough, so I moved to Russia to have a different child.

The prospect of my kids believing that was absolutely horrifying. Perhaps it was the wrong decision, but I made up my mind that I should keep little Anastasiya a secret from Kelly and the kids until they arrived in Moscow. I wanted to discuss it with Kelly first and then figure out how best to tell Kelton and Aurelia. I wanted them to love their baby sister, not resent her.

Stupidly though, I told my dad my secret. And then somehow my aunt Patty knew. And before I knew it, the entire family knew. Everyone except for Kelly and the kids. I was in some very heated arguments because my sisters told me I should tell Kelly. But I knew that in doing so, I would probably not see my kids again. Kelly always had an excuse why the kids couldn't come visit… and I didn't want this to be another excuse. And so I hid it. And I demanded the family not reveal it, saying it was none of their damned business.

I had saved a decent amount of money here and there, sometimes eating nothing but rice and potatoes for days, or even just celery, but I couldn't cover the cost of the tickets. A friend of mine who knew how devastated I was at the loss of my kids bought the tickets as a gift, choosing my tickets over renovating his own home. Now, that's a true friend. I paid for the kids to get their passports and visas… a whopping

$1800, found a place for us all to stay and I made my plans to see my babies! I wanted nothing more. Kelton and Aurelia wanted the same; my little Kelton would cry at night, missing his father.

Little did I know, Kelly found out about little Anastasya three weeks earlier and she hatched one of the evilest plots a woman could come up with to crush me, while simultaneously dashing the hearts and souls of her very own children against the rocks. For three weeks she knew and had no intentions of coming to Moscow, yet she never told her kids. Kelly let them get so excited. She let the family tell them how wonderful our reunion was going to be. She let me spend an enormous amount of time and money getting their visas. She let me plan Aurelia's birthday party (July 25th). She let us make plans.

I broke up with Irina and I had moved out of her apartment a month before my kids were to arrive. She didn't like the idea of spending the entire two weeks with my kids, and I wasn't going to miss a single moment.

Irina didn't want the kids and Kelly staying in her apartment, and at the same time she didn't want me staying at night with the kids in their hotel. I can understand why under normal circumstances, but these were anything but normal circumstances. Instead of understanding this, Irina put me in an impossible position. I was going to spend every minute of the two weeks I had with them, and I wasn't going to let them stay alone on a foreign country where they spoke a different language. And so I left her.

I was at Irina's apartment visiting the baby on the morning of the flight, July 20th, 2018. I received an email from Kelly saying that she knew about Anastasiya, and that she had no intentions of coming. At first, I was in absolute shock. Shock how a mother could weaponize her own kids against their father. But more so, shock over how she could be so cruel to her own children.

The hypocrisy here is that I didn't tell Kelly about little Anastasiya – my reasoning for protecting the children. She claimed to be angry at me because I never told her or the kids about Anastasiya. Perhaps it was the wrong thing, but it was for what I believed to be the right reason. Kelly, in her quest for vengeance, let her own kids keep believing for three entire weeks that they were going to Russia for a wonderful vacation and to see their father when she never had any intention of going.

I suspect her reasoning for dropping the bomb that morning was to maximize the damage. No way to get refunds on the tickets. Spending money on the visas. Getting Aurelia's birthday cake and sim cards for their cell phones. Getting me excited at a joyous reunion. I absolutely begged her not to do crush the kids. I begged her to punish me alone somehow. If she said she would let the kids come if she was able to stab me or cut off my arm, I would have gladly agreed.

I sent both text messages and email messages in hopes she would reconsider but to any of my text messages, she didn't reply. I tried to call and she refused to pick up. My father went to her house to try to reason with her, and she told him to leave or she would call the police. Only god knows what she told those children.

My father told me that the kids were in the room, and she was yelling that their father left them to have a new family. Exactly my biggest fear. I can't imagine the damage she maliciously caused to their mental state because of her anger at me.

My family was all devastated. My sister was hysterical because Kelton had cried at her house the last few nights asking for his father. She repeatedly told him he would see me soon. She sent him off with a packed suitcase and some sweet notes, telling him what a great time he was going to have, and he was so excited. Kelly was angry that no one told her about my Russian daughter.

My father's wife, Debbie, was crying. My aunt Patty was crying. They were so excited for the children's reunion with their father, for which they were begging for the last two years. And my father – my god, he was undergoing chemo and very sick. He was shaking that night, and I thought he was going to have a heart attack. I sat on the phone with him for an hour trying to get him to calm down.

But the worst of it, the kids. I can't imagine the deep sorrow and heartbreak they felt from the lie she let them believe. Me, I was stunned, but I can't say I was surprised. When I met Kelly, she was such a good girl. She wasn't a particularly a good wife, though in her defense, I wasn't a very good husband. Perhaps it was because I always felt neglected by her, or perhaps it was because she was awful in bed; but I was unfaithful to her on several occasions.

But what matters the most – she's not a very good mother. She pushes Aurelia five or six days a week, four hours each day, in gymnastics. And where does that leave Kelton? Kelton mostly sits at the gym, watching Aurelia practice. He's neglected. He's forgotten. I have talked to her several times about it. My family sees it. And it hurts me deeply in my soul that I can't be there to protect him from his own mother. To do things with him. He's such a brilliant boy, and it's being squandered so Kelly can focus solely on Aurelia. For dinner, it's always fast food or Mac and Cheese. And while I am not a neat person, the children are living in complete disarray because she's a slob. Always has been… just ask the guys that raided the house.

Regardless, I always loved Kelly, even after I left. But she was cold. It seems that with my departure, she grew even more frigid than she always was. When she crushed poor Kelton and Aurelia, HER OWN children simply to harm me, the love I felt for her vanished immediately, for I cannot love a monster who is hurting my kids.

My options from Russia are very limited in what I can do. One of them happens to be to write about it in this edition of the book, and hope to god my children will read it when they get older. Knowing that I had no choice but to flee the country. Knowing their father didn't abandon them to have another family. Knowing I love them so much. Knowing that I tried my best, and my hardest to see them. I want Kelton and Aurelia to meet, and to love their sister.

Kelly's father is a cheap bastard that doesn't particularly like Kelton and Aurelia. He's sworn at them, telling them things like they "are a pain in the ass." And when he sold his house, he got the hell out of town, moving to Georgia. Instead of gifting her money, he gives her loans she's got to pay back. She was getting money and support from my parents, my aunt, sisters and brothers; even my very sick father was helping with transporting the kids when she was unable. But she treated them like trash. They never asked anything of her. Not for repayment, not for anything.

I will always be supportive of Kelly. I will always care about her. I will always be there if her Multiple Sclerosis makes her unable to do basic life functions, as was the case with her mother. I would rather the burden of taking care of her instead of that burden falling on my children and disrupting the flow of their lives.

I have a pretty good feeling that after crapping on everyone in my family, she's going to discover how valuable and caring they were. And I'm pretty sure that her "friends" aren't exactly going to go to the lengths to help her like my family does.

If you've learned anything about me in reading this book, you will know I am pretty crafty and it would not exactly hard for me to come up with creative ways to hurt Kelly. But I would never hurt the kids to hurt her like she did with me. My only hope is that Kelly will realize how unreasonable she's been and allow the kids to come visit.

Chapter 46 - Arrested in Russia!

On September 23rd, 2018, I went to the lovely city of Nizhny Novgorod to look at a new Land Rover Defender and to meet with a publisher about translating this book into Russian. I got a room at the Azimut Nizhny Novgorod, with a lovely view of where the Volga river meets the Oka river, across from the beautifully-lit stadium. After a lovely dinner and fantastic evening at some of the local nightclubs, I turned in for the night. The next day, I had a meeting with a publisher to discuss translating my book into Russian, and then I was going to catch the train home.

I woke early on September 24th, grabbed my computer bag and left for my meeting. As I exited the hotel, there were three men in plain clothes standing outside. They flashed their police identification and said in a thick Russian accent, "John Mark Dougan?"

Surprised, I replied, "Yes? Can I help you?"

"Mr. Dougan, please come with us."

They didn't bother to search me, handcuff me or take my bag. They walked me though the parking lot, put me in the back of a four-door Lada Niva and drove me a short distance to the local police station. During the drive, I asked why I was being arrested. One of the police officers, Andrey, said, "There's a warrant for your arrest through Interpol."

I looked at him and said, "You know I have political asylum here, right?" And I took out my asylum document and handed it to him. He was quite surprised and none of the police officers had ever seen anything like it. I didn't understand what they were saying, but I could tell they were confused.

We soon arrived back at the police station. They led me down the hall, past security, and down the stark-grey corridor. We approached the cell block, but instead of putting me in a cell, they brought me up the stairs and into their office.

They had a discussion with the commander, asked me questions, and began making phone calls. They brought me in front of the prosecutor, who was also confused by my asylum document. Apparently, they don't handle people with asylum very often.

During my stay, I had a fascinating conversation with the officers about rights and protocols of the police in Russia. One of the guys who had been a cop for over 20 years was clearly jaded and pessimistic because cops in Russia are treated like 3rd class citizens. And really, I don't blame him.

They aren't allowed to search people when they detain them, and they are constantly subject to false complaints. And unlike the American police, Russian police are absolutely held accountable for their actions. One mistake, and they are looking for a new job or can be arrested. The level of stress has got to take a toll. And while I think the American police have far too many protections, the Russian police don't have enough.

In reviewing the Interpol file, I discovered my suspicions were correct… it was for recording Detective Kenneth Mark Lewis, and they had 19 charges of illegal wiretapping against me – one for count for each recording. The American government wanted me so badly, they completely dismissed the serious felony crimes admitted to by Detective Lewis on behalf of Sheriff Ric Bradshaw and Chief Deputy Michael Gauger, and to charge, arrest and extradite me for obtaining the evidence in the forms of recordings.

Four hours later, the Russian police confirmed that I did have asylum and I was provided a letter by the prosecutor that I was not allowed to be extradited. They were genuinely sorry for the inconvenience, and explained that when I checked in, I used a copy of my American passport instead of my asylum document. As protocol with every hotel in Europe, the copy goes to the local police station, and each guest undergoes a background check.

The Nizhny Novgorod police department received word that I was wanted by Interpol, and subsequently arrested me. Using my asylum document at a hotel is pretty much useless, because no one has ever seen one before. I got the phone number from one of cops and we became good friends. When he needed moving his apartment, I spent the day helping him. And when he came to Moscow with his family, we feasted at the local crab restaurant. To this day, this crazy event led to a wonderful friend. But that's how it is in Russia. It's the strange things that lead to strong friendships.

Even though the Russian government has told Interpol I wasn't going to be extradited back to the United States, that hasn't stopped them from trying. The FBI has repeatedly met with their Russian counterparts in an attempt to have me sent back, but thank god for President Vladimir Putin – a man with a backbone who will tell the United States to pound sand. President Putin has made it very clear that Russia doesn't give up Human Rights activists back to their hostile nations – and when it comes to playing dirty to protect their dirty little secrets, there is no civilized nation as hostile as the United States.

Russia isn't the only place they've been trying to get me. In January 2019, ten FBI agents and US Marshalls showed up at a company where I have been doing contract work. Apparently, they have been watching my bank account and have seen the payments coming to me. Not big payments, mind you… but it's the thought that counts, right?

These agents show up and start asking questions about me to the woman in the office. She has no idea who the hell I am, so she calls her boss – one of the owners of the company - who DID know who I am. The boss told her that if they didn't have a warrant of some type, to give the agents their attorney's phone number, and then to leave the office.

The agents left the office but visited one of the other owners of the company at her home the next morning. The agents were telling her what a bad guy I was for exposing Sheriff Bradshaw and his cronies, that I was disloyal, and that they should cut their ties with me. Except, they didn't give any real explanation of any crime that I committed. Their sole purpose for being there was retaliatory, using typical American-style bully tactics in an attempt to make my life difficult.

I am very thankful that the owners are strong minded because they didn't give an absolute f#@k about what the government wanted.

Chapter 47 - The Epstein Files Rear their Ugly Head

Well, technically, files do have heads. So, I guess this is a fitting title for this chapter. Remember the files I mentioned in chapter 11 that I got from Recarey? Yeah? Well, I didn't. Not until just a few months ago.

In August of 2019, the Epstein case started picking up steam again. I spoke to a few reporters, and even provided one of them with a document I had from the Epstein case where the Town of Palm Beach Police Chief was extremely concerned about the bizarre handling of the case. But I didn't have any first-hand knowledge.

I worked for the Palm Beach County Sheriff's Office while the case was handled by the Town of Palm Beach. Since I wasn't connected to the Town of Palm Beach, the investigation into Epstein wasn't any of my business. I told the reporters as much and then one of them told me Joe Recarey had died. The last time I spoke to Joe was late 2017, so it was a shock to me. I remembered the files, but I kept that information secret for many years. I never told my closest friends or family. Plus, I had no idea what the contents were. I never really looked except for a second or two at the beginning of each burning cycle back in 2010. And that wasn't enough to show anything at all.

In September, I got a call from a reporter, Tom Parfitt, who writes for *The Times of London*. He wanted to talk to me about the Epstein case. I told him that I didn't have first-hand knowledge, just some rumors and things I heard. He asked about Recarey and I told him I knew about his passing and was surprised by his death.

I told him what little I knew about the rumors from the guys that worked the Epstein detail, and from the rumors from the Palm Beach County Stockade regarding the incredibly favorable treatment Epstein was receiving (a.k.a., he must have been paying off the Sheriff). He began asking me about Prince Andrew, and of course, I knew nothing of the topic. He didn't ask me about anything else.

A few days later or September 22nd, 2019, I awoke to find "The Times" published the story:

MI6 FEARS RUSSIA CAN LINK PRINCE ANDREW TO JEFFREY EPSTEIN ABUSE SCANDAL

According to the story, "The Kremlin may have obtained details of claims of the duke's involvement from a former Florida deputy sheriff now living in Moscow."

This was all a shock to me, as nothing in Parfitt's questioning mentioned anything about the files. I was baffled at how he could have possibly known. And frankly, I hadn't given the contents any thought until the moment I read the article. According to the article:

"British intelligence chiefs are concerned that Russia may have obtained kompromat, compromising material, on Prince Andrew over the Jeffrey Epstein scandal.

MI6 is understood to be concerned about the activities of a former Florida police officer who had access to the investigation into the billionaire pedophile and then moved to Russia.

The bizarre case of John Mark Dougan, a former deputy in the Palm Beach County sheriff's office, has provided further evidence that the prince's repeated efforts to distance himself from allegations of sexual abuse are failing to shield him from the fallout of the Epstein case.

A security source said last week there were concerns at MI6 about how much Dougan knows of the original police investigation into the multimillionaire pedophile's activities and what Dougan may have passed on to Russian authorities.

Both Andrew and Buckingham Palace have consistently denied he has been involved in any untoward activity.

Dougan is known to have had contact with Pavel Borodin, a senior Russian government official sometimes referred to as a mentor to President Vladimir Putin.

Dougan was working in Palm Beach in 2005 when a woman walked into a local police station and claimed that Epstein had paid her 14-year-old stepdaughter $300 to strip to her underwear and perform an 'erotic massage'".

So far, the article was technically correct, but it seemed to make the inference that I was in the police station that the lady had walked into. I was not. I didn't even work for that department. The intriguing part was that MI6 was worried about how much I knew. A leak that apparently came directly from MI6 to the ears of the reporter, apparently knowing I had the files about Jeffrey Epstein. How?!? Being that I was not connected in any way to this investigation, I wondered why that was...

```
After the Epstein case was reopened in July this year,
Dougan claimed on Facebook that he had spoken
extensively about it to the investigating officers and
still possessed confidential documents that no one else
had seen.
```

I never made that statement on Facebook or anywhere else. I have no idea where the author got it from, but the closest statement I made to Epstein in July was a video of me riding on a carriage being pulled by a lunatic tiny pony (it's really a funny video, if you haven't been to my FB page to see it). How is it the closest thing to mentioning Epstein? Because there's nothing closer than that. I wrote about grills and my charity BBQ event in July.

Months earlier when Epstein was being investigated again, I did make the prediction he was going to "kill himself" in a comment to my brother, but that's all. Never any mention of any files. The article continued:

```
"Dougan, a former US marine, later fell out with his
bosses, resigned in 2009 and ended up in Moscow. He
made his Facebook posts from Russia.
```

> His intervention alarmed intelligence officials, who appear to have been tracking his activities since he was photographed with Borodin in 2013.
>
> A western intelligence source said Dougan exhibited a number of "classic traits" that made him suitable for recruitment by a "hostile intelligence service".
>
> The source added: 'His knowledge of the Epstein case would have been of great interest to Russian intelligence.'"

Yes, I did meet with Pavel Borodin to discuss bringing my telecom gear to Russia. And, I don't know what "classic traits" they speak about, but I would love to know. I certainly am not an asset of the Russian government, nor have they asked me to be.

The last paragraph, about my knowledge of the Epstein case, well, that one simply fell flat. Until I realized they were talking about the Epstein videos that I burned for Recarey. Let me walk you through the logic here:

1. In 2016, if you remember, the FBI seized all my computers. They had access to everything I had. Including the Epstein files. Now, it was encrypted, right? Well, kind of. My computers were running when the FBI got to them, meaning the encryption key was in memory and everything was unlocked. The FBI was in a position to keep everything decrypted, and they did… since they took the computers out on special carts with batteries to keep them running.
2. While I never looked through the videos Recarey left in my possession, the FBI most certainly did. And they must have been able to identify people in those videos, including Prince Andrew. Prince Andrew MUST have been visible in the videos. Why?

3. Because American intelligence agencies don't share details with foreign intelligence agencies unless there is something that pertains to that foreign intelligence agency. So why MI6? How would MI6 come to learn about these files in my possession?
4. Because one of their counterparts at the FBI was no doubt watching the 700+ videos on my computer (and knowing the twisted, depraved agent clowns that work for the FBI, probably diddling himself) when Prince Andrew came into the picture. But the FBI, they seized my computers, so they couldn't possibly be worried about any videos of Prince Andrew coming to light, right?
5. Wrong! In January or February of 2019, they must have had quite a shock when it was revealed to them that a backup hard drive that was kept at my wife's office was actually smuggled to me here in Moscow, Russia in 2017. And with that knowledge, they knew this compromising information was floating around.
6. This meant they needed to alert MI6 as a precaution. That's the only reason MI6 could, or would have known about the files.

Logical thinking, right? On September 24th, I put out the following press release:

STATEMENT BY JOHN MARK DOUGAN, AN AMERICAN CITIZEN, GRANTED POLITICAL ASYLUM BY THE RUSSIAN GOVERNMENT

The September 21, 2019 London Times story under the headline, "MI6 fears Russia can link Prince Andrew to Jeffrey Epstein abuse," carries this statement:

MI6 is understood to be concerned about the activities of a former Florida police officer who had access to the investigation into the billionaire pedophile and then moved to Russia.

BADVOLF | BY: JOHN MARK DOUGAN
THE TRUE STORY OF AN AMERICAN COP AVENGING A CORRUPT SYSTEM

My name is John Dougan, and I am a former U.S. Marine and Palm Beach County Florida Deputy Sheriff, now living in Moscow. I was granted political asylum here in 2016. I fled to Russia after American intelligence agencies raided my home because I had exposed the rampant corruption and racism within the Palm Beach County Sheriff's Office. Part of my story was broadcast in a 2018 special Russian TV documentary, "Breaking Bad Wolf: One Crazy Journey from Palm Beach Cop to Russian Exile," broadcast worldwide in several languages.

Because of the intense media interest and oftentimes inaccurate Internet speculation, I am giving further information to help put some of what I know in perspective.

Although we worked in different law enforcement agencies, former Town of Palm Beach Police Department Detective Joe Recarey, who was the lead detective on the solicitation-of-minors case against billionaire Jeffrey Epstein, was a friend. I was shocked, as were family and friends, to learn of his unexpected death at age 50 just over a year ago.

Joe Recarey was very aware of my efforts to uncover the breaches of public trust by the Palm Beach County Sheriff's office via my award-winning investigative website. In late 2009 or early 2010, Joe asked me to scan all the documents as well as copy hundreds of DVD disks he had on the Jeffrey Epstein case to keep them safe. He had lost faith in Barry Krischer, the Palm Beach County state's attorney at the time of the investigation. I would meet with him occasionally to get more documents to store, the last time being in 2015.

I have never looked at what was given to me by Joe Recarey, other than the file names, types, and sizes. The FBI seized my computers in 2016 which had everything Recarey gave me. The FBI and other intelligence agencies may be surprised to have discovered that I kept an off-site backup that was sent to me in 2017, after I was safely established in Russia.

According to news reports, U.S. intelligence agencies apparently analyzed the files and communicated with British authorities. If Britain's Secret Intelligence Service, commonly known as MI6, has concerns about any ties between Prince Andrew and Jeffrey Epstein, they got it from their Washington counterparts, not me.

Of course, this means the FBI has seen everything and has more knowledge of the contents than I do because it was not my business to look deep into the files: I was simply acting as Joe Recarey's computer "safety deposit box." It also means that the FBI has the same exact data that I possess and are in a position to know everyone who is implicated in the videos, recordings, and documents. If media reports are accurate, it seems the FBI has knowledge that Epstein files involve Prince Andrew in some manner, since they made it a point to contact MI6 and warn them.

The Epstein data is encrypted in a TrueCrypt/VeraCrypt container and has been given to a few people. They cannot look at the contents because they do not have the decryption keys. Others have the decryption keys, but they do not have access to the encrypted containers. My contacts are on five continents and do not know each other. The Epstein files stay secure and unreadable to everyone. I do not have a physical copy in my immediate possession, because of security reasons. This is to make sure my family and friends remain safe. I have made arrangements that it can only be decrypted in the event of my arrest, if I go missing for an extended time, or in case of my unusual or untimely demise. I have a system in place to connect people with the encrypted containers to those who have the decryption keys.

I have made elaborate security precautions because of ongoing legal issues, threats, and harassment. The FBI has tried to arrest me twice since I've been in Moscow by pushing Interpol via a sealed indictment. Both times they failed. Last year, the FBI sent 10 agents and Federal Marshals to a U.S. company that I do contract work for, unsuccessfully trying to intimidate them.

I will not be divulging any of the information I may know of or possess, because the secrecy of the data I have access ensures the safety of me and my loved ones. I hope the growing concerns and reports about Jeffrey Epstein's international sex-trafficking empire, and his relationship with the rich and powerful people like the Duke of York, will generate official and news media investigations which will uncover all the facts. I am committed to following this story closely.

I did some follow-up interviews regarding the files, but it was for the word to get out that I did have the files but there's a dead man's switch in case of my untimely demise.

On this very day, a true-crime documentary maker and author, Ron Chepesiuk, had flown to Moscow to discuss another project we were working on. I was in Voronezh doing a charity event, and my friend picked him up at the airport. I got back to Moscow the next day and I was being bombarded by media requests. I picked up Ron and we went back to my house, and I shut off my phone.

Ron said, "Well? Do you actually have the Epstein files?" I walked into my closet and pulled out a hard drive and gave it to Ron. Confused, Ron said, "What's this?"

"The Epstein files," I told him.

He looked squeamish and handed it back to me and said, "I don't want this."

I laughed and put it back into the closet. Ron stayed about a week, and we discussed our project and I showed him around Moscow, but we didn't discuss the Epstein case. However, on the last day, we started talking about it and he said the files would have credibility if we decrypted the drive to verify the contents. I thought about it and saw the logic behind his thinking and decided it couldn't hurt. He was already in Moscow, so... why not? I was getting ready to send the drive with the videos away to South Russia, so now was a good a time as ever.

We got back to the house, I stuck the drive into the docking cradle, and I began the decryption process. I laid down to take a nap while Ron was working and when I got up, the decryption process had been completed. Ron and I decided we would select a few videos at random and watch just a few seconds in the middle of each one. For all we knew, these could have been Epstein's weekly workout videos.

But they weren't. We chose seven videos from between 2001 and 2004, and six of them had older men having sex with clearly underaged girls. The seventh one was of a girl fresh out of a short, applying lotion. These were clearly hidden video cameras. Some from an elevated position and some from waist height. It was said that they found hidden cameras in clocks on the dressers at Epstein's home, which would certainly explain the low elevation shots. The people in the videos were obviously unaware they were being recorded. Our goal was not to attempt to identify anyone, but to verify the contents of the videos. Still one man looked familiar to me though I can't place where I know him. Another, I distinctly recognized a man who happened to be the head of a large US media company just a few years ago.

Out of the six videos that showed sex, it all looked consensual... well, as consensual as it can be for someone under the age of 18. There was no one who looked scared or like they were being forced. Still, the videos were perverse and sickening. I dismounted the drive and that was it.

That night (October 1st, 2019), I took Ron to Domodedovo airport for his flight, which left at 2 a.m. After Ron got out of my car, I saw I had a missed call from a reporter in Australia. I answered the call, and she began asking me strange questions about a message I had sent to her. But I never sent her a message. The message she received came from some unknown number. It said Ron was going to land in Heathrow airport and be picked up by MI6.

Naturally, I was worried, and I attempted to contact Ron, but I couldn't reach him. As I drove the fifty kilometers back to north Moscow, I was speaking to the Australian reporter and noticed the same car – a grey Mercedes sedan - behind me for many, many kilometers. Driving on the highway in Moscow isn't like driving on I-95. There are hundreds of highways that branch off in all directions, and the likelihood that someone would follow you for fifty kilometers is pretty darned remote. Plus, I was in my Defender, which isn't exactly a speedy vehicle. Anyone driving a Mercedes at 2 a.m. would have easily sped past me, not hang far behind me for the duration of my trip.

When I got close to my neighborhood, it was about 3 a.m. and the same car was still back there. I had stayed in contact with the reporter during my trip because she was worried about me. I stopped in a parking lot on the south east side and jumped out of the Defender, running across some railroad tracks and through an abandoned building's courtyard. I meandered around some buildings in the area and took cover in a corridor where I could watch to see if anyone was lurking nearby. No one came. I cautiously left my concealed position and walked a bit more, flagged down a taxi and took it to my apartment.

When I woke up later that day, I went back to get the Defender. Before I got it, I laid on the ground and inspected the under carriage well. I saw nothing. Later in the day, just to be sure, I took the car to a friend who does work on my car to give it a better inspection and he didn't see anything concerning, either.

At 11.28 am, I received a telephone call from the U.S. Embassy in Moscow. The man on the other line asked me to come into the Embassy and meet with him. I asked him why, and he told me I had to bring him my passport. He told me that my passport had been revoked and my law, I was obliged to come to the embassy and turn it in. Visions of Jamal Khashoggi (the Saudi Arabian dissident who was butchered at the Saudi embassy in Turkey) started to flood my mind and I told the guy I would certainly not be coming to the Embassy any time soon.

Here's where things get particularly strange: On October 9th, I decided I needed to get out of town for a while. I had the hard drive with me and I was going to bring it to the south of Russia for safe keeping. I got in my car with a friend of mine from Voronezh – she stayed with me to do some charity conferences in Moscow. On our way to Voronezh, I noticed the car was handling a bit strange, and I heard metal rubbing on metal. I assumed it was either a bad bearing or that I needed new brake pads. To me, it sounded like it was coming from the front, so I stopped on the side of the road, looked at the front wheels, and saw nothing out of the ordinary.

A few hundred kilometers later, it got worse. Much worse. And as I looked on my driver's side rear mirror. I saw the back-driver's-side tire was wobbling slightly. I got out of the car and saw all the lug nuts holding the wheel were GONE and one of the lugs had been broken off. We had just driven hundreds of kilometers at 140 kph, and if the wheel had come off at that point, it would have been disastrous. Fortunately, it didn't.

The Defender has an inner hub with five hex-head bolts, and they all need to be turned a certain way for the wheel to fit properly. The mechanics that changed my wheels a few months ago didn't bother to line them up and instead beat the wheel on with a hammer. For this reason, and this reason alone, the wheel didn't fall off. I jacked up the car, checked all of the other lug nuts on all the other wheels, and they were all tight. I removed one lug nut from each wheel and put three lug nuts on the problem wheel and drove to the Voronezh Land Rover dealership to have everything replaced and inspected. After dropping my friend off at her house, I resumed my trip to Sochi. I arrived in Sochi, left the hard drive with a trusted friend in a nearby town and had a bit of a vacation. After a few days, it was time to head back to Moscow.

When I arrived in Rostov-on-Don, I got a room and went to have dinner, a drink and to do an interview with Shaun Attwood, who was curious about how I was doing. I had been speaking to two girls I just met. They spoke English and said they were from New Zealand. Personally, I thought they sounded like they were from Minnesota or Canada, but I don't know what a New Zealander sounds like.

I spoke to the girls for a few minutes and went into a quieter room, away from the bar, to have my interview with Shaun (see the video entitled, "Assassination Attempt on Ex-Cop With Epstein Sex Tapes?"). After the interview was done, I went back to the bar and finished my drink. The girls tried to get me to stay but I had an early morning of driving back to Moscow. I left the bar and I went to the apartment I rented a few blocks away.

I woke up later that night wish a screaming headache. I brushed it off and tried to get some sleep, without any luck. I was in so much excruciating pain that I couldn't stand or even see straight. I had never, in my 45 years, ever had such a headache. And so I had to call an ambulance.

The medics came, gave me some fluids and transported me to the hospital for tests. The result was surprising - I had been poisoned with Ethylene Glycol. I was incredibly lucky because:

1. I caught it in a reasonable amount of time, and:
2. I didn't drink a lot of it.

The cure, as it turns out, it to drink more alcohol… the regular kind found in regular alcoholic beverages. I don't understand the chemistry behind it, but that doctor got me smashed on strong alcohol. Still, the Glycol did some damage and it took two weeks to heal to the point I wasn't experiencing chronic pain.

I ask myself... the lug nuts... was it shoddy maintenance? The Glycol... just a shitty bar? Anything can happen, I suppose, but the timing is incredibly strange. The car following me, the call from the American embassy, the missing lug nuts, and poisoning... the totality is just bizarre. I certainly am not a conspiracy theorist, but this one, I must admit, has me wondering.

Still, the most troubling about this entire situation is this:

The FBI has had these video files since 2016, when they seized my computers. They obviously know the contents of the videos and who is in them. Yet, they have done nothing. Absolutely nothing. Why? Perhaps the people in the videos are too powerful to be brought down. Perhaps there are top level government officials from the Department of Justice and FBI diddling little kiddies. Whatever their reason...

The FBI is Complicit in the Largest, most Prolific, Child Sex Trafficking Ring the world has ever known about.

I would like to think the media attention this created, and my role in pointing out that the FBI was sitting on this evidence played put so much pressure on them, they had no choice but to reopen the investigations. On September 25th, I did an interview and said exactly that, and accused the FBI of covering up for Prince Andrew and other child molesters. The New York Post wrote:

Ex-Florida cop accuses FBI of covering up Prince Andrew's role in Jeffrey Epstein scandal

They quoted me and wrote:

"'I'm certain the FBI is involved in some kind of cover-up over Epstein,' he told the Times of London. 'That could absolutely include Andrew's role, or it could be that senior FBI people visited the house and don't want to reveal that.'

Dougan now lives in Russia after fleeing there in 2016 while under investigation in an unrelated case for alleged hacking.

He claims to still have backup copies of the trove of evidence related to Epstein, including scanned documents — all of which were seized in an FBI raid.

'My copies of the files will never be released unless something untoward happens to me, because they are my guarantee of safety for me and my family in the US,' Dougan said.

The Times reported that MI6, the British foreign intelligence service, fears Dougan may have leaked the Prince Andrew evidence to Russian authorities."

I told people in my interviews the FBI had this evidence and should demand that the FBI do something with it. Facing intense pressure and scrutiny, the FBI announced just three days later, it was going to reopen the investigation into Prince Andrew. On September 29, 2019, the Times wrote,

Now FBI investigates Prince Andrew's links to Epstein"

Whether people agree with me or disagree with me for not making the files public, the confirmation of their existence created a worldwide uproar; people screaming, demanding investigations and demanding the people in Epstein's ring of child molesters is held accountable. Because of the attention drawn to them by my statements, from intense scrutiny I placed upon the FBI, they had no choice to begin investigations. I will mark this up in the "win" column.

Conclusion

A common question people ask me is how someone can be a good cop. My answer is, it's not possible. It's possible to be good, as in you don't go out and break the law yourself, but honestly being a good cop means an equal application of justice for everyone, including other cops. There is a myriad of reasons that make this impossible and will lead to a cop being demonized, ostracized, and subjected to a witch hunt to discredit him or her, tarnishing their reputation and giving plausible deniability to the crooks running the show.

American lawyers are to blame; they have created an environment where the police benefit by lying. With the liability, police administrations and officers do not want to admit their mistakes. They do not want to admit wrongdoing. They lie to cover up truths, which leads to making it acceptable to lie in all aspects of the job.

To make things worse, agencies promote police work and prosecutions as being a competition; to arrest and prosecute as many people as you can, regardless of their innocence or guilt. Police aren't the only ones to blame.

Prosecutors want that checkmark in the "win" column, regardless of their innocence or guilt. This mindset is a real problem – they lie and cheat to get prosecutorial wins, and many innocents wind up in jail, but they take a guilty plea because of the genuine possibility of ending up in prison for incredibly long periods of time.

Let's face it; if you are an average person who doesn't have millions for legal defense, and you are arrested for a crime you didn't commit; you have a real problem. That problem is the full weight of the American government, with their limitless budget and power, bearing down on you like a ton of bricks. When the prosecutor tells you to take a plea of one year or risk facing thirty years in prison, the average person, despite being innocent, is going to take that plea.

The stacking of charges and the deals by prosecutors; it all must end, and the criminal justice system needs a complete overhaul. What's more, the need to appease everyone, the desire to be politically desirable has led to huge incarceration rates and absurdly long prison terms for minor crimes.

Right now, at the forefront, we have Lori Loughlin and her husband, Mossimo Giannulli facing 50 years in prison for their college admission scandal. I'm absolutely not condoning their behavior, but come on... it's absurd. And every few weeks, the prosecutors add more charges to pressure them to plead guilty. Felicity Huffman plead guilty straight away and got just a few days. Now, imagine these were both poor people who were merely accused of committing a crime. An innocent person is going to admit their guilt and take the plea deal and two weeks of jail instead of risking 50 years in prison.

Do you remember Alice Johnson? The black woman whose sentence was commuted by Donald Trump? That poor woman, arrested as a 25-year-old kid (yes, a kid) for passing messages to drug dealers, was slated to spend the rest of her life in prison without the chance of parole. And for what?

Regardless of what you think of President Donald J. Trump, why was he the one that had to commute her sentence? Where were the scores of other politicians? They were hiding behind political correctness. Americans must push to change the system, but it will never happen. The attorneys see to that. Those greedy bastards make money off people's misery and as such, they make the rules incredibly tricky; impossible, for anyone without an attorney.

Then there is the government itself. In the American system of government (and probably every other country), the worst, most ethically challenged people rise in the ranks based on a blackmail / back-scratch system. Bradshaw is a perfect example. He was caught stealing a gun and instead of being fired, his chief kept him. Bradshaw now owed the chief a favor. Maybe that chief doesn't want his own criminal activities exposed when he retires; things that will land him in jail. Who is the chief going to appoint to replace him? Bradshaw – the man he saved.

Between Bradshaw's dealings with the Mafia, his "arrangement" with the Palm Beach County Police Benevolent Association and crimes he committed for his gain, I am sure he has done so many illegal things that if investigated after leaving office, he would spend the rest of his days in prison. That is, if anyone would ever prosecute him.

The cops that don't stand for this behavior; the ones who go against the system and expose the misdeeds, they are hated by their peers and retaliated against by their superiors, who will distort truths, create unfavorable paper trails and do whatever they can to terminate the offender who crossed that thin blue line. In some extreme cases, the bad cops will just kill the good ones. It makes me sad to tell the people that ask that a truly good, honest cop has no chance of succeeding in the United States.

I hear people saying that it's so wonderful in the United States, and yes, it certainly is, but these people cannot believe the government could be so corrupt. What they fail to realize is the two facts are not mutually exclusive.

Yes, America is probably the most convenient place to live. It's beautiful, has almost every climate someone would ever want, and things run smoothly there. In the overall scheme of the world, America is a very new country, borne right before and growing during the industrial revolution. Capitalism and freedom made America what it is today; the absence of large government during the development is responsible, and not the government itself.

To many in the world, America is seen as the "Land of the Free," where people have the right to free speech and the right to be free of baseless search and seizure. The police should not be able to investigate you for years because they don't like your political speech. The politicians used the 9/11 terrorist attack to destroy our protections. The American government can spy on whoever they want, whenever they want, and without a warrant to do so. If they don't like you, they can comb through your entire life until they find a way to put you in jail. America is now more reminiscent of Hitler's Germany than the country I used to call home. Nether the liberals nor the conservatives get it – if you are black or Asian, you are screwed. If you are conservative or religious, you are screwed. If you don't conform to exactly the government want, you are going to have problems.

Over the last half-century, the American government has grown into an oppressive régime. Not content with controlling only its people but controlling and conquering any nation that shares different political views and agendas – ironically, touted as being "in the name of freedom."

There is no other nation in the world so involved in subversion to affect the elections of other countries, involved in their political speech, controlling of their laws and ways of life; and who has toppled so many other governments - as the United States.

The American government's willingness to impose their beliefs and values on other societies – invading 23 countries in the last 30 years - is the antithesis of freedom. Those controlling tendencies have infiltrated the inner workings of the American government, slowly and systematically stripping away the rights of the American people.

Some Americans who don't know better often criticize me for fleeing to Russia, saying I escaped to a land of oppression. The people who make these statements are living 30 years in the past, unaware that America is becoming the embodiment of a brutally fascist dictatorship while Russia is slowly struggling to take America's place as the land of the free. And if you think it's not true, come here. Visit. Don't tell me it's not until you come here. Luckily, it is a straightforward argument to counter them. I tell them:

"Please download the criminal code of the Russian Federation and read it. It will only take a few hours to read and understand; there are just 150 pages of laws that must be followed. When you are done, download the federal criminal code of the United States and give it a read. It will take a while because it's about 10,000 pages long. Then read your state laws. After you find out that almost everything you do in the United States is illegal, let's see if you can come back to tell me I am living in the land of the oppressed while you are living in the land of the free; and do it with a straight face."

If the American government doesn't like you, they can investigate you for any reason – even if that reason is that they feel like it. If they want to arrest you, they can eventually find a reason. They say the average person commits three felony crimes every day. The FBI has made it so easy to arrest someone – all they have to do is ask you the color of the sky on an overcast day. If you say the sky is blue, but it happens to be grey at the time, or if you say it's grey and everyone knows the sky is blue, they can arrest you for lying to an FBI agent. This penalty that carries a five-year prison term.

The criminals on Mueller's Special Counsel did this with Michael Flynn. They could hold that five years in prison over his head to blackmail damning information on Trump.

When I left the United States, I lied to my entire family and didn't tell anyone I was fleeing. I did this so they would not have to lie to the FBI; the FBI would use their arrest as leverage to get me to return. I have never asked them for money for any reason because the FBI could arrest them for aiding a fleeing fugitive. As clear evidence from the Det. Kenneth Mark Lewis audio confessions, the FBI and even state and local law enforcement entities can easily falsify data and twist the truth to obtain warrants, to hack into your accounts and invade every aspect of your life.

The blissfully ignorant American citizens are to blame; all this happened right under their noses. I can only hope they will act to make a change.

Common Questions and Answers

I want to take a moment to answer some questions many people ask me. It seems people have misunderstandings about why I did what I did, why I chose Russia and what I have been doing. So here we go:

Question: Do I get money from Russia for being a refugee or working for them?
Answer: NO! I have never received a single ruble from the government. I don't get food, housing, or anything else. The only thing I have received from Russia is a document granting my asylum.

Question: Do I or have I worked for the Russian government?
Answer: NO! In fact, they never contacted me or made any type of conditions on my asylum. Here, it's live and let live.

Question: Am I pro-Russian?
Answer: I am pro American but I feel an affinity for Russia because they gave my asylum from my government. There are many things I like about Russia, but like anything else, there are some things I don't like about Russia. I will say this though – I've never met an

American who came here and didn't like it. If you think I'm just saying this because I am living here, ask anyone who care to the FIFA world cup. Or come visit yourself. Ron Chepesiuk, as liberal as he is, loved it here.

Question: Do I hate America?
Answer: Of course not - I love America. There's no other reason I would have fought so hard for the right of free speech and protection of others. I especially love the idea of America; what it is supposed to stand for – but that idea has been hijacked by American politicians, attorneys and law-enforcement leaders.

Question: You complain about Corruption in America, but you jumped from the flying pan and into the fire, right?
Answer: Coming to Russia was not about choosing the better place. It was about escaping from people in my government that wanted to see me in jail for the rest of my life, or worse - dead.
Still, America is seen as the "Land of the Free," where people have the right to free speech and the right to be free of baseless search and seizure. The police should not be able to investigate you for years because they don't like your political speech. The politicians used the 9/11 terrorist attack to destroy our constitutional protections. The American government can spy on whoever they want, whenever they want, and without a warrant to do so. If they don't like you, they can comb through your entire life until they find a way to put you in jail. America is now more reminiscent to Hitler's Germany than the original country I call home.

Question: You complain about corruption with American police, but what about Russian police?

Answer: The corruption is completely different. In Russia, some police officers may take bribes, but you don't have cops running around shooting and killing unarmed people because they are scared or on a power trip. If it happens in Russia, the police officer is held fully accountable and thrown in jail like any other normal person. Still, I have never been asked to pay a bribe. I've even tried after I got stopped for speeding, but the cop didn't want it. He just gave me a warning and let me go.

Question: Do I like Russian food?

Answer: Most of the time, no. For me, it's pretty bland. Porridge and Fish Soup? Ewww... I like spicy food from the Caucasian regions though. Plov. Shashlik, etc. I also have learned to make some of my favorite foods. BBQ, Tacos, etc.

Question: Do I ever plan to return to America?

Answer: I don't know. Right now, I can't because I will not be arrested, putting these animals in control of my life. Honestly, other than for my family, I don't really have a desire to return.

Question: If I had to do it all over again, knowing that I would lose my family, would I?

Answer: It's such a hard question to answer. Sometimes when I feel defiant, I say I did the right thing and someone has to take a stand, or else no one will. But when the night falls and I let my mind wander, I dream of my babies, their laughter, their hugs; it's my own private hell, not being able to be there for them. Not being able to watch them grow old. It makes me angry, makes me fierce. It strengthens my resolve and crystallizes this Волк-Одиночка — (pronounced Volk Odinochka), or Lonely Wolf's mission to seek retribution.

Question: Why Russia?

Answer: I have come here five times and it's a wonderful place. Very different than portrayed by the media. And frankly, where else was I going to go with a few hundred bucks left in my pocket? Besides, on an island like Cuba, you are severely limited in your activities. Russia has the largest landmass of any country in the world, so you can go skiing, go to the beach, or go to the desert.

Question: How many places have I visited in Russia? What is my favorite?

Answer: I have been to over 70 cities now! My favorite is hard to pick because they are so different. I like Moscow for the night life. Sochi for the weather. Krasniy Poliana for the skiing, Voronezh because it's a great city.

Printed in Great Britain
by Amazon